"LA COMPAGNIE IRLANDAISE;"

REMINISCENCES

OF

THE FRANCO-GERMAN WAR,

BY

CAPTAIN M. W. KIRWAN,

LATE CAPTAIN COMMANDING THE IRISH LEGION, DURING THE WAR OF 1870 AND 1871.

DUBLIN:
W. B. KELLY, 8, GRAFTON STREET;
LONDON: SIMPKIN & CO.
1873.

PATTISON JOLLY,
STEAM-PRESS PRINTER,
22, ESSEX-ST. WEST, DUBLIN.

To the Memory

OF

THOSE IRISH SOLDIERS

WHO HAVE

FOUGHT AND FALLEN

IN

FOREIGN SERVICES,

THIS WORK

IS

Mournfully Dedicated

BY

THE AUTHOR

PREFACE.

THIS little work pretends to have no merit but its truthfulness. It neither professes to be the labour of a Jomini, nor the production of a Burgoyne. The author leaves all attempts in abler and better hands. It may, however, fill a gap in the history of the late War—by showing the hardships, the famine, and the wants incidental to a soldier's life, and which decimate a regiment more surely than the *mitraille* of the enemy. While avoiding all criticism upon the strategy of the campaign, the author confines himself to the trials through which the contingent of Irishmen under his command actually passed. There is more in warfare than battles, and there is more in battles than mere fighting. There is, in fact, a fund of almost untouched literary lore in the daily life of a soldier on active service, and it is upon this comparatively unbroken ground that this book is submitted to the reader's courteous consideration.

INTRODUCTION.

"Did you hear the news?"

"What news?" we enquired in a breath.

"The Emperor and his army have been taken prisoners of war," exclaimed our informant, looking at us with a pair of eyes somewhat dilated, while his fingers played with a newspaper still damp from the press.

"Impossible," we answered, showing by our incredulity the bent of our sympathies. But our *vis-a-vis* was demonstratively certain, and tossed off a cooling draught by way of codicil to his information. My companion looked as grave as if he had suddenly come under the influence of some neighbouring Squire Humphrey, while he in turn assured me that I looked "the picture of seriousness, tempered with surprise." We had been making a knapsack tour in Wicklow, and had just entered Jordan's Hotel at Glendalough, to obtain what is known in Irish parlance as "a refresher," when we heard the unwelcome news of the disaster of Sedan. My friend was a Trinity man, and thought that a tramp through what Thackeray called the "Garden of Ireland," would enable him to bend to his pious studies with more devoted zeal than he had for some time past been accustomed to. Although an aspirant for Protestant divinity honours, he was thoroughly Franco-Irish in his sympathies, and we had often weaned away the time with brilliant speculations on the probable humiliation that awaited the troops of the "Vaterland" by the soldiers of the *Armée Francaise*. Although of different religions, we wondrously agreed in our general conclusions, and hit off our differences to what Barney Blinds might call "a hair." We jointly agreed that there were more beautiful spots in "the wide world" than what the Beranger of Ireland called "The vale in whose bosom," &c.; that the brave clans of the O'Byrne had good vantage ground in the wilds of Glenmalure against the savage onslaught of the Pale. We made vague guesses at the state of society when saintly men were allowed to hurl pretty girls from off "beetling rocks" without possible trial by special commission as a climax to the deed. But the news we heard at Jordan's changed our thoughts from the past to the present. Our refresher was repeated, and, packs on, we once more stepped out along the beautiful road that runs through the "Seven Churches." I cannot say that I did not enjoy the scene, notwithstanding the calamity to France of which I and my companion had just heard. My friend was, indeed, of a more ardent temperament, enthusiastic in anticipation, depressed in disappointment. To him the charms of the delightful place were lost. There was alternately a vacancy and a fiery expression in his eyes, which would lead an observer to think that he was wavering between utter hopelessness and imaginative pictures of mimic battalions "marching to death with military glee." Once, indeed, when passing St. Kevin's Church, "that topped the neighbouring hill," we halted, and began to speculate upon the probable results of the capture of the Imperial troops, and after an hour spent in vague guesses, we gave it up, and came to the conclusion that we knew nothing about it. But our tour was spoiled. The mild beauties of the vale of Clara had no charm for my sympathetic friend, and when we got near Wicklow, we took the train, and were soon bowling back to town again.

There is a species of madness which is nothing more than ideal enthusiasm, and surely Dublin was ideal mad about France and its disasters in September, 1870. The fortunes of *La Grande Nation* were indeed overcast with gloom. The surrender of Mack at Ulm had been thrown into the shade by the calamity at Sedan, where

70,000 Frenchmen passed under the Caudine Forks. Jena and Friedland had been avenged. The army of France had been gobbled up by the hosts of Germany. As Egypt, the cradle of civilization, was overrun by Ethiopians, nurtured amidst hardier conditions; as Babylonia was subdued by Chaldeans from Taurus and Caucasus; as Persia fell beneath the rapid onslaughts of Arabs, and Huns, and Moguls; and later on in history, as the Roman Empire fell before Franks, Goths, Huns, Arabs, and Vandals, so did Northern France lie prostrate beneath the iron heel of victorious Germany. The Teuton was everywhere triumphant over the Gaul. The hope of obtaining the Rhine frontier for France, had vanished into thin air. The dream of Lavallée, was, for the time being, no more. The Emperor and his army prisoners of war! Marshal Bazaine, the conqueror of Mexico, thwarted at Metz, Mars-le-Tours, and Resonville, and his magnificent army cut in two, as was done a week before, and in the same masterly manner, to that of MacMahon at Woerth. Strasburg, Toul, and Laon, were all in danger of immediate bombardment and capitulation. Paris was threatened, and but a handful of the French regular army remained to defend the National flag. But the spirit of the nation was unsubdued. The Republic had been proclaimed on the 4th of September, and it was fondly hoped that the new government would save the country, as did the Republic of 1792. The nation was called to arms! Behind the Loire the Mobile Guard was organising with wondrous rapidity. Free corps were forming everywhere. A *debris* of MacMahon's army under Vinoy, had made its way to Paris and formed a nucleus for the ill-conditioned garrison. With hardly a regular soldier in the field, distracted in her internal power, a revolution in the capital, France had nothing but her newly-raised levies to resist the most perfectly organised army the world had ever seen. In Ireland sympathy for France became a standard cry. The French consul in Dublin was serenaded by the people, and "killing a Hessian for yourself" became once more a household word throughout the land. Then the idea of the Ambulance originated, and was quickly put into execution. Hundreds of young men volunteered to participate in the cause, and serve beneath the flag which is now emblematical of the old Calvinistic city. A few only could be accepted. Military men knew that the Ambulance Committee made a serious mistake in sending three hundred volunteers to attend on four Ambulance waggons; but like the thief in the *Beggar's Opera*, the Ambulance Committee danced to the music of its own chains. But it inadvertently forwarded what some anxious men in Ireland had in contemplation—an Irish Legion for military service in France. Many of the Ambulance men accepted a passage to France for this purpose. I was assured that if I followed the Ambulance Corps to France, I could form the nucleus of a Franco-Irish regiment out of the men who were prepared to volunteer for the army; and as *Lafontaine* was leaving the quay in Dublin, the last words I heard from among the crowd of men who thronged her deck, were assurances that there were, at least, one hundred of them willing to learn the soldier's glorious trade, under the French tricolour. I promised to follow overland, and that night amused some of my friends by depositing my last will and testament in their keeping. My Trinity friend made an acrobatic spring at my person when I informed him of my determination. My pious friends offered to say a round of prayers for my safety, and my sceptical acquaintancs bade me a hearty adieu over a few bottles of champagne, while many assured me that if I succeeded they would follow in my wake.

" Once form the nucleus of a corps beyond," said an ex-captain of a line regiment to me, a few hours before my departure, " and success is certain. We can send any number of men, and I'll be out with a batch before long." The two following days were engaged in making some necessary preparations, and on the 12th of October, 1870, two days after the departure of the *Ambulance Irlandaise*, I left Dublin *en route* for Havre.

"LA COMPAGNIE IRLANDAISE;"

REMINISCENCES OF THE FRANCO-GERMAN WAR.

CHAPTER I.

"Semper et ubique fideles."

La Belle France loomed through a misty atmosphere on the 14th of October, 1870, and the waves licked high against the chalk coast of Seine Inferieure as we steamed into the harbour of Havre. Spray was tossed in miniature showers over the slip, and now and again fell in tinsel particles upon the people who lined the quay. To me the multiplicity of uniforms was the most attractive feature in view; as Linesmen, Guard Mobiles, Guard National, and Freeshooters moved with easy gait amongst the neatly-dressed bourgeoise of the town. There were peasants in the hereditary *sabot*, that singular wooden protection for the foot, which bears the same proportions to the wondrously neat French boot, that a bluff bow'd Dutch schooner does to an American clipper. But we were soon alongside, and quickly passed up the gangway, at the further end of which a crowd had collected, and where a *gens d'armes* made a vigorous attempt at English by demanding "Vour passport, sare." But it was a gala day in Havre. The Ambulance had been right royally received that morning, the civic and military authorities turning out in their splendour to do honour to *les Irlandais*.

"*Vive l'Irlande*," said a demonstrative-looking Frenchman, as I was about to enter the old-fashioned portico of the *Hotel des Londres,* while I caught the inspiration, and as demonstratively replied "*Vive la France,*" bowing with a new-born grace, which I verily believe Frenchmen have the power of spreading around their name and local habitation. But surprises like misfortunes often come in battalions, and sure enough many familiar and unexpected faces were soon crowding around me. Amongst the rest the giant and finely proportioned figure of Martin Hanley Carey towered over his neighbours. Strangely enough he held a neatly knotted blackthorn in his hand, which he *naïvely* said was forbidden in Ireland, because of its Republican tendency to endanger "the safety of the crown." The Ambulance was, however, the topic everywhere. Dr. Baxter and his men were the heroes of the hour. Amongst the rank and file it was, indeed, the spring tide of their happiness, and before the sun had set, some of them were rolling half seas over in the stream.

"*Vous cognac, vous cognac,*" I heard a bloused Frenchman say to a member of the Ambulance, one of the men who a few days afterwards returned to Ireland, and who with sympathetic affection boldly replied "*Oui, oui,* me cognac, me cognac."

I had a strong suspicion that a stiff hand would be required to keep some of those gentry in order, for it was easy to see there were men amongst them whose arithmetical calculations did not go beyond No. 1. They thought more of their own creature comforts than they did of the honour of the *Ambulance Irlandaise.* Ireland had given France assistance, like Count Frescoe's gift to the organ grinder's monkey "In the sacred name of humanity," and the magnamimity of the work, allied with previous friendship, made friendly Frenchmen excuse the conduct of some few lost sheep of the Ambulance Corps, and generously take the blame upon themselves.

"We love ze Irish, sare," said an old veteran to me, as I endeavoured to explain away the conduct of a tipsy Irishman, who was one of a few who should never have been permitted to serve beneath the red-cross banner of Geneva. But sure enough the sympathetic chord between the two nations had been touched by the presence of the *Ambulance Irlandaise* in Havre, and it had, too, that day given out its most joyous tones in response to the unanimous demands of the people of the town. The Press lavished encomiums upon the appearance of the men, and Dr. Baxter and his surgeons were entertained at the *Mairie* by the corporate officers of Havre, and mutual vows were made, and mutual hands pledged a fraternity of fellowship between the two peoples. For the moment the bourgeoise of Havre appeared to forget the terrible strides that the German hosts were making into the heart of the country. Bazaine was still held fast in Metz; and the condition of affairs was so brilliant for the Germans that they were already building imaginary triumphal entries into the capital of France itself, which was soon to be encircled in the iron belt of the invader. Optimists, indeed, still hung on that powerful retribution—" an armed nation." The condition of European armies, with their arms of precision, has, however, rendered obsolete the faith which was once placed in the irresistibility of a nation in arms. It is means, not men, which now influence the destinies of armies. The necessity for great genius is not so indispensable to success as the admirable working of the minute mechanism, so as to influence and direct the whole. 'Tis true, indeed, that Russia, in 1812, was overwhelmed for the time, but with continued resistance she overcame her disasters, and left even the great Napoleon unable to revenge the defeats he sustained from the hardy armies of the North. 'Tis true, too, that the untrained people of Spain, aided by a handfull of British troops, beat the legions of Napoleon, led as they were by the first captains of the age. So did the Swiss, from their mountain fastnesses, drive out the Austrians in 1499; and again, the raw levies of the Carolinas compelled Cornwallis, and 16,000 English soldiers to surrender as prisoners of war. But the conditions of war have changed since then. War is now a scientific game, at which the expert alone can succeed. The appliances of modern warfare have for ever destroyed the hopes of irregular troops, unless under conditions singularly favourable to the irregulars, or where the geographical conformation of the country renders it necessary for the regular troops to adopt irregular warfare, as in New Zealand, for instance. The "majesty of an armed nation" is, unhappily a thing of the past, so far, at least, as its prowess is concerned, when directed against the trained levies of a great military power. Nor do I fully accept the opinion of some eminent writers, that old soldiers are not so good as young ones. There were men in France, however, who believed that the *élan* of the raw levies, then being trained, would more than match that of the regular troops. I was more than once told that Ney acknowledged, after the battle of Lautzen, that with his Grenadiers of the Guard he could not have done what was accomplished by his youthful conscripts, who were led five times, ultimately with success, to the capture of the salient points, which the older and more experienced men would have given up as hopeless after the second attempt. But all this was not so apparent to cooler heads. People who were not blinded by national animosity, took a different view of the situation.

"You, Frenchmen," said an Irish doctor to an officer of Mobiles, who was building airy castles to be rudely shaken by the current of events, "appear to have forgotten the good old maxim of Sallust, which taught that before entering upon action, there was need of deliberation, and having deliberated, a necessity of speedy execution." But the Mobile was happy in his inexperience, and blew curling puffs from the aromatic weed which he somewhat artistically held in his mouth and between his fingers. The "Moblot," as the Line called its first reserve, had perfect confidence in the prowess of his arm of the service, and appeared to swallow the unwelcome allusion of the Irish doctor with a kind of hospitable benevolence, which hesitated to offend a sympathetic stranger. But all my work was still before me. I had yet to test the sincerity of the men who pledged their word in Ireland, that "the imminent breach and deadly peril" of a soldier's life was more congenial to their nature than the more humanitarian occupation of promenading improvised Ambulances, administering balm, and dispensing comforts to the sick and wounded soldiers of France. I had to find out the whereabouts of the Irish Ambulance, and then to see if they would turn their backs upon a fair fight, or think that distance lends enchantment and courage to what theatrical people call "the pomp and circumstances of glorious war." Pressing on to the *Lycée*, where the Ambulance was quartered, I obtained my first impression of the discipline and conduct of the raw levies by the loose and irregular formation of some of the *Garde Nationale*, who were hurrying through the streets in the direction of the railway. They were equipped as if for active service, and were singing the Marseillaise with a vigour, and indeed with a touch of real feeling, which Frenchmen generally contrive to cultivate in the patriotic chants. But they were a motley crew, armed with old flint-locks, converted to the percussion principle on the Tablet system, badly dressed, loosely disciplined, and in some cases the entire bread contents of their haversacks, jocularly stuck on the tops of the guns, like a piece of putty on a marlin spike. Those were the men on whom the Mayor of Rouen depended to meet the most perfectly-organized army in the world. The capital of Normandy was at that time threatened by the Germans, and this contingent of the National Guard was all that Havre—the "Liverpool of France"—could send to protect the ancient and majestic chief town of Seine Inferieure. As they walked away from the *Mairie*, they must have left a sad foreboding upon the minds of the few invalided soldiers of the Line who witnessed their departure, and one of whom I saw ominiously shake his head with desponding significance, while I heard him almost inaudibly mutter, "*La pauvre France.*"

But I should press on to the *Lycée*. Passing along the spacious Place Napoleon III., with its public gardens and handsome edifices; on through some narrow streets by open spaces, where drill instructors were teaching the bourgeois some of the mysteries of a soldier's trade, I was attracted to a piece of waste ground, where I saw a man with a wooden leg instructing a full company of *Garde Nationale* in the manual of arms. He appeared to be a well-known character, for no notice was taken of his peculiar appearance; and the way he handled his gun, was sufficient proof that the medals he wore upon his expansive breast were won in actual, and not in mimic, warfare. But the *Lycée* was before me, and the unsightly but familiar uniform of the men of the Irish Ambulance now and again passed me on the way. To the people they were objects of interest, and indeed, their fine proportions might vie favourably with the natives of the country they had come to succour. But I soon reached my destination, where the red-cross banner waved its peaceful folds over the entrance to the *Lycée*, and where an Ambulance man paced under the portico of the gate, in the capacity of a sentry. It was, after all, a pleasant sight to witness the ardour with which the Ambulance men entered upon their duties, and the pride too they took in their really charitable occupation. At that time, at least, all Frenchmen were not destined to be soldiers; and if the idea of a National Army is ever permitted to extend to this unhappy land, no doubt many of the men who thought Ambulance work quite good enough for France, would be easily induced to accept a more dangerous occupation for their native sod, and that, too, without the necessary adjuncts of the constitutional shilling of the recruiting sergeant. But charity indeed covers a multitude of sins, and there was a few of the Ambulance men, who much required that special gift to enable them to wipe out their catalogue of irregularities. As a rule the men were well conducted, and looked with satisfaction upon the rules which were put in force for their better regulation and order; but there were about half a dozen whose chief occupation appeared to consist in running the guard, and loafing about the streets full of the assurance that some enthusiastic Frenchman would take them in tow, and drown their trouble in a glass of cognac. However here they were good and bad, and I soon recognised familiar faces from amongst the crowd whom I saw gathered within the spacious building, while the majority of the Ambulance men were engaged in devouring a repast which appeared substantial enough for that fag-end of humanity— a Yorkshire ploughman. But I was peculiarly circumstanced at this same *Lycée*. Some members of the deputation, or of the Dublin Ambulance Committee who attended the corps to France, regarded me with an expression which to me read very much akin to aversion. I was evidently an interloper in their estimation. I had come to Havre to disarrange the plans of the *Ambulance Irlandaise*, and judging from the austere simplicity of one at least of the Ambulance Committee, I was destined to come to grief in some way not clearly defined by the representative man. But sequels are rude teachers, and often destroy the prophetic forebodings of the would-be-wise. My reception by the men of the Ambulance was an additional source of trouble to the representative man, and he gave vague hints that my mission would end in trouble and misfortune. However young blood will have its way. There is a great deal of human nature in mankind, as Josh Billings says, and I fear there is a great deal of combative human nature in that portion of our species which hails from the Emerald Isle. There were about sixty men in the Ambulance corps who welcomed me as a deliverer, and declared that they wanted to be soldiers, and seek the bubble reputation, instead of becoming "ministering angels" to the stricken heroes of *La Belle France*. As I entered the *Lycée*, Frank Byrne, Terence Byrne, Henry M'Crossin, and others of their friends, pressed around me, and declared their intention of volunteering for the army, provided an Irish corps was formed, when they would have an opportunity of marching to the alternate airs of O'Donnel-a-boo and *Amour la Patrie*. But the plot thickened, or, more correctly, the events which military men in Ireland had anticipated, actually occurred. The Ambulance was too large! Three hundred men were not required to attend on four Ambulance waggons, and the doleful news that only one hundred, all told, could be accepted, struck dismay into the ranks of the gallant knights of the red-cross flag.

Prudence, that mother of success, had certainly not marked the acts of the Ambulance Committee in lending to France more than three times the number of men required, and France had too many idle mouths to feed, to think of accepting the services of more than three times the number of men for Ambulance work, which she required. For this failure the Ambulance Committee was alone to blame, and the "representative man" was overwhelmed with misfortune, from which, however, the energetic conduct of Mr. P. J. Smyth did much to release him and the Committee in general. For a day or two the feeling amongst the Ambulance men was justly indignant. There was much dissatisfaction amongst the men who went to France to be Ambulance men, pure and simple. I had already sixty men who were prepared to volunteer for the army, irrespective of the existence or non-existence of the *Ambulance Irlandaise*. They were determined to be soldiers, let the Ambulance sink or swim. Sunday came! The volunteers for the Army paraded in front of their quarters, and marched to Mass, and fell off in detachments and went to other places of worship with singular precision and good order. Yes, your Irishman is surely a soldier by intuition. He can learn as much drill in one month as an English clod-hopper will in two, at least that is my experience in the English service, where as a stripling ensign I first learned the mysteries of that acrobatic performance—the goose-step. The decorum the Irish Volunteers observed that Sunday in Havre was a precursor of their good conduct on many a hard trying day afterwards, and I could not but feel proud of the soldierly gait and erect carriage of the men, who as yet did not know their facings. But events of importance were on the move, the day of trial came at last and forty more men joined the Volunteers rather than return to Ireland to experience "monkey's allowance," which is generally interpreted to mean more kicks than halfpence, at the hands of their unsympathetic countrymen. On my part I studiously avoided asking any man to volunteer, but I welcomed all who did so on their own responsibility. There was no pressure, not even a request, all were free; and the men had the option of accepting military service, take their chance of being selected for the Ambulance, or return to Ireland. Thus the representative man began to look upon me with more favour, as he saw that I just stepped in and saved himself and the Committee from a dilemma. Dr. Baxter selected the best of the men who remained after the volunteering for the army had been completed, and between us we had the cream of the corps, as each set about his own way of carving his own destiny.

But our path was strewn with difficulties. Mr. P. J. Smyth, however, took a more than kindly interest in our welfare. He and I sought an interview with the General commanding the district, and placed the services of the Irish Volunteers at his disposal. But that poor man was in a quagmire of trouble. Everything appeared going wrong, and after an interview which lasted fifteen minutes, we took our departure no wiser than we were. The General didn't know what to do with us, "he had no orders," and he shrugged his shoulders, and indulged in the telegraphy of his arms, by which Frenchmen generally attempt to emphasise their sentences. Another day wore on, and it was the 15th of October, when a singularly dressed man accosted me in front of the Ambulance quarters, and announced himself as a messenger from Colonel M'Adarus, who was then at Caen organising an Irish regiment for service in the field. The

Colonel's messenger was not a distinguished looking man, but he was none the less remarkable. He called himself a Captain Somebody and by way of assurance, pointed to his military *kepi*, with its green band and three gold *galons*, as verification of his assertion. As no one had ever heard of such a man as Colonel M'Adarus, we were still in a dilemma, and hesitated to accept the singular story of an Irish regiment being formed at Caen, upon the mere words of a stranger, about whom we were somewhat sceptical. But we had a cute gentleman to deal with in the Colonel at Caen. He had made a formal application to the General in command at Havre, to the effect, that all Irish volunteers for the army should be sent to Caen, to swell the ranks of the Irish regiment, then in process of formation. And so we received orders to repair to the "City of the Churches," as Caen is called, from the number and beauty of its ecclesiastical structures. The men did not relish this latest move, as they had heard many unfavourable reports of this M' Adarus and his Irish regiment, from men who had returned from Caen, and were *en route* for London. However on the 16th of October, 1870, we received orders to report at Caen, and as there was no help for it, we made our final preparation, and fell in before the *Lycée*, to take our departure. The men went through their formations with admirable promptitude. A few hours' instruction during the previous days had already shown a beneficial effect, and as they stood in line, their ranks were as neatly dressed, as if they had been native and to the manner born.

"You have a splendid lot of men," said an American to me, as he stood before the Company, preparatory to our marching away, and as the Ambulance Corps, too, had gathered around to bid us adieu. The American I had met before, and as he lived in Havre, he was often of service to giving us advice and assistance in our interviews with the officials. He was not, however, impressed with much respect for the young Republic, and often shook his head at me with quiet humour, as if muttering that he had better game on hands than risking life or limb at the cannon's mouth.

"You see," he said to me, with a drawl peculiar to the people who for any time live within the limits of the great Republic, "this country aint worth fightin' for. France made one great mistake, a mistake which she is sufferin' for now, and will suffer for to all eternity."

"And what was that?" I ventured to ask, while he was engaged lighting a fresh cigar.

"Well," said he, looking at me with a cool, calculating stare, "when Napoleon sold Louisiana to the United States, if he had sold the whole of France too, to the same purchaser, why France would be the first country in Europe now."

"But dont you think there is still some hope for France yet, now, too, that she has come to your way of thinking, and exchanged the eagle for the Gallic cock?" I asked, hoping for a favourable reply.

"No, sir, none whatever," said the American, with stoical indifference. "With Paris and Metz hard and fast in the grip of the Germans, and then the other day Orleans and Chartres fell, half the country placed *hors de combat*; why, the game is up, sir, the game is up;" and he stroked his moustachios with that bland assurance which is almost characteristic of his nationality.

"The fight at Orleans has at least taught a lesson to that portion of the French who are so fond of airing their infidelity," I said. "The best abused soldiers in France fought the most heroically while their censors saved themselves in ignominious flight.

"Yes, you are right there," replied the American. "To be a '*soldat du Pape*' must henceforth be synonymous with undoubted gallantry, rather than with imbecility or servitude as it has hitherto been.

'I heard they suffered terribly at Orleans," I said, anxious to pick

C

some information from a man whom I knew to have just returned from the scene of the fight.

"They did indeed," he replied. "Always in advance, they fought from house to house, every street through which they were forced was defended with splendid obstinacy. They and the Foreign Regiment were the only corps that did any work, the rest ran helter-skelter everywhere."

But just then our conversation was interrupted by the arrival of a messenger who held a note between his fingers, and which on opening was found to be the order for our departure. A word or two of command and the men left the *Menage* behind. Their sections of fours were as neatly dressed as if they had been the result of weeks of training, and the men kept the step almost as well as if they had been under instruction a much longer period than is required by "regulations." Indeed the people of Havre thought that those volunteers must have had some previous instruction, and I too, half suspected that the "rising of the moon" had witnessed some of those Irishmen in the glens and valleys of their native heath, going through the forbidden movements of the "manual" or "platoon." But on we marched to the *Hotel de Ville*, inside the spacious railing of which the *Garde Nationale* were on duty, and where we took up our position, waiting for the chief magistrate of the town. He was quickly before us, and in a few stirring words gave a hearty welcome to us all.

"France," he said, "can never forget the generous conduct of the people of Ireland, between whom and ourselves a bond of friendship has ever existed. France saved, the avenging sword of liberty shall repay the gratitude of our nation to Ireland, and let you Irish soldiers of the French Republic rest assured that the people of Havre would ever remember your conduct with esteem and admiration." It was war time, and we were as a matter of course bound to give a liberal margin to the enthusiasm of the *Maire*, and need only accept as much of his flattering speech as was wholesome and welcome to our palates. Shortly after this pretty formality, the people crowded around us in wondrous astonishment, and expressed no small degree of surprise when they heard we came all the way from Ireland to fight the Germans. But still surprises crowded upon us. It would appear that the people of Havre were indeed generously impressed with our conduct. The colonel commanding the National Guard, and about thirty of his officers, came to us, and the colonel addressed me in excellent English, "thanking us all for the course we had taken." His manner and demeanour were characteristic of that well bred ease which often marks the cultivated man of travel. Without being demonstrative or intrusive, he asked if he could in any way assist us, and when he found we were provided with all our wants, bade us adieu in a tone which left a singularly pleasing impression upon our minds. At 10 or 11 o'clock that night we were to take our departure for Caen, and that insatiable monster, "the inner man," had meanwhile to be satisfied. Some of the authorities took us in charge, and lodged the men in the quarters of the *Pompiers*, who are expected to act in the capacity of firemen, but whose general appearance and old-fashioned apparatus, are but poorly adopted to cope with the destroying demon—fire. But they treated the Irish Volunteers with unbounded hospitality. There was no limit to the supply. The *Pompiers* appeared to regard the Irishmen with a feeling somewhat akin to that which must have animated the poet when he penned the lines

> "Eat, drink, and be merry,
> For to-morrow you die."

Mr. P. J. Smyth, to whose kindly interest the Irishmen in Havre owed so much, determined to accompany us to Caen, where his acquaintance with some of the most influential people of that town was of infinite benefit to us afterwards. And here I must tender the thanks of myself, and I am sure, too, every man in *La Compagnie Irlandaise* would support my recognition of the services which the present member for Westmeath rendered to us both in Havre and Caen. Of all our civilian friends who came from Ireland, he was certainly the most anxious to see an Irish Legion established in France. He was our guide and interviewer. He helped on the good work with the officials, and never left us until he saw us settled and done for in Caen. While in Havre he and I were entertained by the *Commandant* of the firemen, who looked at us as minutely as a money broker might look at a suspicious bill in times of pecuniary trouble. The simple elegance of the little parlour into which we were ushered indicated the presence of a female hand, and sure enough the *Commandant* was happy in the possession of a young and charming wife, who with Christian benevolence offered to say prayers for our safety, at which her husband frowned like a sceptic or an unbeliever. But it is so all through France—the women alone are religious, and it is a fine thing to ridicule the Church and its pastors with an ignorant stupidity which is unhappily inseparable from the ruck of a city population. Our host was demonstratively complimentary, and I think insisted upon embracing us in true French fashion, while he forced our faces into too close contact with the vigorous sprouts of beard which stood out from his cheeks and chin like stubble land in harvest time. He went the entire circuit of the war in his denunciations of incapables, and speculated upon the probable future, with as much cool judgment as a man could be expected to show at such a time. He became communicative too upon the history of Havre, the annals of which are connected with early English history at several important epochs. If we were remaining, he would show us where Henry of Richmond embarked for Milford Haven and Bosworth Field; and with generous impulse told us how bravely the Earl of Warwick held the town against vastly superior numbers; and how Charles II., landed at Havre after the disastrous battle of

Worcester, and his romantic escape from England, with the Royal Oak incident in October, 1651. But those gems of the historic past had little to interest us at the time being. The question of the hour was, the conduct of the war in which we were about to take a part, and when 10 p.m., arrived our time was up, and we prepared to take our departure. Inside the spacious court-yard of the *Pompiers*, the Irishmen were once more formed into line, the roll was called, the great gates swung open to allow of our passage through, and with a kind farewell from our host and hostess we marched away. The rain fell in torrents! We had fully a mile to go, and we were all saturated with wet. I had a huge dreadnought as a protection, but I might as well have had a huge newspaper. A wet blanket was indeed thrown over the person, but not over the spirits of the men. On through the sloppy streets, rain above and puddle below, the station was made at last; and amidst a rush of Mobiles, and Franctireurs, a few carriages were appropiated to the Irish Volunteers; the whistle shrieked, and the soldiers sank back into their crowded compartments, impressed with the cold assurance of having a ten hours' drive, on a cold morning in October, with an envelope of wet clothes as their only comforter.

That night the Ambulance men slept snugly housed in their quarters in the *Menage*, with gorgeous beds of straw, warm blankets, a paternal Committee to watch over their slumbers, and happy in the assurance of two francs per day, and the prospect of seeing some of the campaign, but happier still in the certainty of preserving their persons from the effects of what Hotspur's fop called "villanous saltpetre."

That night the Irish Volunteers, drenched with rain, started on their journey to Caen in crowded railway carriages, for a pay of a halfpenny per day, and with a prospect of Mark Mickle's alternative—"a gold chain or a wooden leg, you know." For my own part the ten hours' drive was not much more than an ordinary run

from Dublin to my native heath in Galway; but the men, the rank
and file, some of whom were gentlemen by birth, education, or social
position, crowded, nay packed, into third-class railway carriages
with steaming clothes, they experienced the realities of campaigning soon enough to test the mettle of the best of them. But the
temper of the time was—

> "Mais a la guerre
> Comme a la guerre;"

and the Irish Volunteers accepted the force of circumstances as men
who were really anxious to seek military adventure and abide the
consequences. The man who called himself Captain Somebody, accompanied us on our way, and more than once as we spun through
the swelling hills and beautiful valleys of Normandy, I ventured to
express a hope that everything at Caen was prepared for our reception, and as he had telegraphed that we would arrive about 8 a.m.,
that coffee and biscuits would be ready for the men. The gentleman, however, was vague in his answers, and he always "supposed"
that all would be well when we arrived. But away we rattled passed
Rouen, so full of mediæval structures, on by ruined castles, historic
fortresses, monastic edifices, and immense orchards; on through
Mezidon, pass the place where William the Conqueror defeated the
revolted barons in 1047, at *Val-es-Dunes*; and at 8 a.m., on the
17th of October, we were at Caen, the chief town in Calvados, with
which we were destined to have many associations.

CHAPTER II.

> Her matchless sons, whose valour still remains
> On French records, of twenty long campaigns,
> Now from an Empress to a captive grown—
> She saved Britannia's rights, but lost her own.

OUR entry into Caen was not of the happiest nature. We left Havre with *eclat*, the good wishes of the people following in our wake. We arrived at Caen under a cloud, the inhabitants declaring that they had had enough of " Ze Irish," as they called us. When we arrived at the station there was nobody to extend the hand of assistance to the Irish Volunteers, and we marched to the barrack, which was the head-quarters of the "Irish Regiment," under the escort of a man who called himself an officer in the new corps. He was evidently astonished at the soldierly appearance of the men as they marched with regular gait and erect carriage through the streets and squares leading to " head-quarters." The men made a most creditable show, and in a few minutes were within the limits of the barrack-square. The yard was extensive enough; but heaps of rubbish, and crumbling walls, told very plainly that it was a neglected spot. The barracks were not very spacious, and had not been used for military purposes for a long time past. The morning was tolerably cold, the men had been all night in their wet clothes, and I naturally thought some arrangements would be made to stimulate drooping and exhausted nature. The Captain from somewhere all at once showed his true colours, and to my demand for coffee and biscuits, he gave me to understand that those luxuries could not be supplied until the men " had signed." This caused a natural reaction on our part, and looked very much like a trap to induce the men into a position from which there was no retreat. Presently, however, the "Colonel" appeared, limping through the gateway, his face reflecting emotion of no ordinary character. This was M'Adarus; and Mr. Smyth and myself were somewhat surprised at discovering, in the person of Colonel M'Adarus, a gentleman whom we had previously met in Dublin under the name of Dwyer, but of whose local habitation, or of whose actual name or character we had no knowledge. M·Adarus was gushing with promises, but really he could order no refreshments until the men "had signed." He had already lost a fabulous sum of money in supporting a contingent of men who came from London, and who were ungrateful enough to abandon him, and leave some accounts to be settled, they never having committed themselves to actual service by appending their names to the paper which was to pronounce them soldiers of the *Armée Francaise*. And as the Irish Volunteers were to have no food until they "signed," which Mr. Smyth and myself expressly cautioned them against doing, until we sought an interview with the municipal and military authorities of Caen. In this we succeeded through Mr. Smyth's personal acquaintances, and we soon found ourselves in the presence of the *Maire* and his assembled satellites.

"The fact was, that the Irish had given much trouble," said the chief magistrate to us, when we had pleaded our case. "Numbers of them came here from London to join the army; they were provided with everything out of the public funds, and when the time came for their becoming soldiers, they all refused, and they were shipped for London again, at the expense of the English Consul."

"But that has nothing to do with us," said Mr. Smyth. "We knew nothing of the London Contingent, nor did they know anything about us. There were one hundred men now in the barrack, they were anxious to become soldiers; and he asked if they would not be treated as men who had come to serve, and not to annoy the people and the cause of France.'

Well, we should see the general, and from the general we should see the *Intendance*, but one and all placed us in the same category as the London men, and point blank refused to do anything before the men had signed. M'Adarus had triumphed ! The men had no objection to sign a paper, or any paper declaring their willingness to become soldiers ; but it looked so much like a trap, of which Captain Somebody was the spring, and M'Adarus was the machinist, that it disgusted us all. We saw *M. le Colonel* once more in a quiet chamber in the *Hotel d'Espagne*, and somewhat astonished that gallant gentleman by telling him we would take the men back to Havre, where our services would be accepted as a corps of *Franc-Tireurs*, and thus solve the pretty difficulty about " signing." M'Adarus expostulated, and blandly reasoned, but all to no avail. Mr. P. J. Smyth, upon his own responsibility, provided a meal for the men, and a *feuille de route* for our return passage to Havre, showed the " Colonel" that we were in earnest. We had, too, ceased to have any confidence in this M'Adarus. Nobody knew him, nor from whence he came. He was as much a stranger in Caen as he was in Dublin. How *he* managed to get authority to raise a regiment of foreigners, is still as much a mystery, as is his previous career. But his was an accommodating mind. He was even prepared to accept a subordinate position. If I had no confidence in his capacity for the command of a regiment, he would become a *commandant*, and serve under me. He saw that his ambition was overreaching him. But his attempted reasoning was lost upon Mr. Smyth and myself, and it was only when the men's appetite had been appeased, and after the general in command of the district had made us handsome promises of his assistance, that the formality of " signing" was gone through, and the Irish Volunteers became soldiers of the regular army, for the duration of the war. Then work commenced in real earnest. The commissions of the officers were made out, and I had Mr. F. M'Alevey and Mr. B. Cotter as my lieutenants, while Dr. Macken was entrusted with responsibilities of surgeon to the corps. Mr. M'Alevey had been four years in the French Foreign Legion, and had seen some service in Africa and Mexico, while Mr. Cotter was two years a Pontifical Zouave, and received his baptismal fire at the battle of Mentana. "Colonel" M·Adarus was delighted! We had formed the nucleus of an Irish Brigade. Our names would emblazon the pages of Irish history, like the Dillons, the Clares, the Sarsfields, the O'Neills, and the Burkes of the old Brigade! We were destined to carve our way to glory, as did our fathers at Guillistia, Embrum, Cremona, Mun, Nemur, Lstetudan, Charleroi, Heidelberg, Urgel, Marsiglia, Fontenoy, Ypres, and Valency. So speculated our gallant chief, the "Colonel." But we should first raise to the dignity of a battalion, before we could become either an "Irish Regiment, or an Irish Brigade." The Government in London took special pains to crush "emigration" to France, and recruits for our expected battalion never arrived

In the meantime we were organizing in Caen. Military law was at once established; an *ordinaire* formed; an orderly room improvised; guards mounted, and discipline rigidly enforced. We tried to establish that *morale* which Napoleon the Great declared to be to physical force as three to one. By degrees the people of Caen came to recognise the fact that there was a distinctive difference between the Irishmen who came from Dublin, and the Irishmen who came from London. Those latter men were, doubtless, badly used by M'Adarus, and being left destitute in a strange land, without organization or discipline, may have committed excesses, which generally follows upon want or trouble. But their conduct was in some instances unpardonable. A story crept into the *Freeman's Journal*, which, in the interest of the corps, I was compelled to contradict, and with which I was able to enclose a flattering notice from the *Bulletin de la Guerre*, of Caen.

Head Quarters, 2me Regiment Etranger,
Caen, Normandy, France.

Sir,—I saw the *Freeman* last week, which contained a communication about the Irish Regiment now forming at Caen. That report may lead to some misapprehension if allowed to pass unnoticed. It was evidently furnished by a member of the London Irish, who composed the original nucleus of the corps. With that formation, the regiment has now nothing to do. The London Irish returned to their homes. The 2me *Regiment Etranger* is now, with a few exceptions, composed of Irishmen direct from Ireland. The report you published, was written or dictated by deserters—men who invented grievances in order to screen their cowardice. There is not a man now in the Irish Regiment, who would return to Ireland, until the term of his enlistment had expired. They have already won the esteem of the people of Caen. They have more than redeemed the conduct of the London Irish. I do not wish to cast any unjust aspersion upon the Irish in England, but they were London roughs, rather than London Irish, who came to Caen. There were a few good men among them, and those few have remained, and are now good soldiers. I allow the following extract from the *Bulletin de la Guerre*, to speak for the conduct of the men now forming the nucleus of the 2me *Regiment Etranger*.

"THE IRISH VOLUNTEERS.

"Last Saturday we saw with deep emotion the Irish Volunteers marching through our streets, and heard their deep voices singing their national songs. How well the self-contained attitude of those young men became their martial bearing. They have taught a lesson to our public-house braggarts, whom we saw a few days ago going to have themselves transformed into soldiers. We blush to think that those noble strangers place at the service of France a courage and a devotion which many of her own children have not shown."

I have the honour to be, Sir,
Yours, obediently,
M. W. KIRWAN,
Captain, Commanding.

This put an end to the mischievous rumour that had been circulated about the new corps. Indeed at this time it was all smooth sailing with our little Contingent. We had fully removed the false impression left by the London men. We worked hard at drill, and six hours a day exercise, besides guard and fatigue duty, kept the men pretty constantly employed. Occasionally we had a mimic combat upon the racecourse, and manœuvered for the possession of a bridge which divided the plain in two. We often, too, encountered that not very alarming enemy " an imaginary foe" who constantly occupied some timber in front of the course, and from which we repeatedly but vainly, attempted to dislodge him. We generally celebrated Saturday night by marching through the town keeping time to such treasonable songs as " God save Ireland," or " O'Donnel-a-boo." On such occasions the ladies stood at the windows as we passed along, waved snow white handkerchiefs before their faces, and more than once conquered our hearts by showers of flowers, as Danäe was conquered by showers of gold. Hats flew off in honour of *Les Volontaires Irlandais,* the name we were then known by in Caen. All went well with us while all was disastrous to France. " Metz has capitulated," was on everybody's lips, on the evening of October the 27th, and the last hope of France appeared to banish with the news. It is not my purpose here to pretend to analyze the strategy of some of the oldest captains of the age. It is a sorry impudence that presumes to openly censure the military conduct of such men as the hero of the Malakoff, and the victor of Magenta, or to accept results without enquiring into the cause of the ruin of the conqueror of Mexico. There may be more things in the philosophy of those men than is dreamt of by their censors. There are some men so wise in their own conceits that the labours of a lifetime are by them acquired in an hour. There is so much " after wisdom" in the world that fools pronounce opinions where previously, wise men would fear to tread. There is, in my humble opinion, one or two moves on the gigantic chess-board of the campaign on the French frontier, which justifies the supposition that Prince Frederick Charles was a better strategist than Bazaine, or that MacMahon was out-generalled by the Crown Prince of Prussia. But the one broad and significant fact is, that the organization of the one army was overwhelming in the multitude of its resources, while the organization of the other was disastrously deficient. The officers of the German armies were better educated, the training of the men was more in accordance with the experience of modern warfare; and, above all, the supplies for the army in the field were so regulated, that failure was almost impossible. It was not the French army, nor the French commanders that failed, but it was the self-confident opinion of Marshal Lebœuf on the one hand, and of the French *Intendance* on the other.

No troops ever fought more heroically than the French army of the Rhine. Overwhelmed by numbers, demoralized by insufficient supplies, the fearful havoc they made in the ranks of their enemies attested the valour of their race, and that they were of the same family as the men of Jena, Friedland, Austerlitz, Moscow, Italy, and the Crimea. The capitulation of Metz cast no shadow upon the valour of the French troops, and as Marshal Bazaine has not yet been tried, it is vain to speak of that " supreme effort" to break through the invading fire, of which so much was at one time said. It may have been possible, and it may have been impossible. People speak of making a dash at a particular point, &c., &c., but they forget that to move an army of 150,000 men, it requires a goodly space of ground to permit them to manœuvre and to deploy. Bazaine might have been able during the few first days of the investment to break the investing lines, but the customary phrases about " bursting through" must be accepted for what they are worth —and that is very little.

At the commencement of the war the French army was nominally 650,000 men, or an available soldier to one fifty-eight of the population, while the numbered force of Germany was 1,183,000. But experience proves that nominal muster-rolls are deceptive. At the commencement of the Italian war, France had on paper 639,000 men, but only 230,000 could be brought to Italy, and but 107,000 thousand were placed in line at Solferino. But I digress. Dijon was occupied by the Germans of the 29th also, and just one small success before Paris at La Bourget, was the one item to the valour of France during the disastrous week that closed the month of October. As the hordes of Attila and Tamerlane carried destruction on their way, so did the armies of Germany carry ruin and decay into the fertile plains of sunny France. The House of Brandenburgh had extended its dominion, and the Machiavellian policy of Prussia in the violated treaty of Gastein, in its premeditated attack upon Austria, and in its policy to Hanover, had once more triumphed, and this time had altered, or, at least, retarded the destiny of a nation. The *acme* of glory and dominion which had been reached by Charles V., was left in the shade by the conquests of King William. At this period the fortunes of France appeared to be at their lowest ebb. The people had become somewhat apathetic, and if some man in the trust and confidence of the nation counselled submission, the French would have accepted their defeat, and succumb to the invisible hand of Fate. But a contrary spirit soon animated the people of France. Gambetta aroused the nation to a spirit of resistance; and the cry of *"guerre à outrance,"* was quickly echoed throughout the land

"LA COMPAGNIE IRLANDAISE."

Whatever the world may think of Gambetta's political creed, it must admit that it was he and he alone, who aroused the people of France to a vigorous defence, when her repeated disasters had almost crushed even the martial spirit of her warlike race. A levy, *en masse*, was proclaimed, and every unmarried man between the ages of 18 and 48, was declared liable to serve in the ranks of the army. From all corners of Calvados the conscripts assembled in Caen, and our quarters became crammed with young men who were being formed into regiments of *Gardes Mobiles*,—the Militia of the country.

One corps in particular, made special friends of the *Volontaires Irlandais*. It was a body of Franc-tireurs, principally composed of soldiers of the line, who had escaped the disaster of Sedan, and as lawless a lot of men as it has been my fortune to clap eyes on during my experience in the Franco-German war. They were obedient to their officers, after that easy fashion which is supposed to be the right of free corps in general. Individually they bore a strong resemblance to that class of persons whom everybody has in his mind's eye—a dare-devil. Collectively they were orderly enough, appeared to take pains to avoid that rigid discipline in manual or platoon exercise, which other soldiers so much delight in. In fact, they looked like men in whom that self-reliant spirit which modern military men think so essential to success. Every man appeared to stand out from his fellows, and seemed quite prepared to risk his life upon the hazard of a personal encounter with the hated foe. If confidence was indeed the precursor of success, as it has been often said it is, the Franc-tireurs would have carried all before them. They expected their irregular attacks would demoralize their enemy, and that the achievements of each individual Franc-tireur would form the theme of some future Beranger. To the Irish Volunteers, however, the free-shooters were demonstratively attentive. One day they drew up in front of our quarters, and the captain in command asked me to form the Irish company so as to face the line of Franc-tireurs. I did so, with nothing more than a vague and altogether wild guess at the demonstration that was to follow. The Irish company formed in single line, faced the Frenchmen drawn up in a similar way. The ancient allies were face to face! People of one origin, bound together by so many historic associations, bound, too, in their hatred of a common enemy, I could not help thinking that those Celts differed more in language than in race. But the captain of the free corps harangued his men in a temper somewhat similar to what I experienced myself, only he with native courtesy made "e'en our failings lean to virtue's side." Then came—to the Irish—the objectionable part of the proceeding, as the Franc-tireurs, on friendly intent bent, rushed with extended arms into the ranks of the Irish Volunteers, and as each proceeded to single out his man, he commenced to hug his "brave comrade" with sympathetic fervour. I need scarcely add that the ranks were broken, and that the Irishmen were fully assured of the friendship of the Franc-tireurs, although they might have considered that their friends, the Free-shooters, had a somewhat singular way of showing their grateful affection.

But the captain of the free corps had something in store for the officers of the Irish Volunteers. The evening before he and his company were to take their departure for the front, he gave a little spree in his quarters at an hotel in Caen. Our host had collected one or two officers of the line, a few more of the Mobiles, some Franc-tireurs, and two of the officers of the Irish Volunteers together, in order to discuss the qualities of a bowl of punch, burned with artistic nicety. The captain prided himself upon speaking a "leetle" English. He could indeed say "God Save the Queen," and evidently knew the full meaning of the phrase, as he usually accompanied it by a remark not to be found in the prayers for " her Majesty and the rest of the royal family." In fact Captain Trucot and all his guests were bitter with Irishism, and pledged the toast, *l'Irlande et l'France* twenty times. But the guests took a more vigorous way of showing their appreciation of the sympathy of Ireland for their unhappy country, and one and all stood up and shouted " *Vive, vive, l'Irlande, vive, vive, l'Irlande, encore, encore; Vive, vive, l'Irlande, vive, vive, l'Irlande,*" and succeeded in impressing me with the assurance that they were genuine in the fervent expressions of gratitude and esteem. In all courtesy I could do no less than return the compliment, and I soon found myself standing up, bumper in hand, and demonstratively shouting " *Vive, vive, la France, vive, vive, la France,*" in which I was vociferously joined, much to the annoyance of the proprietors of the usually quiet establishment. After this mutual display of fellowship we recommenced the not less exciting occupation of consuming French brandy, and it was well into the small hours before I asked my new acquaintance to allow me to say adieu.

The following day was All-hallow Eve, and the Irish Volunteers were anxious to celebrate the festivity in the traditional manner, omitting, however, the customary habit of providing fresh colds, or of improvising a means of enabling a man to singe his whiskers or burn his nose, through the simple agency of what is innocently called " snap-apple." The men were indeed anxious to have some reminiscences of the old land amongst them upon the occasion, and by drawing on the company's fund—the *ordinaire*—about a glass of whiskey was provided for each man, and a few nuts assisted them to crack through the difficulties of the situation.

" You see, sir, the men really require a little extra refreshment now and again," said one of the sergeants to me, "for the food they get is not of the best description, nor of the most abundant in quality."

Of this indeed there could be no doubt. Day by day the officer on duty reported complaints from the different rooms, and it was painful to hear of the men constantly complaining against an evil, for part of which there was only a very poor remedy—the *ordinaire*. Sometimes the beef was tough, and one of the wags declared that it was "meet for repentance." As for the pork some of the men said they would take none in preference to the "whole hog." The loaves were often sour and musty, or "early to bread and early to rise," as somebody accounted for the cause. Another wit assured the sergeant of the week that the coffee tasted of earth, "because it was ground," while all agreed that "onion was strength" when given to flavouring soup, which was indeed the principal article of diet. But on All-hallow Eve all those troubles and witticisms found legitimate vent, and the evening was passed in repartee and story. It was such a picture as Davis would love to dwell upon—calm, stern, and patriotic. There was no senseless bombast, no foolish boast, no picture of imaginary deeds by flood and field, but there was what is better, the quiet soldierly demeanour of men resolved to do their duty. That that duty was cast upon a foreign land, some of those Irish Volunteers no doubt regretted, but that coolness which is often indicative of purpose, told that it would be done nevertheless. Since the Revolution of 1798 there was no Irish corps in France. Line regiments of the old Brigade served in the French West India Islands during the American war, others in Germany, during the war of 1756 and 1762, and Lally's regiment served in India; but during the present century no Irish corps followed the fortunes and shared the destinies of *La Grande Nation.* All-hallow Eve in Caen awoke those memories in the minds of the Irish soldiers, and stories of the old Brigade were liberally interspersed in the conversation of the men. I cannot easily forget how promptly the sound of "lights out" was obeyed in the midst of their merriment, and how willingly those young soldiers acquiesced in the necessity of prompt obedience. The last notes of the "Rising of the Moon" had scarcely been thrown back from the outer limits of

"LA COMPAGNIE IRLANDAISE." 35

the barrack square, as if the echo of the place loved the sentiments of the words, and again cast them rebounding on the air, when the bugles blew, and shortly afterwards no sound was to be heard except the measured beat of the sentries.

Day by day we were expecting the route. About the middle of November, we were quite prepared to take our place in line, except indeed, that fourrier-sergeant M'Crossin, complained of being deprived of " learning the fighting part of the business," through his constant attendance at the Quartermaster's stores, and looking after the food. The routine of barrack life was becoming monotonous, and the possibility of returning to Ireland without having smelled German powder, was not of the most flattering description. Drill continued with unabated ardour, and the spare hours on Sundays were occupied by making excursions into the country, where the most ignorant of the peasantry speculated on the nationality of the men, and when discovered, wondered in what portion of France "Ireland was situated." Every Sunday morning, however, the entire company was marched to Church, the Protestants pairing off to attend their own place of worship, while we attended the Church of *St. Etienne*, with its Gothic façades and its historical recollections of William the Conqueror of England, by whom it was finished in 1077.

" Would you like to see the grave of the great departed, Monsieur," said the church beadle, who, with a gigantic wand in his hand, promenaded about the Church during Mass, and accosted me immediately after the sacrifice was over.

I replied in the affirmative, and following my guide, he pointed to a plain grey marble slab in the pavement before the high altar, and said that that *was* the grave of William the Conqueror.

There was an emphasis on the word *was* that caught my attention; and upon enquiring if the remains had been removed, I heard that it had been for a long time empty, and that one thigh bone was all that was left of the once haughty subjugator of the Saxon race.

"You see, *Monsieur le Capitaine*," said the beadle, pointing to the slab, "the grave was broken open, and the beautiful monument erected over it was destroyed by the Huguenots in 1562, the bones were scattered and lost without record, at the same time, while the Revolutionists of 1793, again violated the grave, when the last remnant of William the Conqueror, the thigh bone, disappeared with the rest." My guide was redolent with stories about the Normans and the conquests, and conducted me as far as the door of the Church, while he pointed out the varied objects of interest around the Gothic Cathedral.

Before the door the company had already fallen in, and a crowd of Frenchmen had collected around the spot. From some source or other, the hat was sent around, and the passing members of the congregation were appealed to by some enthusiasts from among themselves, for a subscription for the Irish Volunteers. Before the company could be numbered off and removed from the ground, a demonstrative looking, but respectful Frenchman, came and offered me the contents of his hat, which I, however, firmly but respectfully declined. "The people are so much charmed with the Irish Volunteers, *M. le Capitane*,' he said, "that we wish to give them some recognition of our esteem. "And," he added, holding the hat up to me with about eighty or ninety francs huddled into its capacious crown, "if you will accept this little offering to buy tobacco for your men, we shall take it as a special favour."

At first I was very much disposed to be rude to the man who addressed me, and treat the matter as conveying a possible insult to the men. But the anxious expression on the countenance of the man who held the hat, and the really interested and sympathetic look upon the faces of the people who had contributed the money, assured me that it was given in good faith, and only with a desire of

"LA COMPAGNIE IRLANDAISE." 87

contributing to the comfort of the Irish soldiers. This tempered my refusal of the money, but I once more firmly refused to accept the gift, at which there was some dissatisfaction and more disappointment amongst the sympathetic subscribers. The company was marched away, and still the man almost apologetically followed me, and repeated his assurance, that no offence was meant to *les braves Irlandais*, but in France, each department looked after its own Conscripts, and the people of Caen were anxious to adopt us as their children. The compliments were flattering, but I was obdurate, and not until we got near our quarters did the gentleman leave me, disappointed but not defeated. From a few individuals the collection extended all over the town until the promoters were assured in tones of unswerved determination, that the Irish Volunteers would accept no favours, nor ask any exceptional treatment beyond what was given to any simple volunteer in the Line. This crowned our triumph in Caen! Henceforth we were the heroes of the hour, and the people were extravagant in the excess of their laudations.

But the fortunes of France had changed for the better in the early days of November, and we were impatiently expecting the route. No recruits arrived for the expected Irish Regiment, and we should be content to take the field as we were, an Irish Company, just mustering one hundred men, all told. A ray of hope broke through the pall-like disasters of France, in the early part of November. It was the hey-day of her chivalrous resistance. D'Aurelles de Paladine had converted the loose mass of Regulars, Garde Mobiles, Franc-tireurs, into shape and consistency. He had proved himself at least a man with capacity for organization; and when he recaptured Orleans, and a portion of the army under his command won the victory at Coulmiers, every tongue in France was echoing his praises. Chevially and Arteney added to the rejoicings of the nation, and the cry of "*guerre à outrance*" was again taken up by the press and the people of the country. The excitement in France at this period was more intense than it was since the capitulation of Sedan, and even Europe held its breath when Baccon was carried by the French of the 11th of November, and the army of the Loire was declared to be in full march to the relief of Paris. It was then D'Aurelles de Paladine undoubtedly failed, and lost a brilliant opportunity of assisting, if not of relieving, the garrison of Paris.

About this time I made the acquaintance of a soldier of fortune, such a man as turns up in all modern wars. I was one day giving some orders to the sergeant of the week, when a man dressed in the uniform of a Colonel of the line, suddenly stopped before me, looked into my countenance, and surveyed my *tout ensemble* with a half quizzical expression peering from beneath his partly-closed eyes.

"Are you all English," he asked, with that peculiar "bluntness," which the amiable John Bull regards as a virtue, but which the people of the Continent regard with aversion.

I replied in the negative and I was soon engaged in conversation with the stranger. I dont think it any breach of trust to give his name, which was M'Iver, and as he appeared somewhat proud of his adventurous life, he cannot be annoyed at a slight recapitulation of some of its leading events. He began life, he told me, in the East India Company's Service, and flashed his maiden sword as a cadet in the ranks of "*the* Company," the name it was then so well known by. When the service came under the control of her Majesty, M'Iver went to America, and followed a civilian's occupation until the outbreak of the Civil War, when he sided with the South, was present in thirteen or fourteen engagements, was wounded several times, once through the mouth and back of the head, and at the end of the war was in command of a Southern cavalry regiment. During the four years' service in America, Mr. M'Iver had acquired a love for military adventure. He shortly afterwards sailed for Cuba, where he joined the insurgents, was taken prisoner and condemned to be shot the following morning. But his sands had not yet run! A friendly Spanish turnkey, who like Mr. M'Iver was a member of the Masonic Order, opened the prison gates, and like the Apostle Peter, the shackles fell from the limbs of the captive, and he was once more free. A ship commanded by a friendly American, sheltered him, and the adventurous M'Iver was soon safe on Yankee soil again. But his spirits were irrepressible. The Paraguaian War offered some chances for his enterprise and dash. He sailed for Buenos Ayres, and was entrusted with the organization of the Foreign Regiment that was to be raised for service in the Brazilian army. He was just the man for the post. Brave, energetic, and experienced, he quickly formed the irregular mass of foreigners into a compact body, when some dispute occurred between him and the authorities; difficulties became dangers; he was tracked by two desperadoes, by whom he was attacked in the streets, both of whom, however, he killed with a simple sword-cane, the only weapon with which he was at the time armed. After this, other complications occurred, when once more his American nationality stood his friend, and an American ship on which he took shelter refused to surrender him to the Brazilian authorities. The busy haunts of New York echoed to the footsteps of the adventurous Scotchman once more, and he was speculating as to what part of the world would next become his temporary abode. An opportunity soon offered itself. The Pasha of Egypt wanted American officers to teach his troops the art of war according to modern tactics. M'Iver succeeded in obtaining an appointment, with the rank of colonel, a salary equivalent to £600 per annum, and liberal allowance to any relatives who might survive the departed brave, in the event of his turning up his toes in the service of his Highness the Pasha. M'Iver was off to Egypt, had a gorgeous time amongst the descendants of Apollo and of Diana; and he often told me interesting stories of the land where Syrinx was metamorphised into a reed, where lived the great god Pan, Bacchus, and Hercules; and where with surety civilization was nurtured by the puny race, the record of whose achievements, surprise and astonish our *savants* of to-day.

But M'Iver's adventurous spirit found legitimate outlet only upon the field of actual hostilities. He was quite at home amidst the toil and trouble of "grim-visaged war." He loved the bivouac, the night-march, the possible surprise, and took a soldier pride in all its spirit-stirring dangers.

Then the Franco-German war broke out, and the gallant colonel once more thirsted to "follow to the field some warlike lord." He resigned his commission, left for France, and was then full colonel, on the staff. It is, I know, somewhat customary to form a low estimate of the value of such men as Colonel M'Iver. For my part, however, I rather admire such men. Colonel M'Iver is but a type of many such soldiers of fortune. He never drew his sword against a cause which he believed to be a just one, but was ready at all times to aid any country which he considered deserving of his sympathies. No inducement could seduce him to support oppression, and if he sold his services, they were given in good faith, and with the honest desire to serve what he considered, a holy purpose. It would not do, of course, to accept as holy writ all that such a man, and a stranger too, would say about himself, but I afterwards heard the main features of the singular career he recited to me, verified by gentlemen of undoubted veracity. But I was destined to meet Colonel M'Iver again, and shall only take a temporary leave of him.

In the meantime the days passed heavily with us all. We were impatient to be in the field. Our neighbours, the Franc-tireurs, had already gone, and the municipal authorities gave them a brilliant ovation as they were departing. And then our turn came! There were two or three false starts, but orders came at last, and on

"LA COMPAGNIE IRLANDAISE."

the 16th of November, a month all but one day from our arrival in Caen, we were to leave for Bourges, one of the great military arsenals in the centre of France. It was a joyous morning as the men fell in to take their departure. The few who had friends among the townspeople had already bade them adieu. I had made the rounds of my hospitable entertainers in Caen, and all was ready for the start. The men looked admirable uniformed and knapsacked, but as yet without arms or ammunition. The sun burst through a bank of clouds and shed its brilliant rays upon the jaunty *kepis* of the Irish soldiers, while they stood in line with ranks as carefully dressed as if they were preparing for a field day. Around the gate through which we were to pass out of the barracks, the people of the town had assembled in goodly numbers, while the Mobiles who occupied the remainder of the barracks, drew up to give us a farewell salutation. The sergeant-major reported " all ready ;" a few words of command followed, the Irish Volunteers faced the entrance of the barracks, and in another moment they were stepping out towards the gate. Then a cheer which shook the very buttresses of the old building, rose from the ranks, was caught and repeated by the Guard Mobile, was taken up by the people outside, passed on to the ladies who stood in the balconies on our way, and swelled through the usually quiet streets of Caen. " *Vive, vive, l'Irlande,*" shouted a thousand friendly Frenchmen. " *Vive, vive, les Irlandais,*" saluted the ladies from the windows. " *Vive, vive, les Volontaires,*" shouted the assembled multitude, who awaited our departure at the railway. Then the bugles blew, the whistle shrieked, the spacious station was filled with the cheers of the Irish soldiers, and a thousand friendly Frenchmen said, "Good luck, Irishmen, good luck."

CHAPTER III

"A Christian is the highest style of man."
YOUNG.

AWAY once more over the historic plains of Normandy, and the "road of iron" points straight for the Loire. At all the intermediate stations soldiers of every arm of the service crowded the platforms, hurrying to their various destinations. Ladies promenaded the spaces in front of the carriages, anxiously looking out for the "sick or wounded," and when found, administered to their wants with pious solicitude. At every station there appeared to be an organized system of relief for the victims of the war, or for such as the chances *de la guerre* had afflicted. On through Argentin and Alençon, the inland Belfast of France, and at about 4 p.m. we crowded into Le Mans, with all its picturesque interest, its marks of antiquity, its walls, its churches, and its active industry. Amongst the multiplicity of uniforms which caught the eye within the spacious station of Le Mans, the picturesque uniform of the Pontifical Zouaves attracted attention. Their loose grey costume, so elegantly made, their handsome gaiters, their bare necks and soldierly grace, made them in my eyes the best looking, and as events proved, amongst the best of the bravest sons of France. Their heroic conduct at Orleans had already gained respect for the once despised *soldats du Pape*, and afterwards their valour at Patay and Le Mans covered them with glory, and at the end of the war to be a *Zouave Ponti-*

fical, was to be distinguished for steady discipline and splendid valour. I often regretted that circumstances did not throw our lot in with the gallant Pontifical Zouaves, although we had been assured that we were to be attached to a corps, not less distinguished,—the Foreign Regiment,—which was so fearfully decimated at the first battle of Orleans, when out of 1,500 men they lost 1,000 in one day's fighting. But the road was blocked, and we had a few hours to cultivate the acquaintance of the Pontifical Zouaves, and to see what was to be seen in Le Mans. The men had an opportunity of obtaining any luxury within the reach of their miserable pay, and of adding a few cakes or an orange to the scanty contents of their haversacks. Confined in a square, a crowd of the curious soon gathered around *Les Irlandais,* and more than one of the *bourgeois* asked me if there was anything they could do for the men. I would have been glad indeed if some one more generous than the rest had given acceptable refreshments to the men, without consulting me, but I was often reluctantly compelled to say that "the soldiers had all they required." Our stay in Le Mans enabled me to see the town, and examine the splendid cathedral, with its magnificent choir, which is said to be the finest in France. Along the streets, and in all the open spaces, men dressed in the semi-uniform, usual amongst the *Garde Nationale,* hurried to and fro, and impressed me with the conviction that they were as useless as they were unornamental. Near the railway station, however, I came upon a battery of artillery and two mitrailleuse guns, the working of which an artillery officer close by kindly showed me how to perform.

"You see, *monsieur,*" said the artillery officer, when the hood was taken off the gun, "the mitrailleuse is a combination of many guns in one, a number of barrels in one tube; the trajectory is wonderfully flat, and it can discharge 300 balls a minute at a range of 1,700 or 1,800 metres."

"But have not the Germans a mitrailleuse also?" I asked of my informant.

"Oh, yes," he replied, "the Kügelspritzen. I think it is an American gun, which was called the Gatling, and was adopted by the Germans at the commencement of the war. Our gun," he added, placing his hand somewhat affectionately upon the piece, much as a jockey would upon the neck of his favourite racer, "is thought to be an improvement on that. In the Gatling gun I saw in Paris, there were ten barrels, made something like this, to revolve around a central axis, parallel to the bores, by means of a hand crank. As each barrel comes into position, a self primed metal-case cartridge is pushed into its breach by a plunger, and is held there until exploded by the firing pin. The cartridges fall by their own gravity through a hooper as fast as they can be supplied by hand, and the barrels are brought successively into position as fast as they can be turned by the crank."

"Do you think the Gatling superior to the Montigny," I asked, seeing that I had an officer of the regular artillery to speak to, and from whom I might expect a full account of the various weapons then in use.

"Yes," he answered, "the results of the experiments I saw conducted, were in favour of the Gatling. The Montigny has thirty-seven barrels, and yet it has neither the precision nor the rapidity of the Gatling."

"But the Germans have the superiority in field artillery," I said, half questioning, half assuring the artillery officer beside me. Just then the buglers blew the "fall in," and I was compelled to part with my informant. He, however, introduced me to the captain of a battery, who was going to Tours, and I willingly accepted his companionship on the route, indeed I expected to learn some more information about guns and gunnery on our way to the south.

As I moved towards the railway I met Sergeant Terence Byrne, who was evidently amused at some occurrence that had taken place. His usually calm and amiable countenance was beaming with pleasurable excitement, and upon enquiring the cause, he told me that one of the men had obtained permission to leave the square, and had asked him what was "Give me some more sugar" in French. "I," continued Sergeant Byrne, "told him, and as I understand the man soon afterwards went into one of the *cafes* you must have passed, and asked for a 'tasse' of coffee." As usual, the waiter brought two or three small pieces of sugar upon a miniature dish or saucer, and placed them before the sweet-toothed Irishman, who was however dissatisfied with the quantity, and then put his 'give me some more sugar' into requisition. The *garçon* was hurried at the time, and replied '*tout de suite, Monsieur, tout de suite.*' This, the Irishman only partially heard, and he bawled out that it was not 'too sweet, nor half sweet enough,' forgetting that he might as well be speaking Sanscrit to a Newcastle 'pit man' as English to a French waiter. It required all my authority," continued Sergeant Byrne, "to quiet the indignant Irishman, who, in the end, courteously admitted his error, and parted on the best of terms with the surprised *garçon*." In all probability the poor Frenchman has often since bothered his brains in vain endeavours to guess the cause of the Irishman's indignation, and "*tout de suite, tout de suite,*" became a standard joke amongst the Irish soldiers for many a long day afterwards, and with the victim himself, when the sergeant told him that it meant, "Just now, just now."

But we were soon in the railway carriages again, and as the train moved out of Le-Mans at 6 p.m., mutual cheers passed between the Pontifical Zouaves and the Irish Volunteers. I was glad to find that my acquaintance, the artillery officer, who was going to Tours, was seated beside me, and with Lieutenant Cotter, and Dr. Macken, had the carriage to ourselves, as the train rattled on for "Black Angers," as the once capital of Anjou was called. My *compagnon de voyage*, the artillery officer, was instructively communicative, and upon my inquiring if it was true that the Prussian artillery was so much superior to our own, he gave me a lengthened dissertation upon the various claims of the breech and muzzling-loading gun.

" You see," he said, placing the under portion of the forefinger of his right hand upon the under portion of the forefinger of his left hand, and using them as a kind of mechanical lever to impress the force of his reasoning the more effectually upon one's memory. " The Prussian artillery is entirely breech-loading, while ours is as entirely muzzle-loading. But I do not think it is on that account that the Prussians are superior. It is because of their greater weight, and consequent longer range, that has given the Germans the advantage in all our artillery duels. They have managed to use heavier guns than ours, but I am still of opinion, that for field artillery, or, indeed, for all artillery, that muzzle-loaders are the best. There is a powerful simplicity in a solid gun, which appears, as far as artillery science yet enables us to judge, incompatible with a breech-loader. At Sedan, however, our artillery had practically ceased to exist before the close of the fight. The fact is, the Germans seldom engage our infantry, before they try and crush us with a shower of projectiles. And now things are worse, when the majority of our artillery is manned by Mobiles, who only shoot the cannon, while the Germans aim. On the march the German infantry generally skirt the roads in small parties close together, leaving the highway for the artillery and baggage waggons, an order analagous to that of a battalion in battle. The method is more fatiguing, but the march is effected at once ; time is gained, and the formation of the line is more rapid."

" But are there no breech-loading guns in our artillery ?" I asked, anxious to know if the French depended entirely upon the muzzle-loading system.

"Oh, yes," replied the artillery officer, "some of our heaviest siege guns, throwing enormous shells three feet long, are breech-loaders, grooved on the 'Stead' principle. The German shells are coated in lead, and, in their passage through the gun, the lead is forced from off that portion which is cut by the grooves. They generally use the percussion fuse, which, however, is somewhat defective. If the ground is soft, the German shells often strike without exploding, and it requires the shell to strike its nose against some hard substance to insure an explosion. The Germans, too, carry their artillery reserve men into action on axle-tree seats, by which means they secure a full supply of trained gunners; while we," he added, with a peculiar shrug of his shoulders, and a slight pouting of his lips, "carry them on the waggons, which is by no means as convenient, nor as safe."

"But we have the advantage in small arms, at least," I said, anxious to catch some ray of hope from the general gloom.

"I don't know that," said the artillery officer, much to my surprise. "The weapons we are getting now are of inferior metal, and their superior range only tempts the unsteady Mobiles to throw away their ammunition at long ranges. The German gun is only sighted for 800 metres, while the Chassepot is sighted for 1,200. But it is a doubtful advantage in the hands of troops only partially disciplined. Besides, after 10 or 12 rounds the breech of the Chassepot becomes clogged with a thick, fatty, substance, proving that the cartridges do not clean the barrel *in transitu*. The breech of the Needle-gun or the Dreysa, also becomes coated a little, but not near so much as the Chassepot. The cartridges of our guns, as you are aware, are enveloped in a fine linen cloth, with a superabundance of grease, while the German cartridges are enveloped in paper, which leaves the breech cleaner and more easily worked. After a few rounds from the Chassepot the breech must be wet, either by water, or snow, or by spittle, or even by wine from the men's *beacons*, in order to allow the "*Garde Mobile*" to work with any kind of order. But the trajectory of the Chassepot is flatter, it is much lighter, and it is, mechanically, a much more ingenious weapon, than the clumsy Dreysa.

"But I have heard that the Bavarian Werder Rifle, is much superior to the Prussian Zündnadelgewehr?" I said.

"Oh much," he replied, "Its calibre is smaller, its range is greater, its fire more accurate, and its construction more simple."

But day wore into night, and still the train dashed on through the dark damp atmosphere, while my companions and myself, by common accord, rolled in our regimental great-coats, each seeking a corner of the carriage, and courted the drowsy god. Station after station was passed in the gloom, and ever and anon the shouts and songs from out of the long line of carriages filled with troops, swelled away upon the calm, moist air. Above the rest, the strains of Irish National songs were often distinguishable, and the soul-stirring air of O'Donnell-a-boo, often blended in melodious revelry, with the revolutionary, spirit-stirring, Marseillaise. Occasional stoppages *en route*, gave rise to speculation, and at one place, two of the Irish Volunteers having missed the train, were left behind, penniless and friendless in the heart of France. I often thought the adventures of those men would form an interesting chapter to a compiler of the realities of the war; but I afterwards heard that, one of them was reported shot at Orleans, and that the other was attached to the staff of some Colonel in Tours. The earliest streaks of daybreak, however, still found us hurrying on. Away over the fertile valley of the Loire, on, on, the road of iron still points for Tours, where Gambetta then ruled it with dictatorial sway. But the day had scarcely burst into "all truthful light," when the train gradually slacked its speed, and the numerous railway tracks gave us assurance that we were at Tours, the charms of which I afterwards thought were greatly overrated. A walk about the town gave me an opportunity of seeing the *renaissance* style of architecture with which the city abounds, and of recalling its historic associations, as one of the league of 64 Gallic towns, which under Vercingetorix opposed the devastating march of Julius Cæsar, and as a place associated with Mary Queen of Scots, and her short lived husband Francis. But I had a more interesting spectacle to witness in the chief town of d'Indre et Loire. When the Irish soldiers drew up in front of the platform in the early grey of that November morning, there were enough of stragglers about to note the strange words of command, and to ask curious questions as to the land of our nativity, our local habitation, and our name. We had still a few hours before us in the train, which was not to start until 7 a.m., and the men had to find cold comfort huddled together on the platform, with nothing but a hard biscuit, and perhaps a small piece of sausage, to cheer and warm the inner man. It was the first rough night experienced by the Irish soldiers since they left Havre. But there was not even a grumble, although many a poor fellow was shivering with cold, and could have ravenously devoured the contents of his haversack at a meal, but that for the next two days he would have had to resort to the Indian method of appeasing hunger, and take "a reef in his waistbelt," as one of the men, Timothy Marks, once characteristically explained. Marks was an old soldier, and had constituted himself the lawyer of the company. He looked the creation of Marryat's Snarleyow, if, indeed, the creature was masculine instead of feline. But he was a good campaigner, full of life and obedience, but thoroughly disgusted at all the evidence of disorganization which he saw around him. I saw Marks looking in through a window, and passing some jocular remarks to a crowd of Irishmen who had gathered around him under the shelter of the railway station, and just as I passed I heard the significant remark, "Well, are these such wonderful looking men as to frighten the life of an ordinary mortal," and peeping over the heads of the crowd I saw a number of Bavarians inside the room, their "shoe brush" helmets indicating the land of their nativity. A guard of Franc-tireurs was stationed at the door, a few more moved amongst the prisoners inside, and my uniform having obtained for me an *entree*, I moved about amongst the captive soldiers. I think there were about 80 men in all. The majority of them were lying on the boards, their heads resting on the legs of their comrades, in a kind of mutual support, much as the handles of four cups, can be placed in the bowls of the vessels, to the security and uniformity of all. There were two officers in the group, and although even at the distance of a few yards, their uniform was scarcely distinguishable from that of their men, their erect carriage, and their easy and dignified movements at once proclaimed their positions. One of them was wounded, and the calm, solicitous, but undemonstrative attention which he received from his companion, was touchingly attractive. I do not wish to make an insidious comparison, but I confess to a warm and respectful impression left upon my memory, by the manly, unostentatious, and dignified demeanour of those two young men, one of whom had an undressed wound of a painful and irritating nature.

But the scene had its reverse picture. Amongst the prisoners there was one poor wretch sitting upright in a corner of the room, and indulging in a swinging movement of his body, which can be best described by calling it by the familiar term of a see-saw. He had lost his helmet, and had substituted a night cap which might have been white, but which then resembled in colour, a dried herring. Correctly speaking the night cap had no colour, and might have turned out any shade, if subjected to the process usual of the washtub. Streaks of blood traced channels adown his cheek, and hardened into crustations upon his face, while he all the time kept piteously whining for mercy. He looked the antithesis of Campbell's hero, who "charged with all the chivalry" of Munich at the battle of Leipsic. But that man was an exception to his class. The

Bavarians appeared to feel the calm demeanour of their officers extending to themselves. They were all well and serviceably clad. The strong half boots they wore were a marked contrast to the *paper-machie* shoes, no stockings, and cotton gaiters of the French soldiers; the great coats, too, were warm and comfortably made; while the great coats of the French troops were thinner in material, and less suited for the exigencies of a campaign. I noticed, too, that the Germans had warm flannels under their tunics, while the French had nothing but cotton shirts beneath their shell jackets. The French were gaily, the Germans were servicably, clad. There was more neatness in the choice of colours in the one; there was more practical utility in the other. The Bavarians had been captured at the fighting around Orleans, at the re-capture of which, we should have taken part, but for the distracted state of the military departments, the heads of which appeared to be all in confusion. The Franc-tireurs who had captured the Bavarians, said they would "do for them," as they would be done by, if they had come under the tender mercies of the German foe."

"They would shoot us, *M. le Capitaine*," said a Franc-tireur to me upon the platform of the railway station at Tours; "and why not return the compliment by sending them to their reckoning." But it was the utterance of an irresponsible man, and I afterwards heard that the Bavarians expressed themselves much satisfied with the treatment they received.

But 7 a.m., came at last, the Irish Volunteers filed into the train, and we were soon bowling along through the vineyards of Cher. Vierzon with its associations of Richard I., of England, and of the Black Prince, who pillaged the town in the middle of the fourteenth century, was soon passed and then we quickly rattled into Bourges, our destination for the time being. To fall in on the platform, and under the direction of a soldier who undertook our escort, to move on through the town, with a few idlers upon our flanks, vaguely guessing as to what part of the habitable earth we came from, occupied but a few minutes. The worthy official whose duty it was to provide for our subsistence and quarters, appeared troubled at our arrival, and it required no secrets from his prison house, to see that he was unprepared for the rush of troops that was constantly pouring into the capital of Cher. Bourges was, indeed, full of soldiers ; and their various officers were patiently waiting for the *Intendance*, to allot quarters to their respective commands. Linesmen, Artillerymen, Cuirassiers, Franc-tireurs, Mobiles, and all branches of the army were represented around the *Intendance bureau*. At last we got our papers, and it transpired that we were to be quartered in some sheds near the railway station, and which had just been erected by a detachment of men who left several of their numbers behind from small-pox.

"The *Intendance* is remarkably attentive," said Dr. Macken, placing an accent on the word "mark," which made it unpleasantly suggestive of *petite verole*.

The quarters of the men were by military courtesy called "barracks," but they were indeed unworthy of the name. Gaps wide enough to admit of the passage of a Chassepot, divided the narrow planks of which the "barracks" were built. Through every part of the sheds, the cold frosty air penetrated with benumbing effect. The cold was more severe than I ever remember experiencing in Ireland, and the only protection the soldiers had was a miserable single blanket, about four feet by three. It was satire to call such a rag a *couverture*. It was not large enough to envelope an ordinary man from the waist downwards, while the body was left completely at the mercy of a frost ten degrees below zero. Caen was Paradise to Bourges. The cold, too, continued to increase in intensity, and the misery of the men became proportionably greater. The inexperienced soldiers thought that they had arrived at that "lowest depth," while the experienced gravely shook their heads with ominous forebodings. The officers were, as usual, allowed to find quarters in town, a duty generally undertaken by the orderlies, who foraged for lodgings while the officers were occupied arranging the disposition of the company.

In the meantime the chequered fortunes of France appeared to be changing for the better. No serious defeat had befallen her armies since the army of the Loire had shown such vital energy in front of Orleans. But that fatality which followed the fortune of *La Grande Natione,* still pursued the armies of France even in their victories. D'Aurelles de Paladine had shown that he was a man well acquainted with the theory of war. The disposition of his forces before and after his successes in November are admitted on all sides to have been judicious. But he wanted dash! He wanted that energy of spirit which surmounts obstacles, and removes impediments with unfaltering determination. He was, in fact, too prudent, and showed an utter lack of that keen perception, of that aptitude to grasp an opportunity, of which all great generals are made. D'Aurelles de Paladine had the trump card of all the French commanders during the war, but he proved incapable in the hour of trial. If he was a dashing general, the siege of Paris would, in all probability, have been raised. His forces were superior to the enemy, even after Prince Frederick Charles, and the Duke of Mecklenburgh had reinforced Von der Tann. The after conduct of General D'Aurelles de Paladine has generally been pronounced faulty, and his whole career is a strange mixture of theory and error. From the 25th of November, disaster after disaster overtook the army of the Loire. On the 3rd December, Orleans was recaptured by the Germans, and the troops under D'Aurelles de Paladine were in full retreat towards Bourges Vierzon, and Tours. General Ducrot had crossed the Marne, and had for two days fought the investing army of Paris with varying successs. Rouen was occupied by the Germans on the 5th and the enemy was already manœuvering around Havre. Garabaldi had a small success at Autun; but the situation of France was almost hopeless. Day by day I had been expecting the route. We had became so weary of quarters that I made a personal application to the General in command of Bourges to be sent into the field, and we were under orders to join the Foreign Regiment at Orleans, when the news of the disaster reached us. Why we were detained in Bourges was always a mystery to me. We could have participated in the fighting around Orleans, had the military authorities thought proper to send us to our regiment, instead of allowing us to become "blue mouldy" in our quarters. We had been assigned a place with the Foreign Regiment. We were to form one company in that corps, preserving our nationality as a company intact. Officers, non-commissioned officers, and men, were to be left as they originally stood. But the disasters of the army of the Loire were quickly visible in Bourges.

I was standing in front of our quarters in the early days of December, when the first dribblets of the routed 15th Corps appeared at the further end of the town, having come pell-mell from Orleans. Dr. Macken, Lieutenant M'Alevey, Lieutenant Cotter, and myself, were together, and as the miserable gangs of soldiers huddled passed us, we were moved to compassion for their misfortunes. Many of the men's feet were tied up in the folds of the patches of tent cloth. Clotted blood stained the rags that enveloped them. The clothes of the men, in some cases, hung in tatters from their persons, and old dirty handkerchiefs were tied around many of their heads. Numbers appeared without their packs, and even a few without arms or ammunition. "No eye hath ever seen such scarecrows," said Mr. M'Alevey. "Even Falstaff's ragged regiment with its one shirt made of two napkins tacked together, could not have been a more motley crew. Those Mobiles," he continued, with something akin to admiration in his tone; "are a fine looking lot of men, but I hear that some of them are as dangerous to their friends as to their enemies."

"Yes" said Dr. Macken, "the aphorism of Richelieu, that—

> 'In the lexicon of youth,
> There is no such word as Fail,'

may stir those men to accomplish something yet."

"I like the pithy aphorism of Louis the Eleventh better than that," replied Mr. M'Alevey—

> 'It is not the Lion's skin
> France needs: but the Fox's

It is organization and diplomacy that will save the country."

The defeated soldiers looked, however, hardy enough to encounter any storm. Their faces were bronzed to a sombre hue, but their miserable shoes were melting from off their feet, and their entire condition was wretched in the extreme. But it might be our own fate any day.

The regiment which we were to join had retreated on Bourges, and with the rest of the 15th Corps hurried on to the encampment outside the town. It was to us a matter of much congratulation that we were to form part and parcel of the regular army, and not to be attached to any of the hundred nondescript corps which were organized for the defence of the country.

I must have been "Methodizing" on some such subject, a few days after the retreat of the 15th Corps through Bourges, for I only indistinctly heard a gentleman, who stood suddenly before me, and begging a "thousand apologies," asked if "we were the Irish Volunteers?" I, of course, answered in the affirmative, and immediately found my hand in the unceremonious but friendly grip of my newly-found acquaintance. He turned out to be a man of some importance in Bourges, and eagerly asked the officers to come and accept the hospitality of his table on the following day. "For" said he in broken English, "I am married to an Irish lady, and she has been charmed to see your soldiers march to Mass so regularly every Sunday morning." This sealed the matter. We all accepted the invitation, and found a goodly assembly of the *elite* of the town to meet us under the hospitable roof of our entertainer. The religious demeanour of the Irish soldiers had charmed the Catholic people of Bourges, and they were determined to mark their appreciation of our conduct after a fashion of their own. They knew we were about to join our regiment in the field in a few days, and they resolved upon a religous ceremonial in the magnificent cathedral, on the following Sunday. Our Irish lady friend, assisted by her amiable daughters, and some sympathetic neighbours, had one hundred scapulars of the *Sacre Cœur* made for presentation to the men. The ecclesiastical authorities entered warmly into the spirit of the demonstration. The Prince Archbishop of Bourges received the officers of the corps in the palace, and spoke in warm and generous tones of the attachment between France and Ireland. He spoke of the memories of the Old Brigade, and touched our hearts by the fervour of his utterances. The accomplished prelate appeared to be deeply touched by the memory of the half-million of Irishmen who had lost their lives for France, from the time of the campaign in Flanders in 1691, to the last record of the Brigade at the end of the eighteenth century. Then France was triumphant and held the nations of Europe in perpetual awe. But the "sweet uses of adversity" had "proved Ireland to be the best friend of France in the hour of her humiliation, and France could never forget the generous offerings and spirited devotedness of *Les braves Irlandais.*" And so we were feasted with utterances which fell deep into the crevices of of our memories, and which to this day, the few who heard them, remember with pleasure, and still treasure with venerable esteem.

But Sunday came ! The magnificent cathedral was thronged with the bourgeoise of the town. The splendid flight of steps approaching the finely recessed portal, ornamented with bas-reliefs in

rows of niches, were crowded with people who came to see the spectacle. It was a solemn scene! After Mass was celebrated, the Irish Volunteers were brought inside the spacious railings under the altar. The exquisite colour which was produced by the great quantity of stained glass, threw a singularly mellow light upon the kneeling ranks of the Irishmen, as they bent in pious fervour before the altar. The immense length of the interior of the cathedral, unbroken by transepts, was sufficiently well filled to give additional interest and *eclat* to the solemn ceremony. An old clergyman who undertook the distribution of the scapulars, could only speak a little English, but the utterances of the pious man appeared to sink deeper into the hearts of the kneeling soldiers, as the words were but faintly, and inarticulately spoken. There were, no doubt, amongst the people who thronged the Church some sceptical souls who sneered at the giver and the receiver of what to them was a piece of cloth and nothing more; but the calm demeanour and religious fervour which animated those Irish soldiers must have impressed them with the assurance that soldierly devotion, and Christian piety, ever go hand in hand. As the old priest passed the scapular over each man's head, he made a bold effort to pronounce some English phrase—
"Vous are no longer strangers; vous are Frenchmen," he said, as one after the other received the sacred gift, and felt happier for its reception. Yes, no matter whether sceptical manhood does or does not believe in that sacred influence which Catholics attach to everything calling to mind the life of Him who suffered for our common humanity; no matter whether or not, the non-Catholic would regard those holy emblems as deserving of respect, there is the incontestible fact, that an *Agnus Dei* or a *Sacre Cœur* very often affects the conduct and character of men so much, as to draw them from evil into good. Let non-Catholics call it a superstition or what they may, yet the broad fact remains, that with a certain class of people these sacred emblems work much good, and tend to the puri-

fication of their general conduct. Apart altogether from any spiritual effect which Catholics believe there is attendant upon those possessions, there is the purely secular result of placing a check upon unlicensed thought and act, by the associations of the scapular. The Catholic Irishmen who that day knelt at the foot of the splendid altar in the Cathedral of Bourges, were better men, and certainly were not the worse soldiers for the possession of the *Sacre Cœur*. The effect of the ceremony on the by-standers was marked, and many French soldiers, Regulars, Mobiles, and Franctireurs, knelt in pious worship before the altar, and begged a few scapulars that still remained in the hands of the priest. But the ceremony was soon over, the company left the church, fell in before the massive doorways, and were soon quickly marching through the town, their regular steps, neatly dressed sections, and erect bearing, contrasting singularly enough with the loping gait of the French soldiers.

"Would you like to see the cannon factory?" asked my hospitable entertainer, the husband of our Irish friend, the morning after our reception at the cathedral, and the day before our departure for the field. I replied in the affirmative, and a little walk to the outskirts of the town brought us to the great arsenal of Bourges. Papers were duly inspected at the gate, the governor of the arsenal kindly condescended to show us over the building, and to point out the different phases in the manufacture in field and siege artillery. The casting and boring of brass guns was minutely shown to us by the governor; but there was a listless expression upon his countenance, as if each day might herald the advent of the devastating Germans, who, under Prince Frederick Charles, were reported as advancing on Bourges.

"Your corps is, I believe, the 15th," he said, turning to me as I was watching a great block of brass turning slowly and steadily around. "You will, probably, be retained for the defence of

Bourges, as we cannot afford to let this foundry fall into the enemies' hands."

Upon this subject I was, however, in perfect darkness; and then the governor took up the talking, and I was glad to obtain information from a man who was, no doubt, well informed.

"Of course you know that the army of the Loire is now divided into two commands, and that Bourbaki has been given one half, and Chanzy the other," he continued, as we walked through the arsenal.

"So I have heard," I replied. "But what do you think of Bourbaki?" I asked.

"Well, he's a type of what is known as the *furieux Francais* a man who creates difficulties in order to surmount them; but as a strategist, he is an untried man," replied the governor.

"And of Chanzy," I ventured to ask, fearing however, that he might hesitate to draw invidious comparison.

"Oh, Chanzy?" he said without a shadow of reserve, "Chanzy has shown more military capacity than any general who has as yet been tried on the Loire. It was he who really won the battle of Coulmiers, on the 9th of November, and it was the left wing under his command that fought at Patay on the 1st of December—the only creditable performance of the army of the Loire in several days previous to its retreat from before Orleans. It was at Patay, too, that the Pontifical Zouaves covered themselves with glory; when for hours the gallant battalion, only 600 strong, under the shadow of their sacred flag, stemmed the tide of a perfect avalanche of Germans. Chanzy has turned at bay now, and is, as no doubt you know, fighting with bull-dog ferocity, refusing to acknowledge himself beaten, and leaving a large tract of country strewed with dying and with dead. The Duke of Mecklenburgh and Von der Tann, are pressing him with desperate persistency, but Chanzy is proving himself to be fully a match for his foes, and only the other day he, by a singularly creditable movement, extricated himself from a dangerous position." And so our distinguished informant went on, and seemed quite at home as he discussed every phase of the war.

"Is it true, as reported, that Herr Krupp has manufactured a balloon gun, with a horizontal range of 2000 feet?" I asked.

"Well, I have heard something of it," replied the governor. "And, indeed, I see no great difficulty in the way of making such a gun, particularly as the Germans require them so much about Paris. Indeed ballooning, as an art of war, is still in its infancy. With a telegraphic communication from the aeronaut to *terra firma*, balloons should be of immense service, until counter balloons come and engage in deadly strife in mid air. And 'great will be the fall thereof,' as I think your Shakspeare says, if one of the combatants come headlong to the ground." And the speaker indulged in that quiet humour which often prompts men to smile at imaginary disaster.

But evening was settling in, and we took our departure, after partaking of the welcome refreshments in the governor's house. The cathedral stood before us; its massive body throwing a sombre hue around, while its giant towers stood out against the already fading day, like the huge sentinels raising their anxious heads high above their slumbering companions around. A bitter wind swept the open space in front of the church, and dashed in fretful gusts adown the narrow thoroughfares of the town. Under the shadow of the cathedral I had to part my guide: he to seek comfort in the bosom of his family, I to the quarters of the men, to see that all was right for the night. Yes, all was right with the Irish Volunteers! The cold swept through the embrasures of the wooden structure sufficiently strong and bitter to cause the hardiest campaigner to chatter his teeth in a kind of frosty melody.

"The cows in those parts should give ice cream," I heard a soldier say to a companion, as they bent over the last flickering effort of a fire in the throes of death.

"Yes, that 'ill come to pass," said Timothy Marks, who joined the shivering pair, "when the Millennium, I have heard preached of, comes showering milk, honey, happiness, and whiskey on our heads."

"What is the Millennium, Marks," said a broad-shouldered Tipperary man, Timothy Larkin, as he seriously scanned the countenance of the quizzical Marks.

"The Millennium ? Is it chafing me you are, Larkin," replied Marks, half doubtingly. "Well, at all events, the Millennium is the time when the lion is going to lie down in peace and harmony with the lamb."

"Then, bedad, I think we will have the ice-cream from the cows before that; for I suspect when the lion comes to move, the lamb would be missing," replied Larkin, with the self-satisfied expression of a man who had placed a period to all discussion upon a doubtful question. I paused beside the door sufficiently long to hear just that one repartee from amidst the men who thronged the frail shelter, and then as I turned to leave for my lodgings in the town, the sergeant of the week, Frank Byrne, stood before me with the melancholy intelligence, that one of the company, Laurence Breen, had that day died of small-pox.

The first of the Irish Volunteers had died for France! If Laurence Breen had fell amidst the pomp and circumstances of glorious war; if he had died while facing the foe; while marching to the grave "with military glee," he could not have rendered up his life more truly for France than he did in the small-pox ward of the hospital at Bourges. There is, indeed, a savage, but still human satisfaction in selling life so dearly that, even in defeat, it makes the enemy purchase a Cadmean triumph. But the sacrifice is all the same ; and the record of the "died in hospital," is not, or at least should not be, a less brilliant or less melancholy roll, than the list of " killed and wounded." To go down amidst the intoxicating shout of victorious troops, to feel the dull, heavy "thud" of the messenger of death, while all around

> "Battle's magnificiently stern array,"

spur on the faltering, and give life and energy to the conduct of the brave, may be a more glorious end to a soldier's career, than to render up life in the calm, still exclusion of an hospital ward. "But it is all the same," as I heard somebody say, when speculating upon a similar topic. "Be merry, and wise, and sing,

> 'King death is a rare old fellow,
> He sits where no sun does shine,
> He lifts up his hand so yellow,
> And he pours out his coal black wine.'"

Away with reverie, for the next morning, the 12th of December, we were to be in the field.

Then the hurry of departure followed. The little quarters of the Irish Volunteers was soon alive with the bustle of preparation, and as the men fell in, I detected a really pleased expression trace itself like a wave of satisfaction, along the entire line. Fully armed and equipped for the field, the Irish soldiers looked admirable indeed. Their neat gaiters were as white as the flakes of snow which very gently fell upon the quarters the men had just vacated. Their Chassepots were clean in every part, and 90 rounds of ammunition were safely secured in the pouch of each of the men. Their tins, and pots, and cooking utensils were all in order, and then a word of command, another, and another, and we passed out of our temporary shelter, to take our chances in the field. On through Bourges, marching to the stirring strains of "God save Ireland," while the people of the town gape with distended eyes at the martial bearing of the Irish Volunteers; on through narrow streets where ladies wave an adieu, which the officers return. The Artillery Barracks were reached, one hundred stragglers of the regiment taken up, and then away once more, wading through lanes of gun carriages, through muddy roads, and then the country opens, the men march at ease, and we feel that, at last, our hands are actually on the handles of the plough.

CHAPTER IV.

> "One murder made a villain,
> Millions a hero. Princes are privileged
> To kill, and numbers sanctified the crime."
> BEILLEY PORTEUS.

AWAY over the muddy roads which skirt the river Cher. Away to new scenes and to new associations. Dead and dying horses occasionally dot the way, while groups of famished soldiers hacked at the still warm carcases with ravenous haste. The quivering flesh of poor Dobbin was being hewn into patches by the hungry soldiers of the army of the Loire. The flesh on the hind quarters of the dead horses, was in nearly every case cut from off the bones, and from out the steaming kettles which were everywhere visible, the savoury odour of hashed *cheval* flavoured the sharp keen air. The troops were encamped on either side of the road, and the small dirty weather-beaten tents, skirted our route deep into the woods beyond; columns of smoke from 20,000 camp fires darkened the atmosphere, and hung like a pall over the encampment. The voice of 100,000 men raised around the place, a noise such as an angry sea makes, as it rolls in crested violence against the shore. But our Brigade was at the furthest end of the encampment. On to La Chappelle through broken fields, and thousands of *tentes d'abris* where the brouzed coun tenances of the hardy soldiers, looked with compassion upon the clean gaiters, polished accoutrements, and shining appurtenances of the Irish Volunteers. There was something stirring and splendidly real, in the appearance of the soldiers, between whose lines we hurried on to find our own Brigade. At last our division, the 1st of the 15th Corps, was found, and then our Brigade, the 2nd, and then our regiment, encamped upon a slimy soil, to which the men appeared quite accustomed. Behind the encampment the tall spires of the Church of St. Chappelle reared its graceful head, while the setting sun imparted a dazzling brilliancy to the windows of the church and convent, in which my fancy saw a type of ardent Christian faith, that can make life endurable under the most trying circumstances. *There* was peace and contentment—here was war and misery. *There* pious men trod the paths of virtue to the grave—here men, intoxicated and maddened with sights and deeds of carnage, trod the ground where the soil was fattened with the flesh and blood of humanity. But away with philosophical cant. I have but little faith in "Adversity's sweet milk," when applied to present ailment.

> "Live to-day, to-morrow's sun never yet,
> On any human being rose or set."

We had scarcely drawn up in our *alignment* when the Colonel Canat, with three or four officers around him, was seen walking quickly towards us, and then he extended to me his hand, and gave it an unusually vigorous shake for a Frenchman.

"You are welcome," he said looking up to me with a warm expression tracing its lines around his handsome and weather-beaten face. "I have been expecting you for some time. You should have been at Orleans, only I suppose, as usual, the *Intendance* did not know what to do with you. How many men have you, *Capitaine?*" he added, glancing at the stalwart ranks of the Irish Volunteers with an expression which I thought bore some evidence of admiration upon its lines.

"Just one hundred, *mon Colonel*," I replied, moving with him to the right of the company which I saw he was about to inspect.

"Oh, you Irishmen are very big men. Now, I suppose you know that you are to act as a company in my regiment. You are to be *La Compagnie Irlandaise*, or Ze Irish Cumpanee," and the old man laughed at his attempt to articulate a few English words. A trace of pleasantness passed over the features of the French officers around, and then moved by some spirit of brotherly fraternity which influences comrades in arms, they all shook hands with myself, my lieutenants, and the doctor. And then, too, our new *Commandant* appeared upon the scene. He was a chubby little man, with a countenance brimful of cheerfulness, and his rotundity of person indicated very plainly his antipathy to a rigid observance of the fast. Obesity may not, indeed hardly ever is, the result of gluttony, but then there is a satisfied expression over the countenances of men whose appetite is appeased and whose soul is animated with a desire to carry off the first prize in the estimation of the *cuisinier*. That night, however, the *Commandant* invited the Irish officers to accept the hospitality of his quarters, and the share of the contents of his camp-kettle. Rumour, indeed, whispered strange stories of our *Commandant*, and said that he frequently suffered from the influence of "wet groceries," as one of the men of *La Compagnie Irlandaise* interpreted the common phrase "tipsy." But Herodotus tells us that the ancient Persians had a custom of devising their political (and, perhaps, military) schemes, while inebriated, and of executing them when sober. So our *Commandant* may have been wise in his generation, while he was certainly an exception to all the French officers with whom I came in contact. Yet he had his virtues, upon which, however, he did not place sufficient reliance to bring their own reward. I suppose it was the correct etiquette for the *Com-*

mandant to invite the Irish officers to his table, and that it was equally correct for the Irish officers to accept the offer, as their camp service was not in the best of working order. It may be un friendly to speak disparagingly of a man's entertainer; but if I am to criticize the military capacity of my chiefs, I fear I cannot pass the *Commandant* of the 5th battalion of the Foreign Regiment, without a word of censure. But the entertainment was not an encounter with a deadly foe, and our host conducted the attack and covered the retreat, over the various *entrees*, with splendid judgment and with unfaltering energy. The little cottage was, too, like all French cottages, neat and orderly. A handsome walnut chest of drawers, a large walnut wardrobe, well stocked with linen and calico, two neatly furnished beds, and a look of cleanliness about all the culinary appointments, gave an air of comfort and thriftiness to the kitchen. There was, however, another room, where everything was more handsomely arranged, and ponderous curtains, shadowed a bed which looked deep enough to swallow our little *Commandant*, beyond his depth in feathers. All those things were new to us, but they were familiar to our host. We improved the occasion by finding out our position in the regiment, and it seemed as quite a matter of course that we should be the last company in the regiment.

"You see," said the little man, looking at us with the air of an experienced soldier, "there are five battalions in our Regiment, but only the 1st, 2nd, and 5th, are in France, the other two are still in Algiers, the men being principally composed of Germans, the Government would not trust them here."

To an enquiry of mine, the *Commandant* told me that there were eight companies in each battalion, and that on an average, the number of men ranged from a minimum of 80 to a maximum of 160. This gave the commander of a battalion in the French army more men than the Colonel of an English Regiment, although not half so pompous as the latter dignitary. But the viands were discussed, the candles burned down, our *Commandant* appeared desirous to seeking his couch, and we left for our quarter escorted by our host's orderly.

The night was as dark as Erebus, and it was not without some difficulty that we succeeded in navigating our way among the numerous baggage-waggons which encumbered all the arteries of the village. At last, however, our quarters were reached. Four of us were to occupy two beds in an upper chamber of a dilapidated inn, the under portion of which was crammed with Mobiles, stretched out upon the boards in all conceivable attitudes, from the "spread eagle," to the "teaspoon." A sickly tallow candle illuminated our quarters, and just made its filthy beds perceptible to the eye. M'Alevey rolled over the scanty blankets, and handling the pillow swore, that it was a most unsightly "knapsack for a soldier," and it was not until the witticism had travelled to the roots of my hair, that I acknowledged the "*bon mot.*"

"Never mind, Mac," said the doctor, tumbling into his bed with that ready assurance which speaks of a man determined to look at the brightest side of the picture. "Never mind, Mac," he repeated; "you'll find no difficulty in napping upon it;" and then he rolled the bed clothes over his head, and very soon a vigorous snore announced that he was in dreamland. Mr. Cotter extinguished the light, and all was quiet, save, indeed, what some German author calls "the artillery of sleep."

The *reveille* was sounded under our dilapidated quarters the following morning before daybreak; and so groping in the dark we frequently cannoned against one another, and ultimately hurried out, and made our way to the encampment, where sickly fires were already sending spiral columns of smoke up through the calm, still, cold atmosphere. A hurried repast of biscuits and coffee, the regiment moved on, and we stepped out to take our first long march.

The soldiers of "*La Compagnie Irlandaise*" did not look altogether in holiday attire after their first night upon the slimy soil near St. Chappelle. The stains of the campaign had already begun to leave their marks upon the uniforms of the men, but the jovial indomitable spirit of their race was still visible in their countenances as they stood in line preparatory to their first day's actual work. The bugles blew, and the men moved on, the Irish soldiers in rear, as the last company of the last battalion of the *Regiment Etranger*.

Over the broken fields, torn up with our train of waggons, into the village close by, and then the "halt" was sounded, while the road appeared blocked with troops. We were still only a few miles from Bourges, and the grand old towers of the Cathedral stood well out against the clear atmosphere of Central France. The sky was of a pale blue, and painfully transparent, as it caused the eyes to blink when looking into space. The sun appeared bright in its weakness, for no intervening clouds darkened its disc. Looking across the deserted encampment, thousands of smouldering fires were sending up small columns of smoke, which contrasted against the forest of evergreens beyond; the village dogs were prowling about the place, and an occasional bird of prey would swoop on pinioned wings over the plain. The day before nearly 100,000 men had encamped between the village where we halted and Bourges, and now we were the last of the army of the Loire that had not departed. The road was blocked with troops, and we had to bide our time. "*Sac-a-terre! Sac-a-terre!*" blew out the regimental bugles, and the men took off their packs and passed the time as best they could. Even after so short a march, a halt was needful. The men's boots were so wretchedly bad, that the pebbles worked into them after the first kilometre had been passed over, and every halt was utilised by bandaging blistered feet, or stuffing wads of old garments into the gaping holes in the shoes. I was sitting on a soldier's knapsack, when Lieutenant Cotter touched me on the

"LA COMPAGNIE IRLANDAISE."

shoulder, calling my attention to a pale young Frenchman, who was wrapping his frozen feet in some mashed turnips, which he had begged from a neighbouring house; the flesh was almost falling from the bones and it was only by the aid of a companion that he could finish the sickly task. The shoes were tied under the feet like a sandal, and the soldier took his rifle and limped away, for march he should, every man was wanted, and above all the men who had seen so much of the tough work as he and his comrades of the Foreign Regiment had. It had not come to that with any of my men yet, but that pale young Frenchman was but the precursor of many an Irish soldier whom I afterwards saw in the same plight. Somehow, I gave way to the refuge of thought—reverie—that 13th of December, 1870. I thought not of home, but of friends; not of hearths, but of hearts; not of places so much as of people, and was gone into the reminiscences of the past, when that villanous regimental bugle went off again.

"That's for the sergeant of the week," said Lieutenant Cotter, counting the three notes at the end of the call.

Away down the battalion a murmur of voices was heard, and came nearer, until at last it reached the head of the Irish company. Ah! there was the explanation, as the sergeant of the week appeared with a bundle of letters and papers under his arm. "*Billets, billets*" shouted the Frenchmen; "letters, letters," said the Irishmen, and soon the sergeant was surrounded with a hundred eager faces, each hoping, yet almost dreading, for news from the dear old land. Then followed the oft-told tale—"Mother's dead, Katty's married, or Jimmy's gone away," or perhaps the affectionate little colleen, who had sworn fidelity and love, had ceased to entertain any recollection but "remembrance" of the past, had forgotten her pledge, and told the lover that he should forget it too.

Somehow I fancy that soldiering develops all the sentiments of our nature. In his natural state man is essentially a sentimental being. It is our civilization that makes us cynics; it is our refinement develops the criticism of doubt. But war against his kind is certainly not opposed to the instincts of man, and he becomes less artificial when engaged in the bloody game. There may be nothing of sentimental romance in sleeping in a scooped-out snow-drift, living on half rations, or marching with bleeding feet and broken shoes ov.r the jagged edges of a newly-made road, but there *are times* when it is easier to touch the heart of a soldier than it is that of a man engaged upon a less hazardous game. Napoleon was affected by the whining of a dog over its master's corpse after Marengo, and thought the brute might teach mankind a lesson in fidelity. Bayard was the tenderest and most chivalrous of men.

And so it was when letters were distributed. I thought I often detected a merry eye grow dull, or a joyous heart become sad, after the contents of the *vague-maitre's* bundle had been read and thought over. When men's lives hang by threads, friends become dearer, and the affection of son and father, of husband, lover, or brother, ripen into something akin to adoration. It is not love, for that has been truly esteemed as "a hollow word, the modern fair one's jest;" but it is such a feeling as the angels have when the penitent sinner comes to judgment. War develops many of the good, and many of the bad qualities in our nature, makes us partly fiends, and partly gods. Perhaps, I was a little touched myself that December morning; perhaps the letter marked "*Couvent des Ursulines, Thildonck, Wespelaer, Belgique*," and signed, "Ever your fond sisters," caused me to feel a little queer about the region of the heart, and if a moist eye be a coward's sign, then am I guilty of the crime. If I brooded over the past, if I treasured the affection of those whose letter I received, thought of their future if the chances of war went against me, was it a crime if I left my companion and wished to be alone? I know it is customary in this cynical age to sneer at this "sentimental trash," but everyone to his taste and according to his experience; for me, I just now remember some of the best men I ever knew, and they were not quite free from this feeling. But, to come to the practical, just allow me to put my letter safely into the most secure part of my *portefeuille*, to draw the elastic band carefully around it, safe, but ready when I am again in the humour for indulging in a little "sentimental trash."

"Ten sous on this," said the sergeant of the week, holding a well-thumbed letter in his hand; "Timothy Marks," repeated the sergeant, reading the name of the soldier to whom it was addressed.

"That's me," said Timothy Marks; "but where am I to git tin sous? Is it to save it on a sou a day I am? Bad luck to them. Sure a month's collection wouldn't pay toll for a ramrod."

"Marks," said Lieutenant Cotter, "I'll have to put you under arrest if you use such language."

"I can't help it, sir," seriously replied Timothy Marks. "I haven't broken my fast to-day, except with a mouthful of bad coffee, and yisterday I had only wan male; my feet are to the ground, and you see my uniform in rags; an' thin to want tin sous for my letther! I can't help it, sir! I can't help it!"

I was glad to see Lieutenant Cotter tolerate the poor fellow's plea, for the authorities were not ruinously liberal to the Irish Volunteers, and I was, too, pleased to see Timothy Marks receive his letter, and ravenously devour its contents.

"*Sac-a-dos!*" "*Sac-a-dos!*" rang out the regimental bugle; "*Sac-a-dos!*" shouted the *sous-officier*. "*Sac-a-dos!*" echoed throughout the line. The usual hurry followed; the *alignement* was taken up, the command *en route* given, and away we shuffled, somewhere, anywhere, but out of St. Chappelle. The people of the village appeared to take neither interest or notice of our departure, but just as we were passing the skirt of the village I saw Lieutenant M'Alevey waiting for the company, a handsome geranium stuck in the button-hole of his tunic, and he just in the act of waving a salute to a rather pretty girl, who smiled at him from an adjoining window.

"Flirting again, M'Alevey?" said I, as he smilingly walked beside me, his usually neatly-curled moustachios a little out of order.

"Oh, no, captain! only preaching patriotism to that lady you saw in the window—a sweet girl, with all the passionate idealism of St. Teresa."

"Whew!" whistled a newcomer behind us. "M'Alevey, you'll die a monk or a teetotaller as sure as fate, if you pull through this campaign."

"You are quite wrong, doctor," coolly replied M'Alevey, addressing Dr. Macken, who had just joined us on the march; "I'm too ardent a spirit to be either."

M'Alevey was the soul of humour. Often I had to beg of him to leave me, for his companionship meant a round of laughter, which became painful from its constancy. Sunshine or shower, feast or famine, M'Alevey was always the same jovial, joyous fun-maker; occasionally flirting, but ever the essence of wit, good-humour, and joviality. His jokes generally went the round of the regiment, and M'Alevey had become noted for saying the best things of the day. In appearance he was every inch a soldier, his tall well-knit figure being set off by the medal he wore for the Mexican Expedition. If there was an evidence of vanity at all, perhaps it was in the twist of his moustachios, which he as carefully trimmed in the field as in quarters. To lighten a march or cheer away *ennui*, M'Alevey was the best hand I ever met, and, in consequence, his companionship was courted by every officer in the regiment. He was, however, too much the cavalier. A pretty face or a glass of Burgundy was irresistible to M'Alevey. If he had lived in the time of Charles I., the days of "personal allegiance," abundance of sack, and unlimited license to woo and win the daughters of the Roundheads, M'Alevey would have been a paragon of perfection. His wit, his jovial humour, his successful amours, and his capacity for a modicum of wine, would have made him beloved of all the beloved. But in those days of revolutionized warfare, I fear M'Alevey did not carry the good wishes of all; some, perhaps, were envious of his wit, while others may have been teased at his importunities. The Colonel might think that he neglected his regimental duties for some frivolous pretext; and if I occasionally took a similar view of his rollicking conduct, and witty sallies, I hope M'Alevey will admit that I was not more rigid in my interpretation of the word—duty—than was necessary. But the march from St. Chappelle to Mehun on the thirteenth of December, 1870, went on. Past destroyed vineyards, trampled gardens, deserted homes, and occasionally the *debris* of war material on the road. Sometimes a wearied soldier would fall out and throw himself exhausted upon the snow or mud that lined the *route*. Sometimes a horse, worn with exhaustion, would be unyoked from the baggage-train, and shot upon the side of the road, and as we looked behind perhaps some famished dogs might be seen prowling around its still warm carcass. Occasionally the "*Sac-a-terre*" would sound, and then the troops were, as usual, busy bandaging ugly sores, searching for a mouthful of water, or catching a moment's repose.

Just before the sun was about to leave us, we pulled up beside an inviting looking field, where the warmth of the deep soil had caused the snow to melt from off its surface. The "*Sac-a-terre*" had sounded fully quarter of an hour, and a few adventurous spirits were busy making coffee. They had set themselves industriously to work the moment they arrived. Two or three had gone for wood, some for water, and others were busy lighting the fire. All went merry as a marriage-bell, the water was just boiling, the soldier who undertook the part of cook had poured the coffee upon the bubbling liquid, when "*Sac-a-dos*," "*Sac-a-dos*," shrieked the bugle. "*Sac-a-dos*" shouted the *sous-officiers*. Consternation followed amongst the anxious men who surrounded the kettle full of boiling water. Timothy Marks made use of some sentence which invoked the chaacter of the prince of Pandemonium, while all the time he looked as ferocious as an irritated bull-dog.

"Fall in!" shouted Sergeant Carey.

Around the fire, where all was harmony a moment before, all was turmoil now. Some were for carrying the coffee, others were for spilling it on the ground; a high word or two passed.

"Fall in!" again sternly spoke the sergeant, in language that showed no further tampering with; we rattled away, and the disputed coffee was consumed—I know not how.

I thought I heard Timothy Marks's voice once or twice a little too high, and then I thought I heard the corporal of his squad say a word that silenced him for the while.

"This is the kind of work that makes one think of the comforts of home, captain," said M'Alevey, coming up and walking beside me, and speaking more seriously than I had heard him for some time.

"M'Alevey," said I, a little surprised at the tone of his conversation, "are you becoming touched with home sickness?"

"I don't know that," repeated the lieutenant, "but I was thinking of a family party seated around the family table, the ancestral Bible being read by the eldest-born, and the old man occasionally enlivening the scene by rocking on the cat's-tail."

I saw M'Alevey was in one of his humours, and I was right, for he rattled away, passing the weary hours of the march in jest and repartee. It was now quite dark and as we entered a road that led through a deep-set forest, the shade of overhanging trees rendered it difficult to see a yard beyond one's face. Now and again a murmur or a groan came from something that looked like a human being, beside the route, as we passed along; some poor wretch had laid down in his misery, perhaps to die. The groans increased along the way, and, turning around, I found that two of my own men had disappeared. The pace was begining to tell! The march was forced and why, nobody knew. There was no enemy in our immediate front, there was none near our rear, and yet we marched as if the fate of our armies depended upon our movements. At the moment I could not condemn the evident hurry, for I knew not but there was a cause, but I afterwards found it was quite a usual thing to knock up half the troops with useless hardships. It is all very well for officers who are mounted, or officers who are not mounted; it is all very well for officers who are well shod, well fed, and have nothing to carry, to command the pace; but it is a different thing with famine and fever-struck soldiers; it is different when the feet are blistered, and the friction of broken shoes and pebbles causes blotches as large as five-shilling pieces to eat into the soldier's insteps; it is quite a different thing for the men whose knapsacks are full, and whose haversacks are empty, and who are weighed down with ninety rounds of ammunition. I know well Marshal Saxe was right when he said, "It is legs and not arms that win campaigns," but they must be used at the proper time, and in the proper place. My experience of the 13th of December, 1870, was verified many a day after when I had occasion to hurry in a death-like march, for no other purpose than because the officers thought what they could do, could be done by the men also. French soldiers were hurried when there was no occasion, and thousands of good lives were lost by uselessly forced marches, to use the mildest language. But onward still, past the timber, ankle-deep in mud, through quiet villages where the dim light of tallow candles placed at the little windows makes us feel that we are in the land of our kind still. The limbs weary, the heads ache, and the sick dropping to the rear; but the spirit is still the same—indomitably Irish. They bore their first day's march with wondrous good will. Occasionally, indeed, a snarl from Timothy Marks broke the monotony, and gave forebodings of coming events with more than prophetic truthfulness.

But the lurid glare in our front told us we were approaching our destination. The shattered wing of the army of the Loire was encamped around Mehun. Pressing on, we reached the town about 9 p.m., and marched through its narrow thoroughfares to find the place of encampment beyond. How strange the feeling of being in a town once more. How the lights glare!

"Look at thim fine rolls of fresh bread in the window!" I heard a soldier say, as we passed a confectioner's shop, the steam rising through the grated cellar as incense rises from a Pagan altar to the gods.

"Yis, and you may look at thim, an' that's all you may have for it," said our old friend Timothy Marks, looking with fretful indifference towards the indicated spot.

"You're always looking at the black side of the moon, Tim," said a good-natured young Dublin man—O'Brien. "How do you know but we shall have those rolls for supper to-night, nicely buttered, and crisped before a gorgeous fire."

"Begone, you omadhaun," said Timothy Marks, casting a look of scorn upon his inexperienced companion. "Yis, indeed, it's butter you want on rolls; bad luck to thim, the only roll you'll get for supper 'll be a roll in the mud."

And, indeed, so it was. As we wheeled into the place marked out for our encampment, I thought it resembled what the bed of the Liffey must be. The mud, or clay, adhered in huge flakes, as large as snow shoes, to our boots, and rendered walking "no small joke," as I heard somebody beside me say. The acting sergeant-major was, however, equal to all emergencies, and was one of the first to give a silvery lining to the darkened prospect.

"Come, Tim, my man, there is no help for it; you must only make the best of a bad bargain," said Sergeant Carey, going up to Timothy Marks, who was surveying what he called the "cut of his gib" with the air of a man who was not quite satisfied with his measurement.

"No, I suppose not, sergeant," said Timothy Marks, shaking his head; "there's nothin' for it. Bad luck to thim. There is a big town within half a mile of us, the Prussians will be sleepin' in it before a week, an' their own soldiers are left to waddle in the dirt, like eels in a mud-hole; an' thin they expect min to march and to fight for thim ; the omadhauns."

At first I feared that the remarks of Timothy Marks might create dissatisfaction amongst the men, but I soon discovered that they regarded him as a good-natured grumbler, and then I let him have his say. Old soldiers are always hard to please, and Timothy Marks was no exception to the rule. As for the rest, there was not a word of complaint; the sergeants made the best selections they could of places, consistent with the *alignement* of the company, and the men went to work, pitching tents, gathering wood, or, carrying water, while the guard for the *faisceaux* was being told off for the night. The scanty rations of the soldiers had been consumed in the morning, and were it not for a little help from the companies' purse—the *ordinaire*—the soldiers of the Irish company would have been foodless. Just as everything was in order, M'Alevey came and took me by the arm, and gave the comforting news that the officers might sleep in Mehun.

Just then a rifle shot rang out sharp, clear, and shrill upon the frozen atmosphere.

"That's from your company," I said to Captain Ceresole, who was just passing me at the time.

"I suppose some poor devil has been putting an end to himself. It has happened several times before, and all because of *la misere*," said the captain, giving the last shrug to his shoulders, and moving towards the scene of the disaster. Dr. Macken happened to be passing at the time, and he came with us, and there, sure enough, was a soldier lying in such a manner as to convince us that it was a case of suicide. The doctor pronounced life to be extinct, the ball from the Chassepot having passed through the brain, and slightly wounded a man who was engaged as the *cuisinier* for his guard, a hundred yards away.

"Captain," said Lieutenant Cotter, who was attracted to the spot by the discharge, "isn't that the man whom we saw bandaging his feet at St. Chappelle? see the shoe how it is tied, and I think I recognise the features, too."

"I believe you're right, Cotter; it is the same. Was he one of your men, Ceresole?" I asked.

"Yes, poor fellow, he was," replied Captain Ceresole, "and I regret this very much. *Mon Dieu*, what will his mother do? Here, sergeant, search his pockets. Give me those papers; thanks! Throw his blanket over his face, place a guard upon the body, and tell the sergeant-major to report it to the adjutant." And the captain walked away, opening a letter directed to himself by the "foot-sore Frenchman."

"Capitaine," began the letter, "you know me, Henri ———; when you get this I will be dead. You know I have tried to do my duty, looking for my only reward in your recognition of my willingness to obey. For your kindness to me I give you my dying thanks; you have been a generous commander and a kind superior. When you could, consistent with your duty, you gave me all the indulgence in your power. But, Capitaine, I am afraid of life. I cannot live any longer in the agony I am now suffering. You may think I am not worse than other men; perhaps I am not; but I must be of weaker mind, or physique, for I would rather die than live in torture. You will find that the bone protrudes through the flesh of my feet, eaten off with frost, and the doctor has refused to allow me to go to hospital. I cannot march, and it is better to die. I have, however, one request to ask of you. My poor mother nursed you when you were a boy—tell her I fell in action; if I thought you would not do this, I would die unhappy; but I am sure you will, so I will die easily. Good-by, Capitaine. Adieu.

"HENRI ———."

"Poor fellow," said Captain Ceresole, folding up the letter and putting it into his pocket-book, " I suppose I must tell his mother that he fell in action, but that will be poor consolation for her gray hairs."

I knew Ceresole wished to be alone, and I left him to the communion of his thoughts.

A parting instruction to Sergt. Carey, and M'Alevey, Lieut. Cotter, the doctor, and I waded through streams of water, dodged through baggage-waggons and gun-carriages, and at last entered the boundary of one of the dirtiest places in which it has ever been my lot to pass through. Mehun, oh! may I never look upon your like again! M'Alevey was a capital hand at scouting out lodgings. He knew exactly by the conduct of the people who answered his query, "Have you room for four officers," whether he would persevere or not. If it was a lady who showed the slightest evidence of good temper, M'Alevey would interest her with his conversation, make her laugh with his witticism, and the chances were ten to one that he would succeed in finding a bed where dozens had failed before.

"There's no use going there, M'Alevey, the *Commandant* has just been trying," said I, as M'Alevey left my side and walked over towards a little house that stood in from the road. There was a peculiar twinkle in M'Alevey's eye, he gave the least curl to his moustache, and knocked at the door. From the moment the door opened and a handsome dark-haired girl stood in the passage, I made certain that M'Alevey would succeed, and succeed he did. I could see the stern look she assumed for the moment relax, then a smile traced an expression upon her features, and before many seconds I saw the lieutenant raise his *kepi* as his fair *vis-a-vis* ran off to ask

her father if he could make any kind of a shake-down? With
the young lady's father M'Alevey was equally successful; and a few
rugs placed upon the boards, beside a gorgeous fire, made us comfortable for the night. Mehun was so crowded, that officers who
trusted to their servants finding quarters for them, were put to some
shifts, and in several instances had to return to the camp and find
shelter in a baggage-waggon or under a gun-carriage.

Our host treated us with marked kindness when he heard
we were Irish Volunteers; he was singularly intelligent for his class,
and he understood perfectly that Ireland was washed by the
Atlantic, which I am sure was what many of his neighbours did not
know. To us who went to France full of sympathy for her misfortunes, and who had thrown our lives into the contest—we who conjured up the history of the past—the stories of the Old Brigade—of
Clare at Ramillies—of that heroic burst of Fontenoy—of the stand
at Cremona, or of the efforts of our fathers at Ypres, where the ramparts yielded to the charge of the Irish Volunteers, and covered them
with glory—to us who remembered all those, who treasured them as
gems in the history of our people—and who expected similar recollection of them by the French—it was often amusingly mortifying
to hear some mawkish Frenchman ask—"*Ireland! Ireland! Where
is Ireland?*"

But our host was an intelligent man in his way. He had a vague
idea that Ireland was somewhere on the west coast of England, and
made a wondrously amusing effort to trace its geographical position
with the point of M'Alevey's walking cane. He appeared to think
that Ireland was, geographically, a hump upon the shoulders of Great
Britain, and the poor man looked amazingly satisfied as M'Alevey
acquiesced, or at least hesitated to contradict his charmful innocence.
But my mischievous lieutenant had his eyes in other quarters.
M'Alevey could not be quiet in the presence of a woman—be she
lady or simple maid—without paying her courteous attention. He

made us all laugh rings round, and the little clock beside the bed marked one a.m., before the old man, or perhaps the old man's daughter, could be induced to say *"bonne nuit."*

Our toilets were a little troublesome that night—that is, we took off our great coats and long boots, and, wrapped in our blankets, watched the flames lick up the logs of wood that were abundantly heaped upon the hearth, the heat from which sent the flush of comfort through our veins. Oh! how gorgeous the single rug, that was stretched upon the wooden floor, felt; a little hard, perhaps, but it was dry; and as fatigue is the best of narcotics, we soon forgot our troubles in pleasant dreams of the dear old land.

CHAPTER V.

> By foreign hands thy dying eyes were closed,
> By foreign hands thy decent limbs composed,
> By humble hands thy humble grave adorned,
> By strangers honoured and by strangers mourned.

THE sun was about peeping over the south-eastern horizon, or, in the words of M'Alevey, had "struck a light," the following morning, when a vigorous shake by somebody caused me to awake. Looking around I saw M'Alevey engaged in an interesting conversation with our host's daughter, while I heard him advocating the relative becomingness of short dresses and high-heeled boots. Andy, my orderly, had, by some peculiar power of his own, a power he was fond of calling the "instinct of rason," ferretted out my whereabouts, and he appeared to be seriously engaged at bayonet exercise with somebody who had sought refuge in the flue, but, as he readily explained, he was only removing something that stopp d the free passage of the smoke through the chimney. Lieutenant Cotter was still quiet, but nis nasal thunder grated harshly upon the delicate utterances of M'Alevey, who appeared to be now using such language to his *vis-a-vis*, as Pope might put into the mouth of Abelard when addressing Eloise. To Lieutenant M'Alevey I was often as obnoxious as a fat man is to the occupants of an omnibus, or as a tall man is in a crowd on a procession day, and I fear the recording angel had no prayer to register for his orderly, who had so unceremoniously awaked me from my slumbers.

Crash! crash! down came the sheet of iron with which Andy had too successfully played, and carried along with it a cloud of soot, which enveloped the poor fellow from head to foot, causing him to spit and splutter like a monkey after a dose of genuine S. P. Andy gave a spring to the rear that an athlete might envy, and upset a *marmite*, which was filled with water, over the beardless face of the sleeping sous-lieutenant. M'Alevey sprang into the hall, kicking up his heels like a well-trained circus-horse, while the half-drowned Cotter was calling for the assistance of the half-choked Andy. M'Alevey kept crowing away in the hall just by way of illustrating that he, at least, was "out of the wood," while I succeeded in covering my head with my blanket to ward off the soot, and rolled away from the pools of water that were forming around me. The situation was, however, quickly understood, and as Andy was engaged removing the soot from his person, M'Alevey put his head in at the door, and congratulated him upon his successful attempt at a *reveille*. Just then the proprietor of the house appeared upon the scene and invited us to another room, where we were safe from Andy's attempt to improve the unimprovable, and shortly after we bade our host adieu, and were soon floundering our way back to camp again.

En route we were joined by Mason and some officers of the regiment with whom we got into conversation about military events in general. At that moment some Spiahs cantered by, their white burnouses flowing gracefully over the quarters of their Arab steeds. They looked as if they had copied their ideas of a uniform from a chapter in the Bible. Their snow-white *burnouses* were thrown with easy grace over their well formed shoulders. Mason gave us a long description of their habits when in their native wilds. Their nomadic life, their hospitality, and their social customs. The few of them I met with were singularly reserved, and all possessed that self control which is characterestic of their race. Mason was loud in their praises, and lauded their devotion to France with soldierly fervour.

When Mason had disposed of the Spiahs, he went into eulogiums on the regiment of which we formed a part, and shrugged his shoulders with ominous meaning as he declared that "France was sold." "You know Fouche sent the Duke of Wellington Napoleon's plan of Waterloo," he added with a glance, which I interpreted to mean as being a period to his argument.

"The French will never forget that affair," said M'Alevy, rolling up a cigarette, and lighting a match on the ruffled side of a tin box. "But, apart from that, everything appears 'topsy-turvy,' as we say in Ireland, in the army. You have no logistics of any experience, indeed your entire staff appears, like everything else, to be improvised for the occasion. Your artillery is badly served; your cavalry do not know how to ride, and appear only to hold on their horses because it is 'regulation' to do so."

"That is not the worst," said Mason, pointing to some famished soldiers who were sitting near us; "to be foodless and shoeless, and crushed down with abominably heavy knapsacks; our commissariat broken up; the *morale* of the troops destroyed by continual defeat; that's what beats us up and gives us the finishing stroke. But what's this?" he added, looking along our line of route, to a cluster of men coming towards us. "I declare they are prisoners, and Uhlans, too."

Immediately after we saw twenty or thirty dismounted Uhlans, escorted by some Franc-tireurs, coming towards us. The Uhlans walked with the finished stride of well-trained men. They carried themselves as proudly as if they expected to be the recipients of an ovation, or to hear the stirring words of "Wacht am Rhein" greeting their ears. There was a *hauteur* about their bearing that was almost defiant in its dash. They were, too, men of much muscular development, and kept the step and their dressing in singular contrast to their escort. Their outfit was warm and serviceable, and there was neither the trace of famine nor excessive misery in their countenances. They were, in every respect, good-looking soldiers.

To the alarmed senses of the French peasantry all German cavalry men were alike—Uhlans. Dragoons and Hussars there were none, all were Uhlans, whose audacity and bearing too often, indeed, caused alarm and terror. The Uhlan proper is an ordinary lancer, taking the title from their Polish originals. They are, too, heavy cavalry, and may be fairly spoken of as big men on big horses. They carry beside their lances a sword and pistol, and are distinguishable by lancer-caps called "Chapkey." The German Hussars and Dragoons, however, do similar duty with the Uhlans, and are recognisable by their fur caps and helmets. In the field the armies are surrounded by a perfect web of mounted men, through which no spy can penetrate without great personal danger. Their cavalry, too, penetrate an enemy's country in all directions, miles in advance of the main body, often in twos and fours, and keep up a well connected line of communication with the troops behind. Unlike the French the German cavalry is not loaded down with dead weight, which, as every rider knows, is what kills the horses. A light schrabraque goes over the horse's back, and a pair of shoes, a comb, a brush, an extra shirt, and a pair of stockings make up the equipment of the German cavalry men. Nor have they any dismounted men in the German cavalry. Every man is liable for outpost duty or the shock of a charge.

"There is not a regiment in the French army those fellows hate or dread so much as they do us," said Captain Mason, as he walked by my side, at the same time casting a significant glance at the captured Uhlans.

"Why," I asked, "surely the *Regiment Etranger* is no better than any other regiment in the army; or can it be considered as such ?"

"Yes," replied Mason, "it is, even by Frenchmen themselves admitted to be one of their crack regiments."

"Not even excepting the Zouaves or Turcos ?"

"Not even excepting the Zouaves or Turcos. Prince Frederick Charles, in his 'Art of Fighting in the French Army,' admits that the Foreign Regiment is the most formidable corps in the French service. You see we have all the dare-devils of Europe in our ranks. In some cases, indeed, men whose insensibility to the difference between mine and thine is somewhat deadened, are found amongst the rank and file, and there may be a little proclivity to cram haversacks with booty when in an enemy's territory. But the highest testimony of our worth is that we are always placed in the post of honour, and you'll see when the fighting is to be done, if we are not placed in front, as we were at Orleans, where we lost 1,000 men in six hours' work. It has given the corps some *eclat*, too, that nearly all the great commanders of the day graduated in our ranks; Bazaine, General Fleury, Bourbaki, and MacMahon included."

"Yes; but your African experience is not calculated to develop the capacity of generals for command, as much as it is to encourage young troops to stand fire," I urged. "In Africa you move in small bodies, your warfare is entirely guerilla in its effects. You require no strategy, and but little tactics to overcome the untrained Arabs."

"Very true," replied Mason; "it is a better field for the rank and file, than for officers in command. Campaigning in Africa is, in every essential, different to what it is here. You see in Africa we march in squares, for those wiry Arabs are likely to attack us at any moment. At night the *videttes* and sentries are continually harrassed by the insurgents. It is a frequent occurrence for an Arab to steal through the short underwood like a veritable snake, and, watching his opportunity, spring on the startled sentry, and, before he can make any alarm, the keen knife of his active assailant has despatched him."

"That should surely induce caution, and develop that sense of keenness without which *videttes* and sentries are always liable to fall into snares."

"So it does; and if you saw, *Capitaine*, how quickly the *Regiment Etranger* can turn out in the middle of the night to the cry of *Aux armes*, you would see that all their African experience is not quite lost on them. "But," he added, somewhat sorrowfully, "we have no *Regiment Etranger* now. Those men of yours," said he, looking around at the hardy countenances of "*La Compagnie Irlandaise*," "are now almost the only foreigners in the regiment—Orleans did for the rest."

"But is it true what I hear about your marches in Africa being so harrassing?" I asked, desirous of finding out all I could about a country in which my regiment had seen so much service.

"Perfectly," replied Mason. "It often happens on the march that men fall behind as you see them do here every hour. But their doom is sealed. It is certain death to lag behind in Africa, for the enemy is ever hovering around our flanks ready to murder every man who falls to the rear. You know an Arab never thinks a man dead until he cuts the head off; and more than once I have seen the heads of some of the men of my own company, men who loitered or were compelled to fall behind owing to sickness, cramps, or blistered feet; I have more than once seen their heads before our battalion on our line of march. The Algerians had decapitated the soldiers, then ridden past us, and deposited the head on our route, a grim warning to the foot-sore and the sickly."

"Lagsters must be rare under such circumstances?"

"Not so rare as you would fancy, *mon Capitaine*," replied Mason. "I remember once in the province of Oran my own orderly got sick on the line of march. The nearest station was ninety kilometres in our front, and the poor soldier struggled on until he became exhausted. I allowed him to abandon his pack, keeping his rifle and ammunition alone; the release enabled the sickly man to struggle on ten or fifteen kilometres more, and then his coat was thrown away, and I myself carried his rifle and ammunition. Behind us the clouds of sand-dust dotted the horizon, and away upon our flanks Arab horsemen were stealthily watching our movements. To fall to the rear was certain death, and I can never forget the terribly resigned countenance of the young man as he found himself sinking as it were into a living tomb. He grew weaker and weaker; the eyes protruded, the tongue swelled, the head grew giddy; his companions supported him as long as they could, but his hour had come, his sands had run; he became a dead load, and had to be left upon the Sahara, the sun's rays piercing to his brain, and the savage natives waiting to pounce upon his half-dead body. The battalion was halted for a moment, to allow of a parting word with his companions, and then he was left to his fate, a horrified shriek of despair being the last we heard of him as he found himself utterly alone. Once, indeed, I looked behind, and saw him leaning upon his hand, as he appeared to be gazing around the open desert, while his countenance wore an expression akin to madness. I waved a handkerchief as a parting salutation, and then I saw the abandoned soldier raise his *kepi* from his head, throw it in the air, and sink exhausted upon the sand. In four hours afterwards his head was before us on the road, the face horribly contorted, while the blood clotted around the thorax, in hard sun-dried patches. However," said Mason, with a significant shrug of his shoulders, "it's all a soldier's luck—

"Mais a la guerre,
Comme a la guerre."

And he walked away to join his company, and left M'Alevey and I again together.

Day was lapsing into night, it was *coucher du soleil*. The sky was as varied in its hue as the most varied of mother-of-pearl shell; gold, green, and silver appeared to be blended in the beautiful blotches of clouds that dolphin-like changed their hue at death. It was such an evening as Scott pictures in his "Rokeby," when he makes sunset in the tropics a sight the angels might envy. There was something immeasurably impressive in the solemn stillness of the hour. Beholding a gorgeous sunrise or sunset, man must, indeed, feel the greatness of nature and the littleness of art. What are the boasted works of Nineveh or of Egypt; of Greece or of Rome; of Carthage, or of Athens, or of the wonderful remains of architectural grandeur—

"Whose very ruins are tremendous,"

compared with one glance at the coming or the parting day. Even in Nature itself, there is nothing so magnificently glorious as the effect caused by that orb which obeyed His word when He said— "Let there be light." The Alps are "grand;" Niagara is "sublime;" the Rhine and Killarney are "beautiful;" but sunrise or sunset is alone "magnificent." It is but holding "a glimmering taper to the sun" to make even the semblance of a comparison. Look up, and draw upon your fancy those fleecy castles in the air, changing in character and formation before the attacks of those beleaguered clouds which dash in firm resolve against the buttresses of the structure. Cannot your fancy see the combat between the hostile masses deepen, and the clouds around tinged with the blood of the dying day! It is daylight battling with darkness. The rainbow's hues form but a fractional portion of the many-coloured dyes which for a fleeting moment stamp their impress upon the shaded splendour of the clouds, and yet all these colours harmonise so beautifully that Art becomes but a poor copyist of glorious Nature. But night triumphed! The moon heralded the victory of Erebus, and the sun sank below the horizon, bathed in a sea of glory, and the last ray of daylight, with sickly glare, followed in its wake, faithful to the end. Then the moon, that "sole arbitress of night," shone forth in all its borrowed splendour. The tall shadows of the poplar trees that lined the route were thrown across the way, like spectral shadows across the valley of death. Along the tops of the deep set-brush in our immediate front the moonbeams played in fancied gambols, while the entire plain around was bathed in a flood of genial brightness. The numberless little *tentes d'abris* covered hill and dale, while the occasional challenge of a sentinel sounded clear and sharp upon the now still atmosphere. The star-spangled heavens added lustre to the brilliant canopy above, and a path of light traverses the surface of a small lake close by, and seems to penetrate into its dark, unfathomed caves. The firmament overhead is familar to the gaze, and impresses a feeling of boundless immensity onthe mind. Nearly all those familiar stars above are visible in Holy Ireland; and looking up, I bethought me of that passage in the Old Testament, which asks: " Canst thou bind the sweet influence of Pleiades, or loose the bands of Orion ?" Pitiable, indeed, is that poor pensioner on the bounties of an hour, whose heart is callous to the calls of Faith, or who cannot think with Young, that " By night an atheist half believes a God." To a soldier too, this feeling is keenly perceptible. When active life stands still, and the wearied troops sink upon their slimy bed, and make a pause in their career—a pause which may be prophetic of their end; when Night from her ebon throne, in rayless majesty stretches forth her leaden sceptre o'er the slumbering world, there is a depth of thought, an ocean of Faith before the sentinel as he gazes in respectful awe at the majesty of Nature. Look at the order of that vaulted dome, hung with crape for the departed day; look from out of the narrow heart of man's experience; take one broad, great view of Nature as it is ; look away from the pretensious littleness of humanity, into the mysterious ocean of space, and say if you can " There is no God ;" or will you not rather think that the scoff of an atheist is but a sorry exchange for a Deity offended. But let us descend to mother earth again, and see how fares the men of *La Compagnie Irlandaise.*

"LA COMPAGNIE IRLANDAISE."

The fires were growing dull, and already some weary soldiers sought the shelter of their miserable coverings where they were expected to rest and be thankful. The clayey soil had been, for miles round, torn-up by passing troops as they converged in all directions upon the principal route, beside which we had encamped. The army had departed again, and there was but a few thousand troops behind—perhaps ten thousand in all—awaiting orders for the morrow.

As I passed along the line where the Irish company was encamped, the moon's rays were sufficiently brilliant to enable me to see the industrious patching torn garments or artistically sewing the soles of their shoes to the decaying uppers with pieces of whipcord, some stretched upon the muddy earth with nothing but their miserable blankets around them, often huddled together like pigs in a sty, for warmth sake, and more than once I could not help roundly censuring the penny-wise-pound-foolish-policy of a Government that could sacrifice the health of good men to a system only worthy of a nation of paupers.

"Captain," said Sergeant Terence Byrne, coming up to where M'Alevey and I were standing, "one of the men wishes to speak to you."

The poor fellow who desired to see me was barefooted, and his feet were blueish-red, while he limped over to us, the very picture of *la misere*. He spoke in words of manly bearing, hesitating to blame, willing to endure all that mortal could, but yet declaring his inability to march unless he could be provided with shoes. Just then, *mon Colonel* was passing, his little grey Arab sticking fetlock deep in the clayey soil, and I brought the barefooted Irishman over and pointed out his lamentable condition. He was a kind old soul too. He visibly shivered when he saw the pitiable state of the young man, and, while professing his regret, asked what could he do? There was no shoes in store, there were none at Mehun—not a pair! Thousands of men are not much better, but if he could hold out for the next march, perhaps at St. Flourent we might find something that would at least keep his feet from the ground. It was poor encouragement to the perished young man, for whom, however, we succeeded in buying a pair of shoes at a price which would certainly suggest the practical illustration of there being "nothing like leather."

Night had now fairly set in, and the few officers in camp returned to Mehun—M'Alevey and I to our old quarters, which our host of the previous evening had reserved for our special accommodation Cotter had to find shelter in what his senior lieutenant called a "joint proprietors' establishment"—*i.e.*, a butcher's shop. But it was the same old story with M'Alevey, cracking jokes, telling rich stories of his African and Mexican experience, and making laughter fatigue rather than recreation. One good one he had heard of Mac-Mahon when a colonel in Africa. The now celebrated Marshal was, for an African officer, a rigid disciplinarian. One time on parade he had occasion to reprimand a captain, whose temper got the better of his judgment, and he snapped his revolver at MacMahon's head. The pistol fortunately missed fire, the captain was immediately arrested, and the colonel turning to the *Commandant*, said, "Give that man fifteen days *salle de police* for having his arms out of order." M'Alevey vowed it was true, and his vows were to me as "Bible writ, sound as the Gospel," except, indeed, when he vowed by a woman's eyes, and then he was a darker dissembler than Tartuffe. I always thought he considered love and war as twin sisters, and he blended the two elements in very fair proportions. And so night and morning passed, and I fear M'Alevey lingered a little as we said adieu, and perhaps the dark-haired girl regretted the imperative parting as much as he. "Never mind," he said, as we turned our backs upon the house that had given us the shelter of its roof-tree for two nights; "never mind, you know the old song, captain—

> 'Every town we march through,
> The girls are looking arch through,'

but I wonder where we shall sleep to-night."

"On grand guard, my boy," I answered, "don't you know we are for duty."

"Delighted to hear it; Mehun, with all your mud, I love you still."

But the *rappel* sounded as usual at noon, and the 5th battalion of the Foreign Regiment was for grand guard. In all, the battalion that should have mustered 1,000 men could only show about 300 rifles. The drums beat and the rolls swell out upon the keen air and, for the moment at least, makes even the wearied soldiers stand erect, and forget their miseries. And then a word of command, another, and yet another, and we floundered over the slimy ground, out upon the road, and then away for the post. "Step together boldly tread, firm each foot, erect each head," until two kilometres are passed over, and then the various *petites postes* were pointed out, the command handed over, the old guard relieved, leaving us to occupy the ground. The enemy's cavalry had been seen not far off during the day, and the prospect of a brush had knocked a little *esprit* into the men. But the drizzling rain had soaked into their garments damped their ardour, and left them cowering at their posts in a miserable plight. The pitching of tents was forbidden, the lighting of fires would not be allowed, even if it were possible, and rolled up in their miserable blankets, four feet by two, the soldiers shrank behind some low ditches, or lay in batches upon the open field, while the rain fell upon their half numb forms. For my own part I was comfortable. A little hut close by afforded excellent shelter, and the props that supported the vines, soon made the place as snug as an nut-shell. The *sergent-fourrier*, M'Crossin, shared my shelter, while an orderly attended to a fry for a late meal. But the rain still poured upon the men, and must have thawed the spirit of the best of them. It is not fighting but the elements that soldiers fear. The ring of a rifle has no terror in a soldier's ear, but it is the drenching rain, the benumbing frost, and *la misere* that breaks a soldier's spirit, and makes him indifferent of life, almost anxious for death. Edmund Burke said, indeed, that "every day we live will convince thinking men that there are evils to which the calamities of war are blessings." Well, perhaps there are; but they are not physical evils. To give such new miseries to the world would be like cutting the volumes of the Sybil. If Edmund Burke *felt* a campaign he might alter his theory, for practice is the best of teachers. There was not, indeed, more discomfiture than men could expect amongst the soldiers of "*La Compagnie Irlandaise*" up to the present, but the shadow of the future was even more terrible than the sufferings of the present, and, as time found it, became severe. We were but young in our experience that night upon grand guard. But custom is indeed second nature: a "happy family" show *par example*. Even under drenching rain, the soldiers of the Irish company sought forgetfulness in repose. Sleep overcomes all men. Alexander the Great slept on the field of Arbela, and Napoleon, if my memory is not coquettish, upon that of Austerlitz, and every schoolboy knows that Homer, in his "Iliad," elegantly represents sleep as overcoming all men, and even the gods, except Jupiter alone. What, then, the gods could not resist, surely the Irish soldiers had to succumb to, and under the downpour the men slept, if not comfortably nor soundly, at least so much that they were unconscious to the outer world. But the sentries here were all alive to the importance of being on the *qui vive*. It was often indeed a matter of much trouble to teach some of the soldiers of "*La Compagnie Irlandaise*" the necessary challenge and counter-challenge in French. Some of the men honestly confessed that it "bothered them entirely." Amongst the latter there was one giant Cork "boy," whose rotundity had been sadly diminished since he became a soldier. He was fond of showing his companions his gradual decay as he would clutch his great coat in folds, and appealingly say, while he gave an ominous shake of his head, that he was " going, going, going." He had the form and build of a huge man, but he was as simple as a child, could cry for a lost companion, or lose his life for a friend. But Timothy Larkin had, like everybody else, to do his sentry go, although he could not master his *ralliment*. I was told a good story of this man-child. Tim was a *factionnaire* on one of the outposts, to which an unfortunate French peasant too nearly approached. Tim made a vigorous attempt at the " *qui vive*," which in cooler moments he could, no doubt, have remembered, but the excitement of the instant drove everything out of Tim's head but his native brogue.

" *Qui, qui, qui*—who's there?" challenged Tim, bringing his Chassepot promptly to the charge. To this there was no reply. the poor Frenchman standing as still as St. Paul when he was afflicted with the loss of speech.

" *Qui, qui*—what's there," again demanded the persistent Tim. To the Frenchman the mixed jargon was confounding, and, as he afterwards explained, he thought somehow that he had strayed into the German lines.

" *Qui*, who's there—what's there ?" roared the now aroused sentry, at the same time fixing a cartouche in his gun. The peasant heard the " click," as the garde mobile of the chassepot was drawn back to open the breech, and, in the descriptive words of Timothy himself, " the Frencher bolted ;" but he wasn't quick enough for Tim, who was by his side in a second, and almost transfixed him with his bayonet, when the terrified peasant threw himself into a half melted snowdrift, and lay on his back, kicking up his heels, like a fly pierced with a needle. The sentry was in no good humour, for he believed that he had surely caught a German spy, and, while he shouted for the " corporal of the guard," he kept tickling the

Frenchman with the point of his bayonet, and swearing that if he attempted to stir "one inch" he would "skiver" him. The peasant roared, the sentinel shouted, the whole post was under arms, when Tim was found by the corporal of a French post close by, who arrested the peasant, and clapped Timothy on the back, telling him that he was "very good *soldat*; very good *Irlandais*."

But at midnight the rain clouds passed away, and the wind carried dark masses of clouds across the pale surface of the moon. At regular intervals the lieutenants and sous-lieutenants reported to me the incidents of the rounds, and, just as I was about to stretch upon the damp hearth of the hut, a messenger arrived in haste from the camp, with orders to return at once. In with *petite postes*, there is surely something in the wind now! Back to Mehun, where the troops were all awake and under arms, while along the road leading in the direction of Bourges a stream of soldiers was passing. Our own regiment was filing into the road as we arrived.

"Did you see that, captain," said Dr. Macken, looking away to the north-east; "it was like the flash of a gun. There it is again," he added, as something very like a flash appeared through the gloom.

"It is only the aurora," I replied.

"Going into action," said one of the captains—Ceresole—as his company filed past. "We shall see what your Irish boys will do now."

"All right," I replied; "we'll be with the crowd somewhere."

In the meantime, we had some sick, and it was arranged that they should stop behind and go to hospital at Mehun. One poor fellow named Eustace was very bad with small-pox, and had to rough it upon the earth, the fever eating into his veins with deadly effect. In all, there were five or six knocked up by the trials they had already gone through; but "going into action" acted miraculously upon their fevered minds.

"Pat," said Eustace to his companion, "I'm betther, thanks be to

"LA COMPAGNIE IRLANDAISE." 97

God; I can march finely this morning; is this *my rifle?*" said he, looking at the beautiful weapon with something of fire in his eyes, and with a tone akin to affection for the gun. "Maybe I'll hear it ring at rale work at last."

"Eustace, my man," said I, "you must stop behind. Arrangements are made for you to go to hospital at Mehun."

"Sure I'm well, captain, thanks be to God; I never felt betther in all my life," said the poor fellow, endeavouring to put his rifle upon his shoulder, which, while he held in his hand, acted as a support for his tottering body, and now that the support was withdrawn, he would have fallen to the ground were it not that his companion caught him in his arms.

"*En route, en route.*" Now gird up your loins, my men, for surely that was like another flash in our front. The pace was at the double, but there was no lagging that morning. The weakly fall behind, for the march is killing, but away go their packs into the slimy ditch, and they still hang affectionately upon the rear. Everything that would likely impede the march was cast aside—a dangerous experiment, for soldiers are liable to be court-martialled for losing their packs. But it was "going into action," and once, as I looked behind, I saw the moon cast its brilliant rays upon the fevered countenance of Eustace, who evaded the ambulance, and, with rifle and ammunition, had followed us, as he, and we all, believed that we were going to the front.

As usual the pace was rapid. Rain drops as large as hailstones fell with clattering haste upon the *marmites* and *beadons* of the soldiers, as we hurried on over the slimy route. The air was calm, and still away on the horizon, an occasional flash of light penetrated the gloom, like a rocket through a storm cloud. Many weakly old soldiers abandoned their packs, believing that they were going into action, and thinking that if they survived the day, they could easily obtain another, and if they were placed *hors de combat*, that they

H

would not require the contents of their packs *en route* for their new abode. But on still; on through the dark damp atmosphere, expecting every moment to hear the roar of artillery, or the rattle of small arms in our front. On over roads, ankle deep in mud, and as we reached a village on our way, the earliest streaks of dawn broke through the gloom, and pushed damp dark night from its throne. But it was a false start after all. It was only the Aurora lighting up the northern sky with its brilliant but deceptive reflection. Then the pace appeared to become easier, and as daylight advanced, we trudged away for our destination, which we found to be La Subdery or St. Florent, and as the sun climbed upwards, the heat became another source of unpleasantness for the now wearying troops. At the village we had passed, we heard of the capitulation of Phalsbourg, after a siege of four months, on December 12th, and the only fortress in Lorraine left to the French was Bitsche. Montmedy surrendered on the 14th, but the gallant resistance of Chanzy from the 10th to the 15th, proved that there was mettle in the French troops still. Bourbaki had departed on his eastern dash, leaving our corps —the 15th—to watch Prince Frederick Charles, who was then manœuvring in front of Bourges, the defence of which we were intrusted with. The spirits of the troops were indeed almost broken at this time. The food was bad and insufficient, the clothing of the men fell in tatters, and their shoes were in many cases worn from off their feet.

About this time Gambetta issued two of his famous decrees. He would have a man court-martialled if he fell to the rear, although the tottering limbs might refuse to any longer support the half dead form. If the feet were blistered, or ulcered, or frost-bitten, and a soldier, doubled up with the weight of his miseries, fell behind, he was to be court-martialled, and, perhaps, shot.

"Better supply us with a pair of shoes than a pair of handcuffs," I heard a soldier beside me say to his companion, Timothy Marks, as we again trudged over the broken road; "Better look after our wants than make new hardships for us, for God knows we have enough of them already."

"Yis, indeed; if Mr. Gambetta gave us shoes, and food, and clothes, and lollypops, and good straw beds—oh, yes—sure every man would be a soldier thin. But the omadhawns, they havn't sinse enough to thrate their men like soldiers," replied Marks, the spirit of crankyism making itself evident on his countenance.

"It is the *fournisseurs* that should be arrested and not the lagster," said the other, with a degree of far-seeing justice that caused me to make a note of the words on the fly-leaf of my memory.

But on still! through a country watered with the tributaries of the Loire; hurry on through quiet villages where the *paysans*, in canoe-like *sabots*, stared in gaping wonder at the passing troops; where village girls arch their eyebrows and either pity or joke with the soldiers as they hurry by, where little children look vaguely and wildly into our faces, and little boys wear gay cockades, beat miniature drums, carry the tricolor in groups, and make mimic warfare upon their companions. The sun climbs over the ridge of hills that skirt the eastern horizon, and bathes us in a flood of light. An occasional halt, men falling to the rear, heads ache and limbs weary again, but on still until the sun sinks away over the undulating country to the far west, and night is once more monarch of the scene. But as the longest lane has a turn, our destination was made at last. In the distance, nimbus-like clouds hovered above a clump of trees in our front, and we rightly conjectured that our corps was encamped beneath the shade of the grateful boughs, which our imagination pictured as hanging in picturesque fondness over some bubbling stream, and where wood and water was abundant. At last the confines of a town are reached, and after a little delay, we rattle into St. Florent with its 5,000 inhabitants. Outside the town the troops rested in *echelon* on the slopes of the gently rising ground in the neighbourhood. The low tents huddled together, looked at a distance like flocks of sheep grazing. Not a drunken man was to be seen in or about the place. The wine shops were not quite empty, but they were in no case crowded. A few busy men entered their doors from time to time, filled their canteens with wine, and hastened away. While we halted beside the route, a general followed by six or seven of his staff, entered a *cafe* beside the road, eat what was placed before him in a few minutes, drank his *demi tasse* of coffee, and quickly vanished with his companions. Officers in red and blue kepis, some of whom know the secrets of the gods are more mysterious than augurs. The commissariat continues its purchases, and fourriers are making hard bargains with illiberal shopkeepers. Little herds of oxen, waggons loaded with flour, defile into the streets, and, the bargain struck, are sent on their way towards one camp or the other. But loiterers are not to be seen. The troops are all in camp, and here comes our companions of the 39th regiment of infantry, white with dust, and looking weary and footsore. Behind it, but by another road, arrives a troop of hussars, haughty and defiant, upon their Hungarian chargers. Warlike figures they are, noble in expression, from the captain down to the youngest soldier. They came from afar: their caps of fur, their jackets, saddles, and camp utensils piled up around them and hanging to their horses' saddles, contain the dust of nearly forty miles of travel. Our corps, too, must be again *en route*, and we hurry out of town, pass the boulevards, picketed horses, troops in line, baggage and ammunition waggons, sergeants calling company rolls, on to our division, our brigade, our regiment, and we arrive just in time to hear the command "*en route*" as we rattled away for the small village of La Subdery.

"M'Alevey," I said to my lieutenant, as we marched together a little to the left of the leading files of the company, "you are somewhat sad lately. Your tone of conversation has suddenly changed from the gay to the melancholy. Are you really afflicted with that passion which is 'doomed to mourn,' or has that letter you received yesterday opened anew some old wound in the crevices of your affections?"

"Perhaps," replied the lieutenant, placing his hand, with theatrical grace, upon that portion of his great coat that covered the region of his heart, "I may have determined to devote myself to one Eve instead of to many."

"The richest joke of the day," said one of the officers, Kuess, joining us; "M'Alevey touched by the tender passion—seized with 'an insane desire to pay for a woman's board,' as I heard himself once say,"

"You are a brute, Kuess," replied M'Alevey. "You Poles are as phlegmatic as an Esquimaux."

"You are a little astray, M'Alevey," said Kuess. We Poles when we love, we love but once in our lives. With us love is indeed 'as strong as death, jealousy as cruel as the grave,' as I think Solomon sang. You Irish too often admire the face, or the symmetry of form, and think you love the possessor of such charms. We Poles love the mind, but only admire the face or figure."

"Oh, you are on your metaphysics again," said M'Alevey, with a slight shake of his head, but evidently troubled about the Pole's reasoning.

"Well, I'm giving you the logic of my school of thinkers. The man who loves a woman for her mind, who finds in her ideas a reciprocity of sentiment, who reads in her thoughts a character in unison with his own, that man loves indeed."

"And has beauty, the gift that 'is a joy for ever,' no power to hold a man's love as pure and as constant as what you call 'the love mind?'" asked M'Alevey.

"None whatever," said Kuess, with a determined shake of his handsome and well-formed head. "Beauty may catch, but the mind alone can hold the passion of, the heart. I would not give the value of a round of cartridges for the love of a man whose affections had been moved by the passing beauty of the fairest belle in all your little island."

"Oh, you are a second brute, and remind me of my Byron—

> 'The cold in clime are cold in blood,
> Their love can scarce deserve the name.'"

"Your Byron was a false teacher; he could be no philosopher. I think, too," replied Kuess, "that I read somewhere in a German translation of your Shakespeare that—

> 'Love looks not with eyes, but with the mind,
> And therefore is wing'd Cupid painted blind.'"

"M'Alevey, I'm afraid that last letter accounts for this sudden change in the temper of your reasoning," I said, looking at my lieutenant, who sighed, raised his *kepi*, and smiled with a somewhat pleasant melancholy expression, which I readily interpreted into "yes."

But as day wore on, and fatigue and hunger wore out the endurance of the troops, many of the men were compelled to fall behind, and too often into the custody of the *gens d'armes* who followed us *en route*. Some of the men were by this time entirely barefooted, and limped along the sides of the road with a painful effort. Amongst the rest, poor Timothy Marks was shoeless, and the blood trickled from more than one vicious-looking sore, as he shuffled with unsteady gait upon our flank. He would not give up, no, not as long as there was a stride in his weary limbs, and he carried his rifle, ammunition, pack and accoutrements as gaily as a man could under such painful circumstances. His spirit was not broken, but it was crushed, and he still found time to give a well deserved snarl at the impecuniosity of the authorities, who were so well performing the work of demoralisation, even more effectually than the victories of the Red Prince, Manteuffel, or Von der Tann. But we were promised a rest at La Subdery, where our broken ranks might have time to close up, our men provided with shoes and clothing, and where for a few nights we could stretch our limbs upon gorgeous beds of straw. The thought was refreshing, and knocked some spirit into the drooping frame of Marks and his equally foot-sore companions. Look up! the sun is sinking, and there in the distance beyond the clump of timbers that surrounds the Chateau upon that still distant hill—look keenly, and you may see the steeple of the little village church of La Subdery. It is only a few kilometres away ; a few kilometres over the sharp edges of the little stones that are too abundantly strewn upon the road ; a few kilometres with bleeding feet, hunger gnawing at the vitals, and about 70lbs of, in many cases, useless lumber upon your back ; only a few kilometres, Marks, and you'll be at rest for one night at least.

Yes, La Subdery is before us, and we pass on into its quiet little square, where we halt, and are soon told off to our quarters for the night. The little village was crammed with troops, who were almost bursting through the frail walls of the cottages of the *paysans* and bourgeoise of the place. We were always the last to be provided for by virtue of our company's number in the battalion. There were at all times seven companies to cater to, before we entered into the consideration of our *Commandant*. We were the last to get *billets de logement* and the last to get *vivres*. After a march, too, the work of providing food was often a fatiguing and troublesome duty for the sergeant-fourrier. I have known Henry M'Crossin to be for hours trying to obtain food for the soldiers of " *La Compagnie Irlandaise*," even after a march of thirty or forty kilometres the same day. Like the rest of the troops, even the sergeants were often miserably provided with shoes, and M'Crossin was no exception to his rank. He had often to labour, when other men were taking refreshing naps upon manure heaps or logs of wood, anywhere but not on the cold, wet, and clayey soil. This evening, however, it failed even the energetic spirit and active mind of Sergeant M'Crossin to obtain food for the famished soldiers. The poor fellow became disconsolate, as he was pushed about by the numerous sergeants who were on a similar mission for their own men. He fought hard enough, but he had neither the physical energy, nor the wild effrontery to succeed at all times upon such a mission. M'Crossin would have made a better commissioned officer than he did a sergeant, if, indeed, he had a little more comprehensive military knowledge within his cranium.

"I can't succeed, Captain," he said, as he returned empty-handed; "there is a terrific rush for food, and everything is so wretchedly organised, that I fear I must wait an hour or two."

"Bring Sergeant Carey with you," I said, "and perhaps he may make some impresssion upon the crowd," and soon Carey was stepping towards the stores with determined strides, and a countenance which bore the impress of "do or die" upon its every lineament. I watched him as he was about to enter the door, already blocked with equally eager, but less persistent men, as Carey, followed by his fatigue party, pushed his way through the throng.

"*La Compagnie Irlandaise, La Compagnie Irlandaise*, make way, make way," and soon the surprised throng caught the spirit of the words, and generously replied, "make way, make way, for *La Compagnie Irlandaise*," and Carey quickly returned with rations to the hungry and famished soldiers of his company.

CHAPTER VI.

" He jests at scars, that never felt a wound."
SHAKSPEARE.

" LA COMPAGNIE IRLANDAISE," was billeted at the Chateau of La Subdery. The handsome building stood in the centre of a clump of trees, surrounded by open meadow and pasture lands. It was the residence of one of the *noblesse* of France, and its turreted angles topped the neighbouring timber, and stood out sharp, clear, and bold, against the moonlit atmosphere beyond. There was indeed, no princely demesne, nor deer-park, nor artificial ponds to show the lordly rank of the proprietor—such things are almost unknown in Democratic France—but there was the usual courtly tone about the surroundings, that in itself stamped the Chateau as the property and residence of a man of rank. But the family had gone : " The son and heir to the war, *messieurs,* as a simple soldier, and we hear that he has been promoted to be sergeant for distinguished conduct at the battle of Orleans," said the aged caterer who guarded the place and property of the proprietor. Here was one sample at least, of the ennobling spirit of patriotic love. Here was the only son of a long line of *noblesse*, the heir to what in France is a princely fortune—£10,000 per annum—the little king of a little principality, renouncing all, and in the ranks of the Mobile Guards, standing shoulder to shoulder, a private, with the *paysans* and bourgeoise of his native locality. France, so "fruitful in brave wits," gave the best and bravest of her sons to her country. France, " the land of scholars, and the nurse of arms," with all her wild, passionate faults, stood as one man under the tric lor, even when amidst the darkest passages of that eventful war there was no rift in the cloud of her uninterrupted disaster. The patriotism of the French, at this period at least, is almost unsurpassed either in modern or ancient history. Communists, Republicans, Imperialists, Legitimists, and Orleanists, all, as one man, renounced party, and allowed their differences to stand in abeyance, until they had either sank or swam together. When it is considered that political antagonism in France is a passion—that political faith is too often the only creed of one or more sections of the people—that they regard the triumph of their party with a political madness—it is no trifling sacrifice to renounce all these and stand shoulder to shoulder in the ranks of the common service, for the common cause. This is patriotism of the highest type, and deserves the highest commendation. But there is a sad yet glorious history of the career of the young *noblesse* under the shadow of whose ancestral home we slept the sleep that fatigue induces—the sleep of regenerating rest. Poor fellow, he fell during the gallant retreat of Chanzy towards Le Mans. I afterwards heard the story of his death around which there was something of romantic interest. "It was on the margin of a wood, *mon Capitaine*," said my informant, "the Bavarians were pressing hard upon our flank, with their accustomed tactics, for one of the first features of their military code is 'Gain the flank of your enemy upon every possible occasion.' At this time young Monsieur La Fonte was sous-lieutenant, and during the day his captain and his lieutenant had been put *hors de combat*. His company was covering the retreat, and he halted his men under cover of the timber to check the Bavarian advance. To him the whistle of the bullets were but as sweet music in his ears, for he was a true soldier, a worthy scion of that ancient line. But the enemy pressed closer; La Fonte gave the order to fix bayonets, and just as the Bavarians were about to carry the wood, he at the head of the Mobiles of La Subdery met them in their advance, foot to foot, bayonet to bayonet, eye to eye, and was himself first to spring upon his man. But," he added looking sorrowfully upon the snow-covered ground, " the villanous steel of a German *cochon* entered his heart, and sent his soul to his Maker." But all this was an after event. That night, at the Chateau of La Subdery, we had joyous anticipations of a few days' rest. Take a peep into the hay-loft to which the Irish soldiers have been told off, see how happily the wearied men stretch out upon the heaps of straw that abundantly cover the floor. You can read fatigue in the listless and wearied motions of the men as they sink into the yielding piles. Packs and belts hang from the wooden pegs that protrude through the wall, while the rifles are piled with scrupulous care in the corners of the room. Sleep appears to have already overtaken the majority of the men, while a few whose duty it is to cook the food of their respective squads are making vigorous attempts to light fires in the courtyard of the Chateau. The clothes of all are soiled and torn, while blistered and bandaged feet tell a tale of keen and anxious suffering. But

> " Who breathes must suffer, who thinks must mourn,
> And he alone is bless'd who ne'er was born."

But the caterer, too, had his tale of sorrow. His son had fallen a victim to fell disease, and died in hospital.

" Hé was all I had to look to in this world, *monsieur*, my only boy, his mother's darling, his sister's hope, but

> Mais a la guerre,
> Comme a la guerre,"

said the old man, using the familiar quotation of the time, and looking sorrowfully towards his wife, whose mother's heart looked through her melancholy shaded countenance.

But there is no time for vain regret. The bustle of a soldier's life gives sorrow to the winds. Rest, and be thankful. Rest upon a veritable bed, with luxurious feathers and handsome counterpanes, and genuine fatigue to lull you to refreshing sleep. How gorgeously the soft beds sank beneath the exhausted frames of those who could secure the comforts of that abode. How refreshing it was to take off the boots, from the wearied and blistered feet, and then when partly undressed, to sink into a refreshing slumber upon the yielding feathers. Men after all must experience hardships to appreciate even primitive civilization. Sleep upon the stony surface of a ploughed field in winter time, have the frost eating into your bones, and benumbing your limbs, be hungry for the time, let cold, famine, and *la misere*, obtain full control over your system, and just get one night's genuine repose upon a yielding bed of any material, and if you do not enjoy it, I am no reader of human nature, nor experienced in the same. And then fancy after all your pleasant thoughts, after your happy and refreshing rest in prospective, fancy to be rudely shaken out of your slumbers after four hours' sleep, and hear that the regiment was already away. It was a discordant sound that was uttered into my ear that morning when some one shrieked:—

"Captain, Captain, the march of the regiment has sounded, the battalion is under arms, the enemy is in the neighbourhood!" Then indeed a scene of bustle and confusion followed. But it was only for a few minutes, and we soon burst away, over ploughed lands and vineyards, on to St. Florent again, where the waters of the Ouron course through the usually quiet thoroughfares, and where we were destined to have two days' happy and refreshing repose. It was Sunday too, and the *Angelus* bell sounded beautifully soft upon the calm still air. When we halted for a moment at the outskirts of the village, I remember falling away into one of my dreamy moods, and humming a familiar air about "Sweet bells of music stealing round about me as I lay," when M'Alevey came to my side and asked me if I could'nt "whistle a jig for a change."

"From the sublime to the ridiculous," he added, "as the man said when he made 'the angel's whisper' read 'the angel's whisker,' by the alteration of a letter."

"M'Alevey, you're a harebrained fellow," I answered, amused at his importunities.

"If getting bald is an evidence, I certainly am, Captain," he replied, tracing his fingers around the upper portion of his scalp.

"As I told you—marked for the cloister, M'Alevey."

"No; I have, as Kuess charges me with, an insane desire to pay for a woman's board, and if I pull through the war, I have made up my mind to devote myself to one fair girl alone," said the lieutenant once more placing his hand upon the well polished regimental buttons of his great coat.

"You are incorrigible, M'Alevey."

"No, Captain, you don't understand me, that's all. You see with all our boasted civilization and progress, man neither knows himself nor his neighbours. We have never gotten beyond the idea of 'instinct' for the soul power of animals, nor can we, with all our sciences and refinement, solve the problem of 'why a spaniel wags its tail, or what a lobster thinks.'"

"Philosophical, by Jove. Why, man, your attainments are as varied as Crichton's," broke in the doctor; "but," he added, "what is to be"—

"To be!" replied M'Alevey, without giving the doctor time to complete the sentence, "why it's a verb of course."

"Oh, nonsense, M'Alevey, you'll never be easy, until you don sackcloth, and ashes," replied the doctor, moving towards an officer, the purple facings of whose single breasted tunic, pronounced him to be a brother-follower of the healing god, and both immediately returned and asked me to accompany them to a church which stood before us, and over the door of which the red-cross flag waved its international emblem in peaceful and charitable assurance. "*Secours aux blessés*" was written in large characters upon a white flag, and maimed and disabled soldiers loitered around the entrance, their pale and emaciated countenances, broken limbs, empty sleeves, and ugly gashes, too plainly telling the origin of their troubles. Sisters of Mercy promenaded the spacious aisles of the church, and hung, with tender solicitude, over the hard-breathing soldiers, who whispered their dying wishes into their ears. The seats had all been removed, and the men were arranged in rows, from the door to the altar, and the beautifully clean coverings that were placed upon the straw, were here and there dotted with blood stains. There were no bedsteads, but there was a delicacy in the careful folds of the counterpanes, and neatness in the improvised regularity with which the wounded men were surrounded. The first bed Dr. Macken visited was that of a Franc-tireur, who had been shot clean through the body, the bullet having struck him in the chest, about four inches above the heart, and passed out of his back a little to the left of the spine. The poor fellow underwent the changes of his bandages and syringing of the ghastly wound in his back with the greatest fortitude, only moaning once slightly as the fresh plugs of lint were applied and strapped on. For him as well as for the next four men who underwent inspection there was no hope of recovery. "They are all dead men," said the doctor, as he passed them by. Four out of five of them were shot through the lungs—one of them as handsome a young fellow as ever I set eyes on. Not a man flinched or swooned whilst under the surgeon's hands, although the agony of being moved must have been fearful in every case. But the stoutest case of self-command I witnessed throughout my two hours' visit to the hospital church at La Subdery was manifested by a young man of the Breton Gardes Mobiles. He was a stalwart, broad-chested, beardless lad, with large rough hewn features, and great muscular development.

He had only just been brought in, with a terrific hole under his right shoulder, plugged up by the field-surgeon after he had lost a great quantity of blood, and this was his first inspection since his arrival. He sat up in his bed quite steadily whilst his wound was being uncovered, and never shrunk forward once from the doctor's touch.

"Has the bullet been taken out, my man," said Dr. Macken, looking at the jagged edges of the wound with his eyes half shut, as if to concentrate his sight and to pierce the depths of the orifice.

"I really don't know, sir," replied the wounded soldier, with a degree of coolness that surprised the well-steeled nerves of Dr. Macken himself.

"The report says it has, but I find it has not," said the doctor, after his carefully-trained fingers had tapped the neighbourhood of the wound. "Would you like to have it out?"

"Yes, if you please, sir."

"Will you take chloroform, or do you think you can stand it?"

"Oh, I can stand it, sir, unless you prefer giving me chloroform."

"Very well; lie down and keep quite steady."

The projectile, which had entered the young man's back under the right shoulder-blade, had been stopped by the collar-bone under which it had lodged deep down in the flesh—too deep, indeed to be got at with the probe—so there was nothing for it but to cut down to it from the other side. The operation, which was splendidly executed by Dr. Macken, took exactly one minute and twenty seconds from the insertion of the knife to the strapping-up of the new wound, during which time the young soldier never blenched, nor moved his head, nor clenched his hands, nor even breathed hard. I never witnessed such an example of perfect stoicism before. The projectile extracted proved to be a mitrailleuse bolt quite knocked out of shape by its concussion with the young man's collar-bone, which must have been of no ordinary hardness, judging by its powers of resistance. As soon as the doctor pulled out the bolt and had it washed, he handed it to the young man, saying, "There is something for you to remember the Germans, my lad." Upon which, raising himself, he thanked Dr. Macken as calmly as if having an ounce or so of lead cut out of his body were the most ordinary occurrence of his every-day life, and then he submitted himself to the hands of the *infirmier*, who touched him as delicately as an infant.

The stretcher had been used more than once while we were making the rounds, and more than one body was brought out to be deposited in its last resting-place. Priests were bending with pious solicitude over the sinking form of many a stricken soldier, and cheering their last moments with words of hope and prayer. If you look to the farthest end of the church, just beside the railings, where devout communicants were wont to receive the sacrament, you may see a priest kneeling over a man, whose soul appears about to quit "its mortal frame;" the left hand of the pious man supports the head of the sinking soldier, while a crucifix is held before his eyes, and he clasps his hands in holy resignation to the will of God. A Sister of Charity bends over the dying man, and looks calmly into the eyes which are already becoming glazed with the dim shadows of death. Closer and nearer still bends the *abbé*, and he presses the crucifix upon the lips of the sinking soldier; the eyes of the good sister open a little wider, she takes his hand and applies her well-trained fingers to his pulse, looking steadily into the patient's eyes just for a minute, and then the hand is gently placed upon the bed-covering, the head is allowed to fall upon the pillow; the priest and nun join their voices in prayer—the soldier is dead. In the whole history of human charity there is no more melting picture than the tender compassion, the anxious hope, and the pious care of holy people over the bed of a dying human being. The soldier dies for honour, glory, and risks life and limb for visionary dreams of triumphs in the future; but the priest, or Sister of Mercy who renounces much of the comforts of the world, who can hope for no honour, who can anticipate no earthly reward, and who brave death in the hospital, is, to my mind, possessed of a higher degree of true courage, than the man who merely dies in action. One is mental, the other is too often physical courage alone. One is true heroism, the other may or may not possess that virtue.

But I am philosophizing again! I had had enough of the church-hospital and left my medical friends to continue their charitable work while I walked out of the place into the now busy thoroughfares of St. Florent. Here, as usual, Sergeant Carey was floundering about, doing as much genuine service as an orderly-room full of ordinary men. His splendid figure might be seen darting here and there with rapid but dignified ease. When I came to the door his handsome face illuminated with a smile beamed upon me, and I felt the effect of the influence which his generous voice cast upon my mind. I knew there was something unusual the matter as he advanced towards me holding a fowl in his hand. He got the bird as a present from a woman whom he had just befriended, and he came up to me with the jocular but well-remembered remark:

"Well, Captain, luck has favoured me for once. Here I am getting a beautiful and a delicate dinner for nothing, when the order of events have been, to have nothing for dinner;" and he walked away to attend to some matter of detail, leaving me full of admiration for his irrepressible humour and indefatigable power of endurance.

Our two days at St. Florent wore pleasantly away. The usual routine of a soldier's duty was not uninterrupted by anything which left its impress on my memory. Gambetta had, indeed, come to St. Florent, and was closeted with the municipal officials and the military chiefs for a short time on the first day, and then we once more paraded to take our departure again for Bourges, upon which we now began to look as a kind of home. It was a lovely day as we stood in line in front of our comfortable quarters awaiting the word which was to give us the route. The sun's rays shone with brilliant significance upon the unburnished rifles of the men whose weather-beaten countenances, hardy expressions, and tattered raiments, pronounced the dangers and the trials they had already surmounted. But we were away at last—away over the uninteresting country watered by the Auron—away to Bourges with its happy associations and pleasant reminiscences of days gone by.

I was thinking of our chances, and speculating upon our hopes, as we trudged along the road, through the flat and unbroken country around, when the tall towers of the Cathedral of Bourges again stood out against the cloudless sky. The grand old structure, with its deeply-recessed portals, its bas-reliefs, its rows of niches, its florid Norman ornaments, its unsightly flying buttresses, its beautifully painted windows, and its happy associations, was once more in view. Beneath its very shadow, almost under the protection of its wings, lived the dearest and most friendly of our many friends in France. We were sure of at least a hearty welcome just within the limits of that gigantic shadow-making structure. Yes, there is something in the words of Robert Blair, "Friendship is the cement of the soul; the sweet'ner of life." It is something to know that a generous welcome awaits the weary and the foot-sore; it is something to feel a conscious monitor drawing the sentiments of the heart towards the abode of kind friends, where kindred spirits meet, with kindred longings. It is something to know that in the desert of the heart there is one oasis to which the weary thinker may turn with hopeful longings, and bask beneath the protecting shade of friendship's tree. If only for a moment, it is something to know that, even in the great distance, beyond the seas if you like, there is one hand that will grasp your own in joyous welcome. Part with friends, go on a campaign, hold your life in your hands, and return, even for an hour, and if you don't feel as genuine pleasure as mortal can experience, I am much in error.

But Bourges was still before us. The country was flat and undrained, and the prospect of a comfortless night broke down the spirits of the men. Marks and some others were still barefooted. The pebbles, which were abundantly strewn along our route, created sores, and the frost eat holes, as large as five-shilling pieces, upon many a brave fellow's foot. Sergeant Terence Byrne marched at the head of the company, his honest countenance reflecting the character of as brave a man, and as gentle a Christian as ever wore a side arm, or nursed a stricken enemy. There was indeed no regularity in the steps of the soldiers as they shuffled along, they were marching *a voluntaires*, but yet the tramp and noise at that moment made a singular impression on my mind, as the small hillocks we were passing echoed the tramp of the 20,000 men who were shuffling by.

"Sergeant," I said, speaking to Terence Byrne, "To a soldier's ear there is after all no music like the music of the feet."

"Yes, captain, but it must be of feet that are protected from the jagged stones and destroying frost," replied Byrne, with a significant cast of his head to the rear, where the bleeding feet of the Irish soldiers, cast a terrible responsibility upon the conduct of the authorities, and the military impecuniosity, which was sacrificing the health and lives of brave men to a system only becoming a nation of paupers. But there was irrepressible mirth still in the ranks of *La Compagnie Irlandaise*, Sergeant Carey would have his joke in spite of frost or famine. Once as the weakly were vainly endeavouring to keep up with the rapid marching, I heard him remonstrating, and encouraging them on. Each poor fellow had his plea, either sore feet, or a ponderous and useless knapsack. One indeed complained of the benumbing frost, and soon after I heard Carey advise the lagsters to "Keep up men, keep up, sure the closer you are the warmer you'll be;" and then the men behind gave a spurt into the ranks again, to fall away by degrees, until another word of encouragement caused them to make a still further effort to keep the pace.

But "the noiseless foot of time" brings on the day. The sun works around the arch of heaven, and sinks away into the darkening space beyond. The keen wind ripples through the branches of the poplar trees that everywhere line the way, and speeds upon its mission over the neatly cultivated lands upon our flank. Empty vaulted night brings gloomy forebodings to the wearied soldiers, as they still shuffle on hoping to make their destination before the witching hours. At last, a glow of flame illumines our front; you can see it like a pall of fire in the great distance, and your fancy pictures the tired soldiers crouching around the innumerable bivouacs before us. But on still a few kilometres more, and Bourges is made, and the men throw themselves upon the slimy ground to rest! But no, there is little rest for a soldier on campaign. Fatigue parties have to get wood, more food, and a few make a vain and unsuccessful effort to beg some bundles of straw from a neighbouring chateau.

"Well," said Timothy Marks, looking down at the ground, and scanning the place he had to lie upon as keenly as if it were a bed of thistles; "well, sure it's soft anyhow, there's no danger of getting bed-sores or any other sores from coming in contact with genuine, aisy, soft soil.

"Who knows, maybe, we'll nave worse before the campaign is over," said one of Tim's companions, trying to find some consolation in the present.

"That's pleasant anyhow," replied Tim, as he spread his little blanket on the ground, and unrolled his patch of tent cloth. "Maybe we would have a worse bed than this, but, if we do, I hope it 'ill be on the *other* side of the ground," he continued placing an emphasis on "other" that made it suggestive of "under."

"We'll go to Bourges after we settle everything for the night, M'Alevey," said I to the lieutenant, "when we know where we are to be encamped we shall come and have the comfort of meeting old faces and the luxury of being entertained in a Christian house once more;" and we consoled ourselves with the prospect of a bright vision in the evening. But we were astray in our reckoning. Our clothes were bespattered with loam and tanned with exposure, and our faces were sun-burned and dirty. We were, in fact, *comme a la guerre*, and presented no holiday appearance as we looked at each other and speculated upon the propriety of facing our lady friends. But we could, perhaps, find some place in Bourges where we could make ourselves presentable, and then, after a few instructions to Lieutenant Cotter, who was on duty, we floundered back to Bourges. But the military authorities disposed of our propositions in their own way. There was no admittance to the town without an order from the colonel, countersigned by the general of division, which involved as much red-tapism as would prevent any ordinary mind from even attempting the ordeal. There was nothing for it but to return to camp, and reconciled ourselves with a piece of sea-biscuit and a tin of coffee, and then seek the shelter of our canvas walls.

CHAPTER VII.

"When the nations made queens by our triumphs
  Showered flowers on the conqueror's head
That, that was the moment to perish,
  Be ye envied, ye dead!"

BERANGER.

THE following morning was, I think, the 17th of December, 1870. It was somewhat warm too, and the sun's rays melted the patches of snow into pools of water, and the tramp of 20,000 men had made the encampment a sea of mud. The troops had a strong resemblance to that class of scavengers known as "mud larks," except, indeed, that the soldiers did not possess singularly long boots, nor serviceable clothing, but the clay covered their uniforms and had hardened into patches of dirt upon kepi, great coat, and pantaloons. The men had had no straw the night before, and were compelled to lie upon the muddy earth, with their little blankets under them, and nothing but a miserably small tent to secure them from the freaks of atmospheric nature. Like many other things in the French army the equipment of the troops was in every way unserviceable. The kepi looks neat and janty in garrison. It sets off a soldier to, perhaps, the best advantage, so long as it is kept in order, but on campaign the kepi is neither neat nor serviceable. It loses shape, fits badly, and the peak droops and goes out of form. It is, too, an uncomfortable night-cap, an adaptability that should by no means be lost sight of in a soldier's forage head-dress. In the German army the forage cap is serviceable but unsightly. It cannot lose shape, because it has no shape to lose. It never looks badly, because it never looked too well. The forage cap of a German soldier is in every way more suited for a campaign than the French kepi; still the latter sits more jantily, and looks more graceful on the boulevards, or "during the piping time of peace." The great coat of the French soldier, too, has nothing to recommend it but its colour, which is admirably selected, and, perhaps, the least distinguishable at a given distance of any in the armies of Europe. But the material is bad and thin, and it gives but little warmth or protection to the famished soldiers. The coat of the German soldier is, on the contrary, warm and serviceable. The material is thick and tolerably good. Then, too, the Germans go on campaign with their tunics under their great coats; while the French troops take their shell-jackets alone. There are no flannels served out in the French army, while in Germany under-flannels are one of the essential requisites of a soldier's kit. The French carry small patches of canvas, about five feet square, and by joining four of them together a little tent is made, which, if it were better regulated, would become a really serviceable portion of their equipment. But, above all, the Germans had the advantage in their method of shoeing their men. Every German was provided with boots, into which the pantaloons were put, and which almost effectually secured the feet from frost and pebbles. In France the soldiers are not even provided with socks, and many of the soldiers of *La Compagnie Irlandaise* were compelled to suffer all the hardships of the campaign, in an atmosphere 15 degrees below zero, without a pair of stockings upon their feet, and, too often, the miserably low shoes worn into shoddy. The Germans very often encase their feet in the folds of a long thin stripe of greased calico, carefully wrapped around the member, and which I believe to be the best of all safeguards from the effects of frost. It would appear, indeed, from the respective equipments of the combatant armies that one had studied the art of war in all its details—that the other had not. Through this means the war became a war between rival organisations, as much as a war between men. It became a war of boots, of clothing, of provisions, and of internal regimental economy. Place a regiment of Prussian infantry in our place at Bourges, on the 17th Dec., 1870. Let them be almost shoeless, and the keen air penetrating through their shoddy garments, after a restless night spent on the clayey ground, and place the *Regiment Etranger* for one night in a town, give them boots and good clothing, and one meal of Liebeg's extract of meat, and an encounter might result in disaster to the usually victorious Germans.

But still another night had passed. The *reveille* had sounded once more, and the smoke from hundreds of camp fires gave notice that the morning meal was in preparation. The hurry of the coming *en route* was again on foot, for we had another day's march before us. Beside our encampment the soldiers of *La Compagnie Irlandaise* had surrounded, and vigorously hacked at the hind quarter of a dead charger, like a swarm of bees over a bunch of honeysuckle. Huge steaks were cut from off the still warm carcase, and the sword bayonets of the men rattled against the ribs and flank of the dead *cheval*. It was a sight for an artist's pencil. Famine appeared to give vigour to the men's arms, and the prospect of a meal traced an expression of joy over their countenances.

"Poor fellows," said Lieutenant M'Alevey, as he sat upon a soldier's knapsack sipping a cup of coffee that his orderly had prepared for him; "poor fellows, a soldier's life on campaign is a round of miseries, hunger, cold, and hardship; but," he added, tracing his fingers along the *frisèd* edges of his moustache, and expressively half closing his eyes by a dreamy movement of the eyelids, "but, after all, its joys more than compensates for its sorrows. For my own part

I am never comfortable except when I'm seeking the bubble reputation," and the lieutenant sipped his coffee, and handed a neatly-finished revolver to his orderly to be cleaned.

In the meantime *resistance à outrance* was still the cry in France. Prince Frederick Charles threatened Bourges; the Grand Duke of Mecklenburg, Tours; and Manteuffel, Havre, in order to prevent Chanzy from Vendome, Bourbaki from Gien, or Faidherbe from St. Quentin from relieving Paris. Chanzy had still 150,000 soldiers well in hands, and was now entrenched around the formidable field works before Le Mans. He had, too, 300 well-served guns, but his troops were in poor condition. Bourbaki was mysteriously moving towards the East with 130,000 men, including our corps, the 15th, which was to follow him in the early days of January. But the German commanders were manœuvring to give the *coup de grace* to the armies of France. Already Chanzy was threatened in front and flank, thus compelling him to show two fronts, by attacking him at right angles—the tactics that succeeded so well in the Bohemian angles—the tactics that succeeded so well in the Bohemian campaign. Such a mode of attack itself implies a contempt for one's enemies, inasmuch as it offends against the rule of attacking with inferior numbers, but the German commanders often, throughout the war, set tactics aside, and acted upon examples as much as principles.

The duty of our corps was still to protect Bourges. An unexpected event, however, prevented Prince Frederick Charles from advancing beyond Vierzon, and our marching and counter-marching was all to no avail. No rest for the wearied troops, but continuous and harrassing marches. Even the muddy soil in the neighbourhood of the old Gallic city would have been an acceptable place of repose to the wearied troops, but owing to our want of cavalry our commanders were so ill-advised about the movements of the enemy that they very often found themselves groping in the dark. No rest, but away again; this time for Bresy, a village about 20 kilometres from Bourges. Our Brigade was soon in line, and we quickly left the smouldering camp fires behind.

I suppose I must have been "methodising," as M'Alevey called a moody demeanour, for my witty lieutenant came to my side, and, looking seriously in my face, began to speculate upon the bent of my thoughts, whether they were of "love, religion, or war."

"Neither," I replied, "As to 'love,' I'll leave all that to you."

"You think me light and flippant upon that subject, captain, but ruffled water sometimes take deep soundings. Remember your Byron, and think that I, too, may have 'sighed to many, though I loved but one.'"

"You surprise me, M'Alevey. I thought you incapable of the tender passion. I always took you to be a man after John Keat's idea, a being 'Whose philosophy would clip an angel's wings."

"No," said the lieutenant somewhat sadly, "not always. I have my own recollections, the incidents that have schooled my thoughts to wander to one spot in that dear little isle of ours. But," he added, looking at a handsomely cut cross that stood beside the way "what is this?" and M'Alevey walked over to note the lines that were carved upon its surface.

Just then the *sac-a-tarre* sounded, and I moved over and joined him on his mission.

"We stand on classic ground," said M'Alevey, when he had read the inscription that was carved upon the face of the cross. "Here the English suffered defeat by the inhabitants of Bourges in 1356, see," he added, pointing to the letter :—

"*Croix Erigee en souvenir de la victoire remportée sur les Anglais par les habitants de Bourges. En* 1356."

"*Vive la France*," said Capitaine Ceresole, coming to our side and saluting the cross, or perhaps the inscription, that appealed to his soldier heart.

"*Vive la France et l'Irlande*," said M'Alevey turning to the new arrival, and doffing his kepi with courteous salutation.

"The Saxon bit the dust here," said Ceresole, looking around the hard, flat country, "and, by my soul, a fine place it was for a rout. How our cavalry must have ridden the beef-eaters down over those unsheltered lands. Of course, all your men are somewhat rebellious in their temper to the English?" he added, looking at me through his blue-coloured spectacles.

"Yes, all to British rule over Ireland. Some of us, however, are not to British connexion with Ireland," I replied, and then the *sac-a-dos* sounded again—packs on—and, as we were about to leave the scene, every kepi in the ranks of *La Compagnie Irlandaise* was raised in parting salutation to the—

"*Croix Erigee en souvenir de la victoire remportée sur les Anglais par les habitants de Bourges. En* 1356."

But Bourges is now before us, and we quickly make the outer earthworks of the town. Fatigue parties are still busy, making trenches, building traverses, sloping counter-scarps, working at gabions, erecting barricades, or arranging sand-bags. There is bustle about the arsenal, and the military workshops have the appearance of being in a fever of business.

But we press on through the town, and once more enter the open country beyond. The constant passage of artillery, military train, and soldiers has made deep ruts in the road and there is mud every where. The Irish soldiers look thoroughly hardened, and have the appearance of real work in their dress which is now *comme a la guerre*. All was not indeed smooth sailing in the ranks of *La Compagnie Irlandaise*. There were three or four men in the company who earned the reputation of being growlers, men into whom the spirit of Oliver Twist appeared to have entered, and who were constantly crying for "more, more," of the good things of the service. They were the black sheep of the flock, and stood out in bold relief from their companions. On a line of march it is often a matter of trouble to keep such gentry in order. If a soldier meets some benevolent peasant or bourgeois who treats him to a *carafon*, or a *demi-tasse* too much, the soldier is likely to forget himself, as all other tipsters do, he may be absent from roll-call—if it is in garrison—and and he may lag or shirk his duty, if it happens on the march. In garrison, however, there is the guard-room, and its attendant consequences—fatigue duty, stoppage of pay, confinement to barracks, and all the etceteras arising from bad conduct marks. *En route*, however, everything changes; guard rooms would be too troublesome to carry on pack mules, stopping the soldier's pay might affect his health by depriving him of his share in the *ordinaire*, and there is nothing but courts-martial left to the officers in command. During our campaign in France, I have known a sergeant-major to be shot for stealing a fowl, although the poor fellow was ravenously hungry at the time. But they were exceptionally hard in the Foreign Regiment. I heard of another instance in which a sergeant attempted to strike a soldier; the soldier put his rifle up to guard off the blow; the sergeant's hand was cut; the soldier was court-martialled, and shot. In the other regiments, however, things were better. In the Franc-tireurs, particularly, the men had a kind of free license to do as they pleased. They were the guerillas of the war. Always well clothed, generally well provided with food, their knapsacks carried on baggage-waggons, the Franc-tireurs neither experienced the hardships nor the terrible realities of the campaign. They moved in such small numbers that they were always sure of shelter and food in their wanderings. Their commanders were very often civilians, or national guardsmen, who were not too strict in their interpretation of "regulations," "decrees," or "orders of the day."

With us, however, it was different. We were part and parcel of the regular army, and had all the duties and hardships of regular troops to encounter. Discipline was rigid enough, too rigid at times; "but it is necessary, sir, it is necessary," as the *Commandant* of our battalion once assured me. "What can we do?" he again appealingly, asked me. "We cannot send men to prison, for we want them in the field, and I have ever held it to be a maxim in military law, that you must shoot a man on campaign, for a crime that you would give him fifteen days *salle de police* for during peace," and the *Commandant* extended his arms, shrugged his soldiers, arched his eyebrows, and settled the question to his entire satisfaction. We, however, managed differently. When the soldiers blundered, we gave them extra duty. They had to attend the sergeant-fourrier and carry the *vivres* from town, or they had to do an extra sentry-go, or if on the march they had to carry the rifles of their more careful companions. It was a very handy and persistent means of punishment, to give the Chassepot of some weakly and sickly soldier, who was straining every limb to pull out and be in at the death, to some brawny broad-shouldered man, who had forgotten himself or his duty the day before. But it happened more than once in the ranks of *La Compagnie Irlandaise*. In pure justice, however, I must say, that such circumstances were rare, very rare, amongst us. The men appeared to thoroughly understand their representative capacity—their fidelity to Ireland—their duty to France.

But on still, over ruts, through mud and water, on for Bressy. An occasional halt, a hurried repast, and away again while the sun climbs around in its never-ceasing course. Evening lapses into night, and away before us an occasional light pierces through the gloom, and we draw a fanciful picture of rustic life within the village cottages around. The keen wind moans its requiem through the branches of the trees, and puffs in fretful gusts over and through the deep-set hedges that line our route. Bressy is now before us, a little further we wheel into a field, take up our *alignement*, pitch tents, light fires, cook a spare repast, and sit around the *bivouac*, of another day gone.

CHAPTER VIII

> "Hallo! the pipe's gone out—what then
> We've reached the spot where I'm to die,
> No binding—no! Stand back there, men!
> I'll face death with unbandaged eye.
> Sorry to trouble you, gentlemen;
> But one more service I'll require.
> God bless you, lads, safe home again;
> Mind you aim low—now!—steady!—Fire!"
>
> Beranger's "*Old Corporal.*"

"The *reveille* has sounded, sir," said a familiar voice the following morning, as the owner endeavoured to untie the frozen cords which drew the stubborn canvas of my tent door together. I could hear the man outside stamping and puffing with that jerky uneasiness which indicates intense cold, as he strove on at his task for a few seconds, and it was not until a chilling blast penetrated through the sheep-skin sack into which I had thrust my lower self, that I ventured to peep from under my heap of blankets, and sniff the morning air. The sight was not an inviting one. My orderly, for it was he, had his fingers stuck knuckle-deep into his usually handsome mouth, which you may be sure was somewhat extended by the operation. The flap of the tent, which by courtesy was called the door, was hanging open, and the frosty prospect without was not agreeably relieved by the shivering sentry who cowered to leeward of an adjoining tent. Snow had fallen and hung upon the upper part of my canvas covering, and formed a curtain-like nightcap, through which icicles traced geometrical figures adown the sides of my tent, like tears of crystal from a silver vase. I could hear the cracking of burning wood, and could see the dim glare of a few fires through the canvas walls, as some shivering soldier endeavoured to keep alive the embers in order to facilitate the making of the morning meal; and then I turned a look upon my attendant—a look half of pity, half of amusement, and I suppose it was the latter expression he detected, for, removing his fingers from his mouth, he half apologetically said—

"By gad, it's cowld, sir!"

"So I see," was my reply, as I saw him change his attitude, and for the following moment appeared to have become possessed of the prancing spirit of St. Vitus. But it was cold, and no mistake that December morning, too cold for human nature to rough it upon the bare, frozen earth, left to the mercy of the piercing frost, and the paternal watchfulness of those vultures of civilization—army contractors. For my own part, I was tolerably well; but as I looked at the poor shrivelled being before me, hungry, almost nude, footsore, frost-bitten, and wretched, I could only think that man knows not the limit of his own endurance, and the world but little of the true misery of war. He, with his companions, had been starving "according to regulation" for the past month, and had huddled together in batches upon the frozen earth, with a shoddy blanket four feet by two as their only covering. But this was all over for one night more, and again the *reveille* sounded clear, sharp, and encouraging on the frozen air, and I heard the "turn out men, turn out," of Sergeant Carey, as he poked around the half-pitched tents, ever doing the cork-leg business of the company with wonderful elasticity. But my good-natured orderly was not idle all this time. The night before he had, for safety's sake, left some chips just within my tent, and I could see him now vainly endeavouring to light a fire, and occasionally, baffled and vexed at his unsuccess. Gusts of wind dodging around the camp blew streams of smoke into his well-bronzed face, and more than once made him retreat with weeping eyes, and tempt the poor fellow into a half-choked utterance which he was never taught under the shadow of his native Galtees. Andrew, or "Andy," as his companions used to call him, did, however, succeed in his task, and soon he left the fire to take care of itself, and, *beadon* in hand, ran off for water, which I had the discomfiture of seeing smothered in smoke, by the accidental turning of the villanous log which formed part of the support upon which the *beadon* rested.

"Andy, you have done it this time," said I, as I caught an expression upon his face which might be interpreted to mean "there is no help for spilt milk;" but he applied himself to resume his task, which resulted this time in complete success, and soon a sickly fire, more smoke than blaze, rewarded his forty minutes' labour.

"Here, try a pull at this," and I called him into the tent for a sip at the contents of a brandy flask, which I contrived to have accommodatingly at hand.

"That's fine, sir," were the first words he said, when he recovered from the gasping sensation which novices in the art of drinking from a bottle experience. "My throat was like the crust upon the inside of a chimney," and away he went to grope amongst tins and little bags, for coffee and sugar, for chunks of dirty beef and lard, to prepare the morning meal, before we were again *en route*.

But the camp was all alive now, and just as I threw over the piles of blankets, which were barely enough to keep the heat from escaping, Sergeant Carey popped his head in at the door with his usual "Good morning, Captain." To me it was always a pleasure to see Sergeant Carey, for his was the very soul of a soldier. It has been my lot to meet many men to whom in periods of trial I surrendered all the friendships of which my nature was capable, but never did I meet the equal of this incomparable man. Gay, indefatigable, and obedient, kind to the willing soldier, severe upon the shuffler, the soul of honour, a very prince among men, Sergeant Carey has left upon my memory associations of friendships and esteem, which death alone can destroy. But here he was, looking as happy as if he had had an hour's rest, or as if his almost empty haversack contained anything but a morsel of the tenderest portion of an aged horse. Amongst the officers of the regiment Sergeant Carey was known as "the sergeant with the grand beard," this same beard being now decorated with icicles as large as the cartridge of a Chassepot or a Snider.

"Good morning, Sergeant," said I, returning his salutation; "is it cold outside?"

"Well, sir," said he, looking down at his singularly frozen beard with an expression of what, I suspect, had just a little tinge of admiration, "my beard is my thermometer, and I see that it marks fifteen below zero, just," and he stroked the said beard, or rather the icicles which were appended thereto. I always thought there was some peculiar property in Carey's beard, for the particles of frost nestled in it with a tenacity which I had not remarked in the beards of other men.

Now, I thought the contents of my flask might help to thaw the frost from off this remarkable beard, and by the manner Carey accepted the invitation to try its effects, I think he had a somewhat similar belief. Poor fellow, it was like dropping a piece of carbonic acid upon a block of ice. But it does a fellow all the good in the world upon a bitter morning, when hoar frost covers hill and valley, and nestles upon shrub and tree as beautifully delicate as daylight upon the waste of waters.

"Ah, that's the stuff, Captain, for a campaign," said the Sergeant, when he had paid the penalty of the drain in the shape of a vigorous shiver, such as a spaniel gives when it emerges from a pool. "If they gave us some of that instead of their regulation doses of soup, and nothing in it, twice a day, they might expect a man to march thirty-six hours out of forty."

Just then the regimental call sounded beautifully shrill upon the morning air.

"That's for the sergeant-major," I said, as the four notes at the end indicated the rank of the man for whom the bugle sounded. Without a word Carey placed his kepi upon his head, left the tent, and I was once more alone. It was still dark, and all around the fizz of damp green wood struggled through volumes of smoke, from which a soldier shrinks more surely than he does from a vigorous fusilade. The little lamp attached to the tent pole gave sufficient light to enable me to make my easy toilet, which consisted of finding my kepi, and buckling on my sword. If we had time, I might indeed, indulge in a wash, but that was not always a comeatable luxury.

"The company is to parade under the command of an officer, Capain, immediately," said Carey, who had just returned. "A man to be shot, sir."

"How is the company to turn out?"

"With arms and ammunition, but without sacks, sir."

"All right! muster all the spare men, I'll come myself." And away he rattled, and soon I heard the clash of bayonets as the men unlocked the rifles from the *fais-ceaux*. It was bitterly cold, and as the men fell in, wet, hungry, and wretched-looking, more fit for the hospital than the field, more like shadows than like soldiers, wanting in everything save the indomitable spirit of their race, I thought the limit of their endurance had been reached. As I looked along my already diminished company that misty December morning, I could not but think that it is the miseries, and not the dangers, of a soldier's life, that should form the brightest chapter in his history. But away with reverie, the battalion was ready to march, a word of command, and we rattle along the broken ground, over a ditch or two, out upon the road, "pick up the step," and away for the place of execution. Just then I thought I would have time to inquire into the nature and the crime committed by the condemned man. Had he outraged person, stolen property, or committed an act of insubordination? Nothing of the kind! He was a boy volunteer, and had simply disposed of some of his kit for a few francs in order to buy food to appease his ravenous appetite. It was said, indeed, that it was merely one of his regulation shirts that he had sold, but for the truth of that I could not vouch. But how firmly and coolly he stood amidst the circle of fixed bayonets with which he was surrounded, and even found time to piteously joke that he would have "no knapsack to carry on his next long march." But just at the limits of our camp, where some chasseurs-a-pied were shivering on grand guard, into a field, and there before us we saw the foremost companies of our regiment forming three sides of a square. We soon arrived at the fatal spot, too plainly indicated by a wooden peg driven in the ground.

It was a solemn moment! It was, too, the first military execution we had seen in France, and the sickly sensation of a new horror crept over us all. But the drums beat, and the bugle flourished as the escort arrived, and the youth took his place beside the fatal landmark. He cast one look around, as if searching for some familiar face, and as the sun shed its earliest rays across the belt of landscape, the shadow of their gleam fell lightly upon his calm still countenance, and then the stilness of death followed. An officer unrolled an ominous looking sheet of foolscap paper, and there was no sound in heaven or on earth, until he read the sentence of the court-martial. All the while the gentle bearing of the youthful soldier influence men's hearts, and makes them wish strange things indeed. But the crisis soon approached, as the boy-soldier—I cannot say culprit—took off his military jacket, and threw it gently on the ground, showing the figure of a firmly-set young man. He took his place so near the wooden peg, that I thought it would transfix him as he fell, and forgetting for the second that he would fall a corpse, I thought of the pain the contact might cause him. No minister of God attended him to soothe the last moments of his life. He was of another creed and of another country; France was not his home. He took his stand alone, and carried himself with the calmness of a true soldier as his eyes were bandaged. He made no motion, he spoke no word, and obeyed the order to "kneel" more like a Christian martyr than a man on whom the shadow of a crime could rest. The firing party took position ten paces from the fated youth; the officer in command raises his sword for "aim," lowers it for "fire," and the fair young Polish soldier is a corpse! But the bugles sound again, and as I turned round to give some orders to the men, I detected more than one moist eye, and saw the firmly-set, proud features of Sergeant Carey half averted from my gaze. I remember, too, many a day after, the daring gallantry of the very men whom I had seen that morning visibly affected by the execution of a boy. I knew these very men to be brave almost to rashness, and even, under a murderous fire, cool almost to apathy. Yes, if you want men who will "march to death with military glee," take the tender-hearted and the gentle, take men who will "not wantonly tread upon a worm."

It was customary, I heard, for the regiment to march past the executed man in single file, but we were quickly taken away after the sergeant of the firing party had given the *coup de grace*. Open columns of companies, "*par le flanc droit, droit !*" and the long, thin line of red-breeched soldiers was gaily marching back to camp again. Of the dead man we thought no more.

> "Cover his bones over with stones,
> He is only a soldier whom nobody owns."

His grave was dug, and before the sun had climbed the skirt of timber which lay behind our encampment, he would be buried in the graveyard of the handsome little church that topped the neighbouring hill upon which Bressy was built.

But the day was well advanced, the steel grey clouds, away upon the south-eastern horizon, were fringed with streaks of silvery daylight. Magpies in ominous numbers perched about the deserted encampment to pick the scanty remnants of the soldiers' spare repast ;. villagers strolled about the place, and slid along the frozen ground in their canoe-like *sabots*, pitying and praying, but selling their *comfitures* all the time. The tents were struck, and *beadons* and *marmits* were everywhere in requisition, and emitted steam from onion soup or garlic. The famished soldiers were vainly trying to "manufacture" a morning meal.

As we drew near the place where our tents had stood, I saw all in preparation for the baggage-waggon. Andy looking radiant at his success in the *cuisine*. Breakfast ready ; never mind the sinewy steak, nor be too fastidious as to its hue, a ravenous appetite makes all the difference in the world.

" Where is Lieutenant M'Alevey, Andy ?" I asked ; wondering at what delayed my lieutenant from his meal.

" Begorra, I don't know, sir ; but I think he is in that direction," replied the mischievous Andy, casting a dangerously-knowing look towards the right of our battalion.

And sure enough, Lieutenant M'Alevey was in *that* direction cracking jokes with a pretty *vivandiere*, whom he compelled to laughingly retreat from the storm of his witticisms. But M'Alevey was soon by our side, endeavouring to fix a sinewy steak upon the point of an improvised fork.

We were joined by Mr. Cotter and Dr. Macken, and notwithstanding the toughness of the beef, succeeded in appeasing our voracious appetites with its savoury morsels. Hunger is, indeed, the best of all sauces. Physiologists say that a variety of food is good for man; if that be so, soldiers in the French army on a campaign are not provided with all that is beneficial or best for their creature comforts. But it is wonderful how even the once fastidious epicures, who, perhaps, abused innocent *garçons*, and swore at the favourite cooks of their metropolis, how they quickly accommodate themselves to the necessities of the times, and devour horse steak with all the relish of a *gourmand*. Latterly, the French military authorities have, I believe, increased the quantity of rations which was allowed to the French soldiers during the late war. Frenchmen, as a rule, are very poor eaters indeed. A moderate Irishman would eat a French peasant out of house and home. At best the French troops had not enough to eat; the men were scarcely ever satisfied. As for the Irish soldier, it was literal starvation—they never had enough. Were it not for the *ordinaire*, to which each man had to contribute three sous every five days, they would not have been able to march. Of this, however, there could not be much to complain of, as all were treated alike. Even the officers had no more than enough, although provided with extra rations. Two lieutenants had the rations of three privates; a captain had the rations of two privates; while *Commandants* had the rations of three privates, and so on in proportion to rank. It is not to be supposed that officers have better appetites than their men, but there are always hangers-on in proportion to the rank, and waste does away with much of the food. But man, of all the animals, can bear the greatest privations. The soldiers of the Irish Company bore the traces of hunger upon their countenances, but the constant marching and counter-marching, with the bustle of campaigning, hardly gave them time to brood over their condition.

"I don't think the Irish soldier has degenerated in his digestive organs at least," said Dr. Macken, as if he was expressing the opinions which were at that moment coursing through our minds.

"*M. la Medicine, par example*," replied Mr. M'Alevey, as he significantly nodded towards the doctor, who was engaged devouring an enormous steak off a tough old charger.

"Well, you know," retorted the doctor, "it has often been remarked that a people are never cognizant of a decline in their own physical or moral degeneracy. The Romans under Julius Didianus, believed themselves the equals of their predecessors under Augustus. Yet," he added, delighted to have mounted one of his hobby-horses —Ancient History—" of the two periods that of the Imperators was immeasurably the more brilliant. His——"

"Oh, stop, for mercy's sake, doctor, don't run into the graves of the contemporaries of that time. We"ll guess the rest about that golden age of Latin poetry, but, in the meantime, allow us to consume our portion of this ancient *cheval*, without sprinkling it with the dust of Virgil or of Livy."

"But," remonstrated Dr. Macken, "I was about to draw a comparison unfavourable to your chivalrous self."

"Impossible," replied M'Alevey, "I am the Bayard of modern warfare, gentle in quarters, a lion in the field, only," he added, *sotto voce*, "I would rather my greatest enemy to be kicking me down Sackville-street, than to be in a real combat."

"No doubt," replied the doctor, "you consider yourself equal to your progenitors, just as Didianus considered himself the equal of Augustus. You think yourself equal to the deeds of Clare at Ramillies or Fontenoy, or of that wondrous achievement of the Irish regiment of Dillon, when they scaled the almost impregnable position of the Tyrolese, but you are in error *mon ami*."

Further *badinage* was interrupted by the arrival of one of Dr. Macken's hospital sergeants, requesting the doctor's presence at the field Ambulance, and he soon left us in full possession of the contents of our camp-kettles.

But we got the route before we had finished our repast. Then indeed there was a scene of hurry. As the head of the column began to move, orderlies rushed about in frantic haste, while sergeants were busy putting their companies in order. But we were in time. In France the battalions alternately march either with the first or last company in front; if this were not the case, we would have always been in rere of our battalion on the line of march. In our turn, however, we led the battalion, and when the *Commandant* placed himself at the head of *La Compagnie Irlandaise*, we saw that we were to march by the left, and it was our place to be first away. Back to Bourges again; back over the same road which we had traversed the day before.

The day was fine, and the march uninterupted with any peculiar incident beyond the one common to all marches—blistered feet, men falling away, some sinking on the road, some groaning with pain, dead and dying horses, broken boots, and hungry men with empty haversacks. Behind us the road was dotted with soldiers who had fallen out of the ranks, and who lay upon heaps of stones or logs of wood—perhaps to die. Gambetta's decrees about courts-martial had been found a failure—they were not practicable. And so the day wore on, and it was well into the evening; darkness had settled over the fertile soil, when in the distance the lights from Bourges attracted our attention, looking like fire-flies in the dark unhospitable night. Another hour brought us to the town, and then we wheeled into a field, through which a small stream coursed merrily along, but where the soil was reeking with wet, and yet where we had to make our bivouac for one night more. My tent, however, was nowhere to be found, there was something wrong with the officers' baggage. Andy, poor fellow, had succumbed to *la misere*, and had fallen out on the march, so Sergeant Carey undertook the task of hunting up the officers' baggage. For fully an hour he floundered about the carts, paying no attention to remonstrances of the sentries, pushing his way where less bold men would hesitate to enter. He was indeed a wonderful man, he could do what he liked in the regiment, his commanding form and vigorous mind overawed the privates and *sous-officiers*, while his magnificent beard and soldierly bearing secured for him the good wishes of every officer in the regiment. Although an humble man, I hope it may be my lot to meet again in life so true a friend, so tenderhearted a man, and so chivalrous a soldier. But it was no use; it failed even Sergeant Carey, and we were compelled to huddle into a nook at the suburbs of the town, where we had the comfort of what M'Alevey called, "the soft side of a deal board."

CHAPTER IX.

"At Christmas play and make good cheer,
For Christmas comes but once a year."

SHAKSPEARE.

O WITHERED, indeed, was the "garland of war" for France in the last days of December, 1870. Even hope had almost fled. Like Francis the First, when he wrote from the Imperial camp, near Pavia, France as one man might say "All is lost, save honour." The garrison in Paris was nearly starving, Le Mans had fallen, Tours had been captured, and Bourges might be occupied any day. In the north, Havre was threatened, and the poor levies of General Zougard in Normandy could make but a sorry resistance against the veteran soldiers of the Red Prince. In the East Von Werder was pressing the siege of Belfort with persistent, and indeed, gallant valour, which the little garrison as gallantly withstood. In the army the French officers looked upon the war as virtually over, and, for a while, I even feared that *La Compagnie Irlandaise* would serve its term and return to Ireland without having seen any more of actual work.

"Yis, indeed, an' a nice figure we'll cut goin' back to the ould sod, without as much as having a German trophy to bring home; bad luck to thim, they might give us a chance anyway!" said Timothy Marks, as we marched out of Bourges the following morning, and took the road once more to Mehun, and its associations of misery and mud. Mr. M'Alevey might, indeed, find some crumbs of comfort amidst the heaps of accumulated filth with which it abounded. I thought he took more care of the twirl of his moustachios, and that now and again he passed his fingers along their *frized* ends to make them stand out, *a la militaire.* Nearly all the men allowed their beards to grow; indeed shaving on a campaign is a disagreeable ordeal, and might be generally dispensed with, in nine cases out of ten, to the comfort and convenience of all. It was late when we reached Mehun, and there was no straw to be had either for officers or men. All had to rough it on the ground. Our baggage turned up, tents were pitched, and after a hasty repast, we threw ourselves upon the ground to sleep as soundly, as if we had the luxury of a spring mattress or a bed of down under us. The officers were, indeed tolerably well off; each of them had four of five sheep skins sewn together in the shape of a bag, and with the addition of a blanket and a great coat, were able to sleep very well upon their campaign beds. The men, however, were, in a pitiable condition. For my own part, I would not ask an Irish dog to go through the hardships incidental to the winter running campaign in the French army. Life has nothing more horribly dramatic. To die of misery like a dog in a ditch, is not the end which men anticipate when they volunteer for foreign service. The accident of battle is nothing. For that, all soldiers are prepared; but to be worn out with famine; to be in torture from bad boots, with great sores eating into the flesh; to be harrassed with perpetual and useless marches; to be nearly naked in an atmosphere ten and fifteen degrees below zero, while stretching upon the frozen ground, the rain or snow pouring upon your person, is a fate I should never like to see a band of Irishmen encounter for any nation but their own. With officers it is of course different, they can provide for themselves, and, they take very good care that such provision should be as ample as possible. Nor do I think it right that officers should suffer as much as the rank and file. If it were so, they too would become invalided or *disparued;* and a ship without a helm is a ship without a head. But there were some of the

Irish soldiers who would have their joke, come weal come woe. Timothy Marks was, as usual, the medium of the "green powder."

"Well," said Tim, looking down at the ground and scanning the place he had to lie upon as keenly as if it were a bed of thistles, "well, sure its soft anyhow; there's no danger of getting bed sores or any other sores from coming in contact with genuine, aisy, soft soil."

"Who knows maybe we'll have worse before the campaign is over," said one of Tim's companions, trying to find some consolation in the gloomy present.

"That's pleasant anyhow," said Tim, as he spread his blanket upon the ground, and unrolled his patch of tent cloth. "Maybe we will have a worse bed than this before the campaign is over; but if we do, I hope it will be on the *other* side of the ground," he added, with an emphasis on *other* which made it unpleasantly suggestive of *under*.

But the wearied troops were soon trying to catch the luxury of a few hours' repose. The tattoo sounded, and an occasional challenge from a *factionaire*, the neighing of a horse, or the cracking of a burning piece of wood that was piled upon the fires to keep them lighting until morning, were the only sounds to be heard. Next morning we were away to Vierzon, where the cavalry of Prince Frederick Charles had been making a raid, and where the Prince himself was expected to make an attack in person, in order to cut communication between Tours and Bourges. The morning was bitterly cold, and the encampment was sheathed in snow, through which the troops struggled on to the road.

"Captain, do you know it is Christmas Eve," said M'Alevey, as he walked beside me, his usually merry-looking face wearing a somewhat sad expression. And, indeed, so it was, Christmas Eve, 1870.

Christmas, with all its associations of home and happiness! Christmas, with its carols, and with its comforts! Christmas, with its reunions and its merry-making, its stories, and its pictures of hope, bright, joyous hope, in the happy homes of the dear old land!

Around the hearthstones in holy Ireland the scattered members of many a family were once more seeking the shelter of the parents' wing. How the thoughts flew homeward, homeward to the loved ones whom we might never see again. Even M'Alevey ceased his merriment, and I could trace deep thought upon his face as legibly as if it were written in characters of iron. But how different the Christmas of the soldiers of *La Compagnie Irlandaise*.

This was a Christmas of famine and of frost: a Christmas when blistered and ulcered feet appealed to Nature for relief: a Christmas of misery when man's thoughts were so much wrapt up in the folds of his own agonising pain that he cannot think of anything but the present. There are stages of human wretchedness when we think of ourselves alone. There are certain conditions of life which absorb all our thoughts, and make us even more selfish than Nature, in her ordinary way, intended us to be. As we wheeled into the place marked out for our encampment at Vierzon on Christmas Eve, 1870, there were few, if any, of the men of the Irish Company upon whose frame the rigour of the campaign had not made sad havoc. The ground, too, was as hard as frost 17 degrees below zero could make it. Our portion of the encampment was ploughed land, and the little mounds of earth had hardened into iron consistency and rendered walking a task of difficulty and danger. This was the coldest night I ever felt in France. Sergeant Carey, who had served in the Crimea, said that the cold that Christmas Eve at Vierzon was more intense than he ever felt it to be in Russia. The keen frosty air almost cut into the system, and the faces of the men became blue and puffy, as the warm current of blood became suspended. Around many a half-pitched tent some companion of a frost-bitten soldier might be seen endeavouring to coax vitality back to the feet of his suffering friend, by means of friction. The ground was too hard to permit of the wooden tent-pegs being driven through its granite-like surface. The tents were in no cases well pitched, and the men lay in heaps under the covering, moaning and shivering with pain and cold.

In the Crimea, even during the first winter, it was a sitting campaign, where the troops settled down to their work, often without changing their quarters for months. The soldiers always had tents, and often stoves. Beds were improvised even in the earliest days of the Crimean war, and clothing was, at all times, immensely superior to that of the poorly clad Frenchmen of 1870. In France, however, with the thermometer 15 or 16 degrees below zero, it was a running campaign, and there could be little or no provision made for the settled comfort of the troops. It was indeed *la misere*. It was to the men of *La Compagnie Irlandaise* a Christmas full of sorrow; a Christmas of famine, of frost, and of disease. Eight of the men had already succumbed to the chances of war, and I couldn't help thinking, as I left the encampment that night to seek shelter in a peasant's cottage, that this Christmas Day would find some of the Irish soldiers frozen to death, and I was somewhat discomforted the following morning when Sergeant Terence Byrne came to my quarters and said—"Eight men died from cold, sir, last night."—until upon inquiry I found it was eight men in the battalion, not in the Company. I never ascertained whether the figures were an exaggeration or not, although I am sure they were given to Sergeant Byrne as correct.

My new orderly thought the cold severe enough to cause the milch cows to give "ice cream" at their milkings, and save the necessity of manufacturing that article of luxury. But my attendant was pretty comfortable, as he busied himself preparing our Christmas breakfast. M'Alevey succeeded in buying a fowl from the proprietors of the cottage, and his orderly was busy dissecting its somewhat aged limbs, and throwing them into a pot full of water that steamed upon the stove. Our host—that is, our host from necessity—was interested, too, in our comforts, and was busy preparing some onion soup for our morning meal. I often wondered how cheaply the French peasantry could live. A few onions roasted, with a little grease upon a pan, a crust of toasted bread, and three or four pints of water added, will do a family for a meal, provided they get their *carafon* of wine, and a morsel of bread in addition. Our host, too, was communicative about the late Uhlan raid on Vierzon, and took pains to trace, with a wavy motion of his arm, the route of the daring cavalry soldiers of Germany. He showed us some souvenirs of the fight that took place among the vineyards, and just before his door two Uhlans bit the dust, "and here are their caps and sabres," he added, bringing two lancer caps and two cavalry sabres from an adjoining room. "You see," he continued, "where the vines and cereal crops of last year were sown, just on the margin of that clump of timber; well, a squadron of Uhlans were driven in amongst the vines by a body of Franc-tireurs who occupied the wood, and the horses plunged and reared amongst the vine props, until some of them become impaled by the pointed sticks."

Christmas Day passed with the usual routine of camp life. There must have been thousands of men amongst the troops who did not even know that it was the anniversary of the coming of the Messiah. There is not much religion in a Frenchman's heart. The Legitimists alone are piously inclined.

"It is we, sir," said a bourgeois to me, as we were about striking our tents at Vierzon, on St. Stephen's Day, 1870—"it is we, the Legitimists of France, who are the upholders of moral law throughout the country, and wherever you see the *fleur-de-lis*, you may be sure that religious training, and the path of virtue follow in its wake."

"By the way," I asked, "what is the origin of the *fleur-de-lis ?*"

"Well," replied the bourgeois, "authorities are divided as to whether the celebrated emblem is derived from the white lily of the garden, or from the flag of Iris, which, as generally represented, resembles it both in form and colour."

"But I think.I heard that it had something to do with an old custom of the Franks at the proclamation of their kings."

"Yes, it is so supposed," he replied. "In olden times it was the custom to elevate the new king upon a shield or target, and place in his hand a reed or flag in blossom, instead of a sceptre, and from thence the kings of the first and second race of France are represented with sceptres in their hands, like the flag with its flowers, and which flowers became the armorial figures of France."

"The story is quite as absurd as your other stories of kingly virtues and Divine right," said a bloused peasant, who stood by the side of the *bourgeois*. "I suppose you'll expect us to believe that this *fleur-de-lis* of yours came down from heaven, or that an angel gave it to King Clovis at his baptism, and the like—bogh !" he added, tossing his head contemptously aside, "Frenchmen have outlived such rubbish, and the least that is said of legitimate virtue and Divine right the better."

Just then a corps of Franc-tireurs passed by, their theatrical uniform and easy carriage giving them the appearance of being, in every sense, the class of soldiers their name implied.

"A fine lot of fellows," said Dr. Macken, who came and stood beside me. "Prussia should be the last nation on the face of the earth to object to the establishment of Free Corps in any country. The history of 1806, should be enough to make every man in Prussia denounce the severity with which these men are being treated by the German troops. Do you remember, Captain," continued Dr. Macken, "that it was owing to the want of irregular battalions that Prussia collapsed in 1806, while the authorities, both civil and military, did all they could to make, not free-shooters, but assasins of their countrymen ?"

"I forgot my Allison," I replied, "but would like to hear the circumstances from you."

"Oh, I don't remember much," said the doctor, "but I believe it is a fact, that in 1807, Prussia attempted to organize bands of assassins to destroy the French, and that one of the distinctive features of those bands was that they wore no uniform of any kind, so that they might pass unknown after they had accomplished their foul purpose."

"But the French Government has acted wisely in ordering that all bands of Franc-tireurs shall be attached to an Army Corps on active service, and they thus obtain the protection of regular troops," said Mr. Cotter, who joined us in our conversation.

But the free-shooters passed along, and orders came for the brigade to march into the town, where the troops were to be billeted. It was joyous news for the men of the *Regiment Etranger;* at last they were to have the comfort of a few days' repose. The weather, too, cleared up; the air, although intensely cold, became crisp and dry, and the troops enjoyed their straw beds, and a comparative abundance of food, with epicurean relish.

In the meantime the German successes were, more and more establishing successive military lines across the country. With the exception of Paris, Havre, and a few places in Normandy and Picardy, the entire country, north of the Loire was in their hands. On the 27th of December, Mount Avron, an outwork, constructed by the French on the north side of Paris, was successfully bombarded by the enemy, who occupied the fort the following day, and in a few days following they silenced Forts Rosny, Noisy, and Nogent, the advanced works of the French on their north-eastern front. Everything pointed to a speedy termination of the war. Hitherto it was our fortune, or misfortune, to be away from the scene of the heavy fighting. At Caen we were delayed expecting recruits who never arrived, else we should have participated in the fighting in and around Orleans. At Bourges I had to go to the General in command, and request to be sent to the front; five days elapsed, nothing was done, and during these five days Orleans was re-captured, and those hopeful combats of Chively, and Artiny were fought. Our regiment participated in all those fights, and were it not for the positive imbecility of the authorities, we would have shared the glory of those victories also. And then when we joined our regiment, day by day we expected to be attacked in force by the army of Prince Frederick Charles. Bourges lay right before him; as a strategic position, he should attack the place if he intended to advance. Bourbaki had taken the greater portion of the army to the East, fully expecting that our corps would have the task of defending Bourges against the hitherto successful Prince. But Frederick Charles advanced no farther than Vierzon, leaving us in possession of all the numerous roads leading from Bourges to the South, and of the railway communications along the Loire to East and West. But it was the fortune of war, and yet it was more painful to see the company decimated by hard marching, by famine, and by frost, than by the bullets or bayonets of the enemy. But we had all a joyous time at Vierzon. We were more than a week housed within its limits, except, indeed, when our turn for grand guard left us exposed to the piercing weather. All this, however, made the men thoroughly experienced with their work, and they soon learned the mysteries of erecting *gourbies*, and of providing shelter in the most approved fashion. Yet it was cold, harsh, trying work. In summer, indeed, it would have been enjoyab'e—the necessity of being on the *qui vive*, furnishing sufficient excitement to cause every man to feel an interest in all his surroundings. And then the patrols in the early grey of the morning, when at any moment from thicket, bush, or sheltered timber, a volley might be thrown upon the party, or a charge of Uhlans, cause them to form a little square, to resist the desperate onslaught. Yes, grand guard is pleasant enough in summer, but it is quite another thing with a thermometer fifteen degrees below zero, with hunger and hardship in full possession of the vital powers of men who are expected to be ever active and vigilant. I contrived, however, to make room for the sergeants, on the main post, inside the little *gourbie* which was erected for the officers when at all practicable, and Carey, Donnellan, the two Byrnes, and Henry M'Crossin, often partook of the shelter of the interwoven branches. Donnellan was a magnificent specimen of a man. He was about eight-and-twenty years of age, six feet two, high, and with shoulders broad enough to be the envy of a prize-fighter. He was, too, a singularly handsome man, and the grace and ease of his every movement gave him an impressive manner. Educated for the English Army, he served many years in the 4th West India Regiment, and was beloved by every officer in his corps. When the West India regiments were disbanded, Donnellan was placed on half pay, and soon after commuted, and then ultimately went to France and enlisted in the ranks of the *Regiment Etranger*. He was in every sense a noble specimen of an Irish soldier. His conduct at the battle of Orleans brought him under the notice of his *Commandant*, and he would have received a commission for his gallantry, but his knowledge of the French language was too limited. His bravery was the theme of many a tongue, but with that native modesty, however, which is so charming in the real soldier, he was dumb upon his own merits, and it was only in action that that gentleman soldier showed all the cool gallantry of his race.

"At Orleans, *Capitaine*," said his ex-*Commandant* to me, " Donnellan behaved with much bravery. He was one of the last to retire across the bridge, and even knelt down in front of all our men to take deliberate aim at the advancing enemy. There was nothing of rashness, but there was everything of cool daring in his conduct, and I hope to see the Cross of the Legion of Honour decorate his chivalrous breast before many days." But famine and fatigue had done their work upon his frame, and his attenuated figure attested the hardships which he had endured, and yet he was uncomplaining, doing his duty to the letter, and showing brilliant example of how a delicately-reared gentleman can endure all the privations of a hard campaign, better, aye a hundred times better, than some growling street rowdies, who seldom had a whole meal in all their lives. I remember one morning, long before dawn, taking Donnellan, three file of men, and a corporal, out on patrol; we marched fully a mile beyond the outer limits of our grand guard, and entered a country somewhat undulating, and dotted with clumps of trees. The air was cold, snow covered the route, and now and again we halted, and tried to detect some sound that might indicate the presence of the enemy, whom we knew to be close at hand. We had entered a narrow defile, skirted on either side by a thick set hedge, while the trees covered the ground which rose on each side of the road to a considerable altitude. It was just such a place as would induce an enemy to lie in wait for their foes. The corporal and two men marched in front, while Donnellan and I with the remainder were about one hundred yards behind. Suddenly the little advance guard halted, and over the snow-beaten route we could just trace their figures siding off into the ditch beside the road. There was something in the wind, and the corporal in advance with laudable foresight, made no indication of his suspicion, knowing that we could see his movements.

"There is something up, Donnellan," I said, "move over under the ditch—silence—hush;" and just then a low whistle sounded away over our heads, and appeared to come from the airy eminence which nearly overhung the road. The whistle was scarcely audible, and were it not for the rarified state of the atmosphere, would have been altogether unheard, and yet it was certain it could not have been more than two hundred or three hundred yards from where we were.

"Did you hear that, Donnellan," I said in a whisper, as the men crouched low under the ditch, "move the *garde mobile* of your rifles very gently, don't make a noise or they may hear the click, steady, hush!" and the men had put a cartridge into the breech of their rifles with as little noise as it was possible to make.

"There is a valuable invention open to some one of mechanical brains, Captain," said Donnellan, "if they can make a rifle come to full cock, without causing that tell-tale 'click.'"

"Yes, there is; but here, Donnellan, take one of the men, and move quietly to where the Corporal is, and see what is the matter." and soon I saw the party return along the bush, moving as stealthily as a cat about to pounce upon its prey. Just then the low, guarded whistle, again sounded upon our ears. Our position was anything but a comfortable one; a mile from camp, in a narrow defile which may be occupied by the enemy, who were at that moment, perhaps, surrounding us. I gave the order to retire, keeping close under the thick-set bush, and almost hugging its thorny branches, as we stole under its welcome shelter. Every step was taken with caution, and just as we were about to pass into the open country beyond, a shot from a rifle woke the stillness of the morning with its ominous sound. In an instant my little command were upon their knees, and not till then did I order to "fix bayonets," expecting every moment to hear the rush of cavalry, or the tramp of infantry, in front, or beside us. We were well sheltered in our rear, and could inflict some punishment upon an enemy advancing along the more open road. Then another shot came in our immediate front, and another, and then a small volley hissed through the the trees around us, and the firing became pretty general all along our entire line, At that moment we thought that a portion of our line had been attacked, and that the enemy was between us and our post. To venture into the open road might expose us to the enemy, and to remain where we were until daylight might lead to our capture.

"I think we had better venture to rejoin the camp, Donnellan," I said in a whisper to my sergeant, who was as cool and as calm as if he were about to take a promenade along some sequestered lane in his native county—Galway. "Put the men out in single file, about six yards between each man, and we will trust to chance and move on rapidly for our post." If the enemy occupied the woods around us, the moment we stepped from out the friendly shelter of the hedge, a volley was certain to be thrown upon us, and the whistle which we all heard, left little doubt upon our minds that such was the case.

I shall never forget how coolly Sergeant Donnellan stepped out upon the road, his rifle at full cock, and his finger upon the trigger. There was not the shadow of emotion visible in his countenance, which I could plainly see as I turned around and looked into his handsome face. Any second himself or his companions might be sent to eternity, and that too, under circumstances, which lack all that soul inspiring pomp and circumstances which make men risk life for military fame. It is at such times that the true soldier is tried. The men, too, behaved with a coolness, which did infinite credit to their inexperience. But on we pressed, peering into the darkness, listening for the least audible sound, when suddenly from out the gloom the joyous challenge "*Qui vive*" sounded upon our ears.

"France," I replied, as I heard a dozen hammers placed on full cock, and saw dark blotches, which I took for men, lining the road before me.

"Advance and give the *ralliement*," and then Sergeant Donnellan went in front and over the pointed bayonets of a dozen Frenchmen, he gave the countersign for the night, and then a hurried conversation took place between myself and the lieutenant in command of the party. We were still nearly a mile from camp; dawn was just breaking; there was a little cover on the spot; I took charge of the squad, and remained there until daylight had fairly set in, and no enemy in view. The cause of the firing I never heard thoroughly explained, but always suspected that it was some Franc-tireurs who, in their eagerness for spoil, mistook us for Germans, never waited to challenge, and when they discovered their mistake, made off as best they could. We were soon scrambling through the vines before our *petits postes*, and stumbled across Sergeant Terence Byrne, whose little command we in vain attempted to surprise. The hardships of the campaign had told with much effect upon the frame of poor Terence Byrne, but that indomitable mind appeared to force his exhausted body on to further efforts of trial and endurance. His life, too, had been somewhat of an eventful one. Tried and convicted for complicity with the Fenian movement; it was he who gave that well-known rebuke to Judge Keogh, who with unquestionable bad taste, attempted to make the prisoner's fate more bitter than it was, and to outrage the feelings of this honest man, by calling him a " low " conspirator.

"Not low, my lord, but humble," was the quiet rejoinder, and a truer word never escaped the lips of a man. Terence Byrne was humble, but he was as much incapable of " lowness" as was his lordly censor. Whatever the world may think of Fenianism, as a worthy or as an unworthy political movement, whether it deserved denunciation or applause, there can be little doubt but that it produced men whose motives were of the purest cast, and who were actuated with the one political desire—the regeneration of their native land. They may have been right, or they may have been wrong, that will, in all probability, ever remain a matter of opinion; but that they were honest, no one but a political bigot can deny. In *La Compagnie Irlandaise* there were several well-known Fenians, and their general conduct, their love of order, their high sense of duty, their unfaltering fidelity, their steady zeal and their chivalrous courage, won from me, and every officer of the battalion, the highest praise.

Fate, in its unwavering course, ordained that two, at least, of those men should not die a soldier's death, and Sergeants Carey and Byrne returned after the war to sleep in Glasnevin; but the memory of their unassuming conduct, of their indefatigable zeal, and of their splendid courage, has left a retrospective shadow of generous recollection ever present with their names.

CHAPTER X.

> "For I am as a weed
> Flung from the rock, on Ocean's foam to sail,
> Where'er the surge may sweep, the tempest's breath prevail."
> SHAKSPEARE.

We loitered at Vierzon until the 4th of January. We had our grand guards to mount, our reconnoitering to perform, and our picquet duty to do. The weather, however, became fine, and duty became a pleasure. The Uhlans of Prince Frederick Charles were feeling their way around our position, and the necessity of being constantly on the *qui vive* made outpost duty a desirable pastime. We had become tired of inaction, and then the sight of a detachment of German cavalry knocked such spirit into the hungry soldiers, that they forgot everything but their foes, and their well-filled haversacks. There is nothing in warfare so pleasant as skirmishing; admitting that Hobbes was right, and that "every creature lives in a state of war by nature," and that man merely tones the desire for blood into what is called " civilized warfare." There is a pardonable pride in dodging from bush to break, and picking off one's enemies at a respectable distance. I know of nothing so absolutely pleasant, if, indeed, there be any pleasure in war, as a nice, quiet, respectable skirmish. You are posted behind a rock, or you are sheltered under a slight inequality in the ground, an occasional bullet whistles past your head, and then you venture to peep out, and send an occasional bullet in reply, and if your man is tumbled, the pleasure is all the keener. Nay, you feel a positive sense of joy when the poor wretch throws up his arms, and you are relieved from watching the place that sheltered him. In after life you may now and again think over some widowed home, where the name of "father" is murmured by prattling babes, whom your handiwork has left upon the cold charity of the world; or your fancy may occasionally run riot with your feelings, as you picture a sorrowful mother, weeping in agonized suspense for the boy that your hand has sent to his last account. But at the time, just when you watch the effect of your shot, and see the successful result, and perhaps hear the dying shout of the stricken man, there is a positive and complete feeling of satisfaction takes possession of your senses. When "war to the knife" is the order of the day, as it was at Saragossa, when summoned by the French to surrender in 1808, the wish to kill is the first desire of a soldier. In fact a man never feels himself a true soldier until he has either killed or maimed an enemy, or until he believes he may have done so. Men go into a skirmish without much misgivings as to the issue, while they experience the excitement of a combat without the broader phases of its dangers. But in great battles it is different; men enter them with dread, and that latter feeling, for a while at least, sickens the heart, and destroys the sense of pleasure which the probability of pulling through with a whole skin, undoubtedly gives the soldier marching into action. About Vierzon, however, we had a pleasant time of it, and it was with some regret we left it to return to Bourges. We had one more night at Mehun, *en route*, but it was merely a rest, for at three a.m., we were again away for Bourges, which we reached early on the morning of the 6th of January. I had heard at Mehun, that we were to follow the army of Bourbaki, and we speculated in joyous anticipation of the high handed way we would pay those lordly Germans back in their own coin, if we succeeded in carrying the war into Baden-Baden. Some of the officers were particularly sanguine, and I well remember Ceresole coming to me, as we halted outside Bourges, and saying:

"Your Lieutenant will have an opportunity of flirting with German frauliens, before the month is over, perhaps he would prefer them to French society.

"*Jamais, jamais,*" replied M'Alevey with well affected indignation, while he attempted to look as wise as Solon. I suspect, however, that just then M'Alevey did speculate upon the theme, and I thought too, I detected a merry twinkle in his eye, which would find expression in spite of all his efforts to look wise and indifferent.

But we passed a miserable day and night. The men pitched their tents upon a hill outside the town, and between some fieldworks which had been constructed to protect the place. It was as bad as Mehun; mud, mud everywhere. Even the wood could not be made to burn, and it fizzed and smoked, but would not kindle. The officers were allowed to go to the town, and one and all eagerly availed themselves of the permission. So we floundered our way to Bourges, and were soon sheltered beneath a comfortable *auberge*, which was already crowded by our comrades. A cup of coffee was quickly swallowed to the dregs, and just as I was about pouring some brandy into a small glass that was placed before me, some one placed his hand upon my shoulder, and in a somewhat familiar tone said, "Ah, we meet again, Capitaine."

I looked up, and there stood M'Iver, his arm in a sling, and his face ashy pale. He extended his only serviceable hand, which I cordially shook, and after pressing him to refreshments, I heard the main features of his career since I had seen him in Caen. But he was silent in reference to himself. His arm and hand in splinters was proof enough that he had been hit somewhere, but he just mentioned the fact, no more.

"Oh, its nothing," he said, moving his arm slightly, "a ball shattered the bone a little, struck in at the elbow and came out at the wrist But," he continued, "where is M'Adarus? I met him some time ago at Tours, and I'd like to meet him again."

"I don't know," I replied, "I hear he has joined the staff of General Chanzy, but I neither know nor care."

"Then you are not friends?" said M'Iver.

"No, no; we regard M'Adarus as an impostor. He is not known in Ireland, nor is he known in France."

"Just as I suspected," replied M'Iver. "Do you know that he first introduced himself to me at St. Lazare, in Paris, and he said that he had served in the East India Company's service. I was glad to meet one of the old Company's servants, and I did all I could to make M'Adarus tell me the corps he belonged to, but it was no use, and he ever after avoided me. I came to the conclusion, that if he ever was in the East India Service, it was as a private and not a Major, which rank he says he held. Besides," he added, sipping a cup of coffee nicely flavoured with brandy, "besides I know other reasons for believing that he was not an officer. The fellow does not know simple trigonometry, is uneducated and vulgar, and I too, believe him to be a downright cheat. I have met whole families like that gentleman in my travels," and M'Iver tossed off his coffee with cool indifference. We parted shortly afterwards, and I did not see M'Iver until the war was over, when he was doing Paris, and vowing vengeance against M'Adarus for some rumours that gentleman had circulated about the adventurous M'Iver.

But we had a miserable night of it at Bourges. The rain fell in torrents, the mud was ankle deep, the men were wet, cold, and hungry, and yet there was nothing for it but to lie down and dose the time away. The morning of the 7th was just the same, rain rain, all day long. The troops were meanwhile being hurried away by rail, and the Irish Company had to bide its time. Every one of the men were as wet as a saturated sponge. From dawn to dark they stood under the downpour, and the water was oozing out of their boots, before it came to their turn to embark. The fires would not light, and even the luxury of a cup of coffee could not be provided. The *ordinaire*, indeed, supplied them with a glass of brandy each, and that with a bit of dry bread or biscuit, was all they had for thirty-six hours. Wet, cold, with gnashing teeth, and hunger gnawing with fatal effect at the vital energies of the men, they at last took the train at 10 p.m. on the 7th of January, and crowded into the compartments with steaming clothes, empty haversacks, and broken spirits. We were away for the East, away to where we dreamed of brilliant exploits, and perhaps retrieved fortunes for poor France. Away through Nevers, where we once more strike the Loire, and where the hedgerows around the country take the thoughts back to the domestic scenery of holy Ireland. On through Autun with its classic associations, and where at one time the most illustrious youth of Gaul were educated. Here I had an opportunity of seeing a perfect mine of Roman antiquity, the noble amphitheatre, the beautiful Roman gates, with their posterns and double arches below for carriage-ways, while above the arcades of open arches, ornamented with pilasters, form a gallery over the gateway leading to the round towers which at one time flanked the walls; and then on still, until Chagny is reached, and the great mines and iron basins of Creuzot Epinac, &c., are close at hand.

At Chagny we had some days' delay, but were still confined to the carriages. The road was blocked with troops, and we could not get on. The relaxation of the muscular action, consequent upon continued rest, caused the men's feet to swell alarmingly. There was not a man in the Company whose feet were not bursting through the frail covering called "shoes." Every soldier in *La Compagnie Irlandaise* was compelled to cut his shoes, in order to give freedom to his cramped feet. Sores were caused in consequence of the edges of the cut portion of the shoe rubbing against the foot, and festered feet, bloated from the want of exercise, afflicted every one of the men. But there was no help for it, we should be away again; away through Dijon, Dôle, Besançon, Baume-les-Dames, and on through the beautiful valleys of the Vosges, where the overhanging mountains, lean with threatening grace over the road underneath. But on still, and then our destination—Clarval—is reached. The houses are somewhat Swiss in their construction, and oil lamps are suspended on ropes, which stretch from house to house across the narrow streets. It is 8 p.m., and we wheel into a field; the men light fires to cook their food, while we prepared to be again away for the front at midnight.

"Well, Captain," said Dr. Macken, as we sat around the bivouac, the light from the fire throwing a lurid glare upon the features of M'Alevey and Cotter, who were engaged consuming some tough beefsteak. "Well, Captain, we shall soon be into it now, I hear we are to march for Montbelliard at 12 o'clock to-night, and that we are sure to relieve Belfort, and then carry the war into Germany. But, Mac, what's the matter with you, old boy?" continued the doctor, seeing M'Alevey somewhat dull.

"Well doctor, I was just thinking of a circumstance that happened in '63, when I was in Mexico, and when I lost the dearest of my comrades, and who knows," he continued, "whether we four shall ever see another night together in this world."

"Oh, never mind the future, but tell us about the past, this comrade of yours, who was he and where and how, did it all occur?"

"Oh, I'll tell you some other time," said M'Alevey, sipping his coffee, and carefully wiping all traces of it from his ever neat mustaches.

"Tell us, Mac; perhaps your prediction may be fulfilled, and you may not have an opportunity again, so out with it," replied the doctor, as he laid his tin cup upon a log of wood, lit a cigar, and composed himself in anticipation of M'Alevey's story.

"Well, I'll tell you," said M'Alevey, "just hand me a cigar doctor—thanks—*une allumette*—thanks, encore. Now, listen, and I pledge you my word every syllable of what I am going to tell you is true, and if you take the trouble of consulting the Regimental Book for the first quarter of '63, you will find it recorded therein.

On the 9th of February, '63, the 2nd *Regiment Etranger* embarked on board the *Wagram* man-of-war at Mers-el-Kiber for Mexico. The inhabitants of Oran turned out *en masse* to see the troops embark, not that the sight was in any way novel to the good people of Oran, for it was the third time in less than ten years that they had seen the same regiment embarking at the same place, for the Crimean and Italian campaigns. There were no loud hurrahs or *vivas*, either by the troops or people, but there were was a good deal of fervent hand-shaking, and kissing, and sobbing between the young fellows of the regiment and the mademoiselles and señoritas, just by way of showing that no ill feeling existed. At six o'clock, p.m., the *St. Louis* and *Wagram* got under weigh, and next day we passed close under the frowning guns of Gibraltar.

Of the voyage out I need say nothing, except that we touched at Madeira and Martinique. Never can I forget the beauty of the scene which met my view when I went on deck one morning, and found the ship at anchor, in the beautiful harbour of Funchal. The sun had just risen from his ocean bed, and shed a flood of golden light on the gentle hills and gardens with which the town is surrounded. Not a breath disturbed the deep calm of the broad Atlantic, which lay like a huge mirror beneath our ship. Not a cloud o'ercast the beauty of the sky. Earth, ocean, sky, all three seemed wedded in one eternal bond of love, and peace, and beauty. On a black, rocky precipice, surrounded by the ocean, stood Chateau Loo, with its grim old cannon scowling envy, as it were, at the natural beauties of the place. It looked that morning, I thought, like some monster that had suddenly risen from his ocean cave, and forgot to return; or like some hideous goblin, that had unexpectedly burst in on a scene of fairy enchantment. At noon I was granted permission to go on shore. The town when you enter it, is not very handsome; indeed the only thing in it worth seeing is the Franciscan Convent, which contains a chamber, the walls and ceiling of which are covered with human skulls and thigh bones, the relics of holy men who have died on the island. To Madeira the climate is everything; the icy cold of winter, and the scorching heat of summer are here unknown, for spring and autumn reign continually, and produce fruits and flowers throughout the year. The hedges are formed of myrtle, rose, jasmine, and honeysuckle, while the most delicate flowers which are nursed in our green houses at home, grow here in wild abundance.

"About the 10th of April, we dropped anchor under the guns of St. Juan de Ulloa, and for the first time cast eyes on Vera Cruz, and in my opinion a more God-forsaken looking place there is not in the world. The town is built on an arid plain, and the whole coast as far as the eye can see, presents nothing but barren sand hills to the view, with here and there a patch of grovelling brushwood, that but helps to make sterility conspicuous. Far in the distance behind the town rises the mighty Mount Orizaba, with its crown of eternal snow. At a short distance from our ship lay a small island of white sand, utterly devoid of vegetation. It seemed a complete forest of wooden crosses; when I enquired as to the meaning of these crosses, I was told that the place was used as a cemetery for sailors who died of yellow fever, while to crown the misery and desolation that seemed everywhere to reign, the bay and beach was strewn with the hulls and masts of seventeen large ships, that had been wrecked a year or two previous, during a gale from the north. On the morning of the 11th, the regiment disembarked, and at evening parade the Colonel informed us in a brilliant speech, that the regiment would have the honour of protecting the communications, and escorting convoys between Puebla and Vera Cruz. Now of all the fatiguing and disagreeable duties which a soldier has to perform in campaign, that of escorting convoys of war material and provisions, is by far the most disagreeable and fatiguing. If the roads are good and dry, you are smothered with dust, and the pace is killing; if they are bad and wet, you are bespattered with mud and filth, and owing to the slow pace, will, perhaps, be marching half the night. To this hour I shudder, when I think of the misery and hardships I suffered in La Terre Chaude. Every day there was a downpour of rain, and such rain, you would think the very sluices of the heavens had been opened. Suddenly the rain would cease, and then the sun would shine out with such rays of boiling heat, that I have more than once seen soldiers drop dead by the side of the waggons. In Africa we were burnt brown, roasted if you will, but it was a dry, healthy heat. In La Terre Chaude, we were boiled, steamed as it were, in a pestilential vapour. The earth is literally teeming with insect life, and night and day there is a continual buzz and whistling that almost drives you mad; lift the first stone you see on the way side and you will find beneath it either scorpions, or enormous centipedes, or coral snakes. At night the air swarms with fire-flies and mosquitoes, sleep you cannot, you dose away the night in a broken nightmare, and when the first streak of dawn appears, you are awoke with such screaming and yelling, as if ten thousand devils had broken into the camp; snatching your gun you hurry out of your tent, and find the camp surrounded by a cloud of green parrots, that shout and scream the louder, when they see your red cap and breeches. But to my story. The first battalion to which I belonged, was echeloned in detatchments of two and three companies, on the road between Vera Cruz, and Chicehuite. Now you must not imagine that Chicehuite is either a town or a village, for there is not a human habitation within many miles of it. It is a huge mountain, at the base of which there runs a rapid river, and over which the road to Mexico passes. In a military point of view the position was a very important one, and was strongly guarded. I was lying in my tent one evening in May, with my hands rolled in a handkerchief, and smoking like a steam engine to keep the mosquitoes from my face, when my friend, Sergeant Morzikie entered. He was about twenty years of age, tall, well built, and considered the handsomest man in the regiment.

"' Where the deuce are you going so late ?' said I to him, for he was in marching costume.

"' Just come to say good-bye, Mac, the mail has arrived at Vera Cruz, with important despatches for headquarters, and my Company is going to meet it, as large bands of guerillas have been seen lately near Cameron. So good bye, old fellow,' said he shaking me warmly by the hand, and turning, he hurried rapidly down the mountain.

"That was the last time I ever saw my friend alive, for two years we had lived in the closest friendship, and during all that time he had been my *camarade de camarades*. By birth he was a Pole, and had been educated for the Church, but preferring the more active life of a soldier, had joined the Legion to try and win his baton. Next evening about the same hour that I had bid my friend farewell, I was half way up the mountain, parrot shooting, and had just sat down to rest myself and enjoy the fine view of the country which the place commanded, when suddenly I heard the clear sharp note of the trumpet sounding the *générale*. Starting to my feet, I listened with breathless attention, and in a moment after, the chorus was taken up by a dozen others, so that the entire mountain echoed with the alarming cry. Seizing my gun I ran furiously down the mountain, and found the troops already under arms. I had barely joined my Company when the trumpets sounded the regimental march, and off we went, whither I did not yet know. As soon as we were fairly started, I turned to the person next me, and asked the cause of alarm. By him I was informed that the Company that had set out the night before to meet the mail, had been surrounded at Cameron by guerillas, and had been engaged all day.

"'God grant,' said I 'that we may not be too late to assist the poor fellows,' and a shudder passed through my body when I thought of my friend Morzikie. The distance from Chicehuite to Cameron is thirty-five English miles. We marched all night, and at four o'clock in the morning halted and made coffee, and when the sun had well risen, started once more on our weary march. Within a mile of Cameron we came on the first token of the tragedy that had recently taken place. Seated under a tree, stark naked, and almost dead with loss of blood and thirst, we found the drummer of the unfortunate Company; a bullet had gone clean through his chest and out at his back, and three of his fingers had been chopped off from a sabre cut. A little brandy was given to him, the doctor hastily dressed his wounds, and one or two soldiers unpacked their sacks and gave him the clothing he so much required. When he had recovered sufficient strength, he told us his Company had been attacked about four in the morning in the plain of Palo Verde by about one thousand guerillas, the greater part of whom were mounted. 'The Company,' said he, 'immediately formed square, and then we fired volley after volley into their ranks almost at close quarters; seeing they could not force our ranks they retired, and called on us to surrender, but Captain D'Anjou sternly refused. We then retreated on Cameron, fighting our way foot by foot. During the retreat we lost about twenty men, and the lieutenant and sub-lieutenant were both killed. We reached Cameron about eight o'clock, and barricaded the doors and windows of the house we occupied; we fought till black dark, fought till there was not a single cartridge left even in the pouches of the dead men. The Mexicans then burst into the house, and I remember nothing more till I awoke this morning and found myself naked lying among the other dead men."

Such was the story told us by the poor drummer, and alas! it was too true. Leaving him with the doctor and a guard, the rest of the troops pushed on to Cameron. There I saw such a sight as I pray God I may never witness again. Sixty-two of our dead *compagnons d'armes* had been been collected by the guerillas, and placed in a deep straight fosse by the side of the road. Shoulder to shoulder in the ranks of death, and divested of every article of clothing lay the brave fellows, every man of whom I knew personally. A bright warm sun was shining on their ghastly features and cold stiff forms; most of them wore an expression of pain, and some of them had their arms extended, and their hands tightly clenched in a fighting posture.

"The Company when it left Chicehuite consisted of eighty-eight men all told, of the entire number only five were left living at Cameron, of whom the drummer was one; the other four were taken prisoners and conducted to Jalapa, where they were well treated, and were afterwards exchanged for Mexican prisoners. More than three hundred guerillas bit the dust at Cameron. When we left Chicehuite we brought but one day's rations with us, and were compelled to return at night without exchanging a shot with the assassins who had slaughtered our comrades. We could not even perform the sad office of interment, as we had neither pick or spade. When we returned to Cameron two days afterwards to bury the dead, the sight which met my view filled me with horror. Owing to the great heat decomposition had set in, and their bodies were swollen to an enormous size. Already had those horrid birds, the zopilotes, commenced to prey on their naked bodies. But I must draw a veil over the digusting scene. Since then I have stepped over the dead and dying on many a battle-field, and have seen men shoot one nother down amid the horrid din of artillery, but the sight was not half so horrible or terrifying as the silent dead of Cameron. I must not conclude without informing you that the drummer lived, notwithstanding the serious nature of his wounds, and that he received the Cross of the Legion of Honour. The regiment was also publicly thanked in the General Orders for the bravery displayed by this Company, and a short time afterwards we left the 'hot earth' for the siege of Puebla."

"But did you distinguish your friend the Sergeant, amongst the number of the dead at Cameron?" asked the doctor, when M'Alevey had finished his story.

"Oh, yes, but cease, ask me no more; the recollection of his bloated, distorted features, clenched hands, vividly distended eyes, with the flesh torn from the bones by the zopilotes, has left upon my mind a picture I cannot contemplate without a shudder. But," he added, starting to his feet, and buckling on his sword-belt which he had unloosened, "there goes the *générale*, and we shall soon be off again."

It was just midnight when we commenced to move away, and for seven hours we floundered on in the dark, through mud and snow; on through the cold, damp, dark night we kept at it until seven the following morning.

It was just daybreak. We had halted beside a canal that skirted the beautiful valley of the Doubs. Away on the eastern horizon a bud of light swelled upwards and tinged with gray the nimbus clouds of night. Those particles of dust clouds heated by contact with our atmosphere, and known as "St. Laurence's tears," occasionally darted across the heavens, like rockets through a storm cloud. The wind ate through the miserable clothing of the men, who had thrown themselves shuddering upon the snow-beaten route, and tried to catch a few moments of repose. The Doubs came bubbling down as if the spirits of the stream were murmuring their thanksgiving at having escaped the frozen grasp of King Frost. The tall ranges of the Vosges reared their venerable heads high into the upper strata of the air, as if observing all that passed below. Cascades trippled adown the steep sides of the hills and rushed madly into the river, and a miniature fall close by, made mimic thunder in our ears. The great poplars that lined the road threw shadowy bars across our path, like spectral forms across the valley of death. The snow was falling in downy flakes, and hardened into patches of icy crystals upon the wearied troops, who lay almost unconscious and indifferent to everything save honour. We had now been about seven hours on foot—an all night march—and just as I sat upon a log of wood that lay beside the road, I heard a sound, distant, but yet a sound of cannon, booming upon the morning air. air. It was the first hostile shot I had heard in the East, and it set me thinking, too. The work had begun for the day, and if our troops did not gain ground before the sun had set behind the south-western hills, *La Compagnie Irlandaise* would be in action. Who knew but a brilliant revenge awaited the army of Bourbaki? Who knew but we might form part of the "Army of Liberation?" We had heard good news at Clarval. We had not heard of the occupation of Le Mans by the Germans on the 12th inst., but we had heard that the left wing of the army under Bourbaki in person had carried Villersexel on the 9th, and that General Werder was hemmed in between the two wings of the *Armée de l'Est*. We had heard, too, that we had been running the enemy for three days, and everywhere along our route there was evidence to show that the Germans were in retreat before us. But there it sounded again, sure enough the ball had begun, and the booming increased, as dawn merged into daylight, and we were again *en route*, this time really for the front.

"Did you hear that, Captain?" said M'Alevey at my side, as we trudged along, a few minutes afterwards, haggard and hungry. "There it is again;—

"It is, it is the cannon's opening roar,"

and the joyous lieutenant affected an attitude suggestive of the drama.

"*La musique de la guerre,*" said one of the Captains of the regiment—Caton—who had fallen out, and was now passing on to his Company in front. "Your Irish boys will soon be into it now."

"It is time," I replied, looking back at the famished and drooping men of *La Compagnie Irlandaise.* "Another such month as the one we have passed through, and my 'Irish boys,' as you call them, will have gone to glory without seeing any more of the Germans. The fact is, Caton, I am tired of this kind of work; with us it has been all famine and frost and no fighting."

"Well, this is the last move on the board," said Captain Caton, somewhat depressingly, while his hand instinctively played with his revolver; "if this fails the game is up; but the fire is growing hot," he added, as the booming increased until the cannonade blazed away in almost continuous discharges.

"Jimmy," said a soldier at my side, when Captain Caton had passed on to his Company in front, and Lieutenant M'Alevey had fallen back to his place in our own, "Jimmy, if the people in the 'ould dart' only knew where we were going this blessed 15th of January, shure a few of thim might say 'the Lord presarve thim from harm,' in our favour."

"Amin," said he who was addressed as Jimmy, "Amin, Pat. The Lord presarve us from harm, but, above all, may the Lord save us from dishonour."

"Niver fear for that. He hasn't given us strength and courage to live through the misery of the past two months only to disgrace the ould land now——"

But the speaker suddenly broke into an exclamation of pain, at the same time he limped out of the ranks and, as I heard afterwards had to fall a little behind, while he bathed his feet in snow, to wash away the pebbles that had eaten into the obnoxious-looking sores around his instep. Bad shoes had, indeed, become the greatest curse to the troops. The sand and small stones had gotten over the miserably low uppers of the shoes, and had chaffed the skin until it became sore, into which the frost gnawed holes as deep and as wide as five shilling pieces. In some instances the men cut out that portion of the uppers that rubbed against the excoriation, and then, exposed to the cold, the sore enlarged, and became offensive, even to the smell. Others boldly threw away the wretched excuses for shoes, and tramped it barefooted and bleeding over the beaten track. A few cut up their cotton gaiters, and lapped their feet in the folds, much as a surgeon bandages up a splintered arm. It was painful to watch the efforts made at shuffling over the ground, for walk the troops could not, except, indeed, a few who had by some means contrived to have a pair of shoes that were not of regulation pattern. The clothing, too, was hanging in tattered patches from the persons of the men. For four months they had lain night and day in the one suit of clothes, and the cleanest *sous-officier* in the regiment could not have been free from loathsome vermin. But "in the deepest depth there is a lower still." The worst had not come yet! Had it not been that we were going to the front hundreds of men of the *Regiment Etranger* would have lain down beside the road, perhaps to die. But the music of war stirred the blood of all. Even the weakly pressed onward then, and the men of *La Compagnie Irlandaise*, who, an hour before, were faint almost to death, stepped out with a vigour that showed there was mettle in them all. Not that men are anxious to court danger, but that they are anxious to see it. The feeling a man has going into action is, I believe, undefined, and almost undefinable. It is a mixed feeling of dread and duty; but it is duty first, and dread afterwards. Every man is by nature a coward. The fear of death is natural to all men. The man who says " I fear not" is a hypocrite, a coward, or a fool. It is not courage, but a high sense of honour that makes good soldiers. Physically one man may be braver than another man, but it is a deep sense of responsibility, and keenness of honour, that keeps him longest at a post of danger. The man who "fears not death" is incapable of command, and can never be anything more than a butcher in warfare. There is nothing in nature more contemptible than a man, whose indifference to life verges into bravoism, mere animal courage, devoid of honour, and stripped of every vestige of sense of duty. Bayard and Ney were the tenderest and most chivalrous of men. Napoleon and the infidel Frederick the Great, were as gentle in garrison as they were gallant in the field.

But the day advanced. The road lay through an undulating country, and the stripes of evergreen timber traversed the snow-covered ground, like threads of emerald over a bridal veil; sometimes climbing up the slippery sides of a hill, and then sliding into the valley below. Occasionally a soldier would slip and fall, and then the stereotyped jokes about "Minding the pieces," and other popular phrases, were sure to be repeated by some of the less quick-witted of the men. The sun was almost in the meridian when the spire of the village church of Arcey suddenly appeared above some trees that stood before us. It seemed to bring a feeling of security to all. It was Sunday, too, the day upon which the bloodiest records of human strife are marked upon the pages of warfare, and who knew but we were marching to another combat that would live in history to add one more record to the bloody calendar? We knew that 100,000 men were in our front, and out of that number death could reap a sufficient harvest to immortalise the day. The village was soon gained, and as we reached its high position the booming of the guns became more constant, and somewhat louder still. Beside the route the old people of the village knelt in prayer, and like Moses, upon the rock of Horeb, they asked Him to bless the effort of our arms. The "Angelus bell" was sounding as we hurried on, and Mass was being celebrated for the repose of the souls that had that day fallen in action. The little boys who stood beside the road looked vaguely into our faces, with, I opine, a suspicion that they should one day be companions in our work. The effect was singularly humanizing. For the moment it took some of the rough edges of the brutal part of our nature, that had been developed and almost cultivated by the hardships of the campaign. I could pity the sceptical mind that was not moved by the pious, but still almost antithetical contrast, of religion and war. But we made our destination for the night; and frost-bitten, hungry, and haggard, the men had to find cold comfort in a bed of mud, and a cup of coffee with a little sea biscuit as their only food. The Capitaine-Adjutant-Major appeared to have selected the dirtiest place around the village for our encampment, or rather for our halting-place for the night, and for no other reason than the highly objectionable one, that thousands of troops had been there before us, and had converted it into a mud hole. Tents were not allowed to be pitched, and the troops unrolled their four feet by two blankets and tent patches, and lay in heaps upon the slimy surface of the earth, cowering and shivering like a drove of pigs huddled in a market-pen. But the play was going on in our immediate front now. On our right a stripe of timber stretched away over the adjoining slopes of the Vosges, and on our left an open country undulated towards the scene of the combat. Sheltered behind a friendly swell in the ground, and placed in position, a brigade of our troops was observable from where we lay, and which must have been the rear-guard of the army engaged, for towards dusk they advanced beyond the rise, and disappeared into the gentle sloping valley beyond. Away upon the left a battery of artillery was belching in the direction of the village of Montbelliard, and as it too pressed forward, with its regiment of Mobiles behind, tirailleurs in front, and cavalry upon its flank, the joyous news came in: "*Une grande victoire!*" "*Une grande victoire!*" We were nearly up at last! I was looking through a field-glass, and was trying to take in the position of our troops, when the focus rested on the battery that was playing upon the left of the position, and while looking at the gunners working the pieces, a concussion shell burst amidst the battery, some men fell as if struck by the pieces, the first soldiers I had seen fall in the East.

"Distance lens enchantment to the view," said the ready-witted M'Alevey, coming to my side. I handed him the glass, and turned to make arrangements for the night. The fourrier-sergeant, M'Crossin, was, as usual, foraging for provisions over the village. Sergeant Carey was busy doing the general business of the Company, and Sergeant-Major Dunsford had gone to attend a "call" that had been just given at the command of the *Commandant*.

The village church at Sainte Marie, the place where we had halted, was crowded with dead. M'Alevey, the doctor, Mr. Cotter, and myself, went over to see the victims of the war, as they lay cold and rigid in all the quiet philosophy of death. Their faded honours were for ever gone. Grim and ghastly they looked with the clothes torn from that portion of the wound where the "fell sergeant, strict in his arrest," had entered. I remember a somewhat unpleasant sensation possessing my mind, as I looked on the array of dead within the village church at Sainte Marie, when M'Alevey, who stood by my side, broke the silence, and almost inaudibly said:

" Straightened by circumstances," as he looked down at the dead bodies that were heaped upon the spacious floor.

" M'Alevey, you're mad to joke upon such a subject," said Cotter, affecting to be shocked at the utterance, just as a music master might be annoyed at the grinding of a street barrel-organ.

" Not at all, sir; not at all. I'm only a little insane upon the jest question; will you try a pinch of snuff?" and M'Alevey offered the acceptable powder to myself and the now appeased Cotter.

" There's a beauty," said M'Alevey, pointing to a hideous-looking German, whose clothes were opened at the breast. A large hole, around which the clotted blood had hardened, was observable, just over the heart. He was dressed in the blue uniform of the Prussian line, and could not have been long dead, for the plain, large, flat buttons, common to the army, looked as if they had only been brushed that morning. Beside him lay a youthful Franc-tireur, who must have been an Adonis in life. The contrast was from the hideous to the handsome.

"*Mon Capitaine*," said a young man at our side, who was dressed in a uniform that corresponded with that of the dead free-shooter, "This was my companion, he was killed by that ugly German, and I killed him," he added, pointing again to the hideous-looking Prussian soldier before us.

"When ?" I asked, interested in the story.

"Yesterday, *mon Capitaine*," near the ditch you may see running eastward from the skirt of the village, as we were pushing on the flank of the enemy who occupied the place."

"Did you know him long ?" asked Lieutenant M'Alevey.

"Yes, yes, *mon Lieutenant*," replied the young soldier, "we were reared together, went to school together, fought together, and I wouldn't care if we had died together." There was a Christian seriousness in the young man's words, that interested us all, and M'Alevey drew from him a story of which, as well as I remember, the following is the substance :—

Pierre and Jacques Vileroy were cousins, and had been piously instructed, when boys, under the guidance of an uncle, who was a *curè* in one of the quiet villages that lay beside the Doubs. They had been educated together, and that mutual friendship common enough in boys had grown into a feeling of brotherly love. They were two of a common age, and by a strange fatality the only cross in life they ever had was, that they had both become attached to the one *fille*. It must have been a boyish love, for neither the dead free-shooter, Pierre, nor his living cousin, and companion of yesterday, could have been more than nineteen or twenty years of age.

At the outbreak of the war they joined a company of Franc-tireurs that had been raised in their department, "only forty kilometres from where we are," said the young man pointing in the direction of his home. Since then they had been in six fights, and upon one occasion the dead Franc-tireur had saved the life of the young man that now mourned over his corse. "We had begun to feel the recklessness which, I suppose, is consequent upon a continued escape from danger, and when yesterday morning we were ordered to dislodge the Germans from their position behind the ditch, we imprudently charged over a narrow field that separated us from the enemy; many of our comrades fell, but Pierre and I pressed on, he, being the quickest runner, keeping ahead of me, and had crossed the ditch while I was still ten yards behind it. I saw him stop and take aim at a German who was running before him, and who fell dead; then this soldier turned upon Pierre, their bayonets crossed, I stopped and took aim, shot him through the heart, but not before he had run his bayonet through the bowels of my brave cousin," and the poor fellow wept tears of pious friendship as he looked down upon all that remained of his friend.

"Come," said M'Alevey, vividly affected by the simple story of the free-shooter, "let us go," and the doctor and I followed him him out of the church and sought the shelter of our quarters, where our orderlies had dressed and prepared a couple of fowl to help to appease our voracious appetites.

"Here's to the old land," said Dr. Macken, holding up a cup of wine, after we had devoured the fowl, and had taken the bones by both ends. "The old land" repeated all, and once again cups clashed to the fervid prayer of "God save Ireland!"

"And the girls we left behind us," chimed in M'Alevey, looking as full of merriment, and seemingly as secure in the possession of a whole skin in the work before us, as if he was to be a spectator, and not a combatant in the expected drama of to-morrow.

We were snugly housed in a deserted cabin, with our companions of the regiment crowded into the adjoining rooms, and chatting gaily about our successes. A knock is given at the door, M'Alevey invites the person outside to "come in."

"Orders, sir," said the Sergeant of the week, handing over an order from the Brigadier:

" ' *Officiers, sous officiers, et soldats:*

" 'The General commanding the 1st Brigade of the 2nd Division 15th Corps late Army of the Loire, has to congratulate the 5th Battalion and that portion of the 2nd Battalion of the *Regiment Etranger* now in Sainte Marie with the spirited energy they have shown under the privations through which they have passed, and the order and discipline that they have observed under the trials of the last ten days. The General commanding cannot speak too highly of the admirable conduct of both officers and soldiers, and the manner in which they have borne the hardships of the campaign assures him that the officers and soldiers of the 2nd and 5th Battalions will to-morrow equal the gallantry of the 1st Battalion and that portion of the 2nd in our front, who have this day covered themselves with glory.

" ' Signed   " ' *General de Brigade.*' "

"Bravo, bravo," said Dr. Macken, as he emptied the contents of his cup.

"Bravo, bravo," said M'Alevey, as he significantly turned around and arranged what he called the "cow's feathers" in gentle lairs for his bed. A word of instruction to the sergeant, and I, too, set about preparing my couch.

Another knock at the door. "*Entrez ;*" and an Artillery soldier, looking neither neat nor natty, the servant of an officer, made a thousand apologies, but asked us if we had a morsel of candle to spare "*pour mon Lieutenant.*" There was none to be had, but the lieutenant of Artillery afterwards told every officer in his battery the answer

M'Alevey made the garçon, when he asked him if the "light of love" would be of any use, and offered the servant a match. M'Alevey's wit acted upon our drooping spirits as the wand of Prospero acted upon the barren wastes and backwoods, which it turned into golden fields and smiling gardens. Sometimes, indeed, he would make an attempt to be sage, but was never sad. He once told a Frenchman that he took him to be a Chinaman, and being asked the reason why, said, because he had "often seen faces like his painted on a tea-chest." But now he covered his head with his blanket, and was soon snoring as vigorously as if he were asleep—a circumstance it was not at all times easy to determine.

CHAPTER XI.

> "He hath bent him o'er the dead
> Ere the first day of death is fled—
> The first dark day of nothingness,
> The last day of danger and distress,
> Before decay's effacing fingers
> Have swept the lines where beauty lingers."
>
> THE GIAOUR.

"COME, arouse thee, arouse thee, my brave Irish boys," said M'Alevey, the following morning, at four a.m., accompanying the invitation with no gentle pressure of his hand. "The men are falling in, captain, and we have only time to roll up our blankets and be off."

"Has anybody been here?" I asked.

"Yes, Sergeant Frank Byrne; come doctor, come Cotter—

> 'March to the battle-field,
> The foe is now before us,'

and M'Alevey made one of his ridiculous attempts to sing a ditty, he having as much taste for music as, to use a somewhat boorish illustration of his own, "a pig has for dancing."

It was not very cold, but the numb, sleepy, and half-dead feeling one has when turning out so early after a fatiguing march the day before, was not easily shaken off. Our blankets were soon rolled up collar fashion, and swung across our shoulders, our belts buckled on and then out into the field where the men had lain during the night. A more pitiable sight I scarcely ever saw than were the men of *La Compagnie Irlandaise* that morning. They looked more like spectres than human beings. The dirt from the clayey soil covered nearly every portion of their uniforms; the heavy dew had soaked through their overcoats, had penetrated through their jackets, and left them shivering, gnashing their teeth with wretchedness and cold. As they stood in line they were doubled up, as if by the weight of their misery, and the very lepers of Lebanon would not have exchanged for such a fate, transient though it should be. But they were all up, for those who had fallen behind on the march the day before, had struggled into camp during the night, and now took their place in line—this time for a march really to the front. There were, indeed, familiar faces absent, amongst the rest, the "Snarleyow" of the company, our old friend, Timothy Marks, who had succumbed to frozen feet, and was, no doubt, cursing French military regulations, as only an old soldier can. But the head of the column soon moved on, a shuffling of feet was heard upon our right, the men were numbered off, and moved along to a low word of command, shouldered their rifles without any order, and followed the battalion without another word. The *Commandant* had become tired of formalities, another instance of the thorough negligence of the officers in command.

Along the route the oblong traces of shot and shell were visible in the snow, as they had torn up the earth, much as a man might scoop a hole in a mud hill by one long sweep of a shovel. To the right and left these marks were everywhere to be seen, leaving their dark blotches upon the ground, like ink stains upon a schoolboy's copy-book. Too often beside the suggestive shot and shell marks, blood crimsoned the snow, and eat holes through its yielding surface, while the warm current must have trickled from the wounded. It was quite dark above, but the reflection from the snow-covered ground threw a light upwards, that enabled one to see some distance around with tolerable clearness. We had still about fourteen kilometres to march, as our troops had driven the enemy into, and around the villiage of Montbelliard, where we heard the Germans were strongly entrenched, and in the attack on which we were to be employed. The feet of many a poor fellow were festered, blistered, and frostbitten, but it is no metaphor to say that the spirt of Longfellow had entered the hearts of all, and that " Excelsior" was on every man's lips. As I looked around I saw more than a dozen of my men limping into action. We were not, indeed, without three or four who were shabbier hypocrites than Pecksniff, darker dissemblers than Tartuffe; but there was none of it that morning, all walked, or limped, or shuffled as best they could to "see the show," as I overheard a soldier say half-an-hour before we were at our destination. I heard indeed more than one groan from the ranks of the Company, and the utterances of men in pain were common enough along the way, but their spirits were pitched to straining point, and onward, upward was the thought of all. Sergeant Donnellan marched, as usual, at the head of the company, and set an example of vigorous limping that inspired the action of many a less determined soul.

"Donnellan," I said, moving up, and walking beside a man whom I was proud to call my friend, "Donnellan, did you rest at all last night."

"Very little, captain," he replied, hesitating to blame even a government that was killing himself and his companions "according to regulation."

"The treatment the soldiers are subjected to is scandalous to a civilized country calling itself a military power," I replied, "but I cannot let the men know my opinions, though I may tell them in confidence to you."

"As you have broken the ice, it is scandalous, sir. As you know, captain," he said, half turning his head towards me, "as you know, captain, a regimental dog in an English garrison wouldn't be treated, as I see some of the rank and file, yes, and even some of the sergeants in the *Regiment Etranger* treated every hour in the day. Men don't volunteer to fight famine; an empty haversack demoralises a man more than a shower of *mitraille*."

"I can understand a deficiency of stores occasionally," I answered, "but even when the regulation quantum is served out, an ordinary man has not enough of food to sustain life during a campaign. In garrison it might indeed do very well, for there is no waste, but in the field it is starvation and nothing less. More than that our men are still at a disadvantage. They cannot economise their food like Frenchmen, nor make palatable soup of grease and hard crusts. The fact is, Donnellan, the whole system is unsound, and I cannot believe that the French have ever studied the art of war."

"It is strange," replied Donnellan, "there is good material and bad method in the organisation of the French army. Look at them now," he continued, drawing my attention to the soldiers who limped on before us, ragged, foot-sore, and famine looking out of their eyes, "how can such men fight?"

"Very true Donnellan, how, indeed?" See how that man's tin cup rattles against his *beadon;* the thing itself, simple as it appears, might betray the movement of troops. On a quiet night the clash of tins may be heard miles off. And, then the meat should be condensed; the Germans can make their soup in thirty minutes, while it takes our men three hours. Clothing the same, and boots worse than all. The fact is, Donnellan, the whole system is rotten."

"Then, again," said Donnellan, pointing to a dead soldier who lay beside the road, "look, captain, a dead Prussian, and, as usual, barefooted. Our fellows always strip the first dead German they meet of his boots, as they are better and stronger than the miserable *papier-maché* shoes supplied to themselves." And so I found afterwards, for all the dead of the enemy whom I saw were barefooted.

"There is another, and another," I replied, as we climbed up a hill behind the village of Dung, where the dead of the enemy lay right and left of the road, all barefooted. Baggage waggons, ambulance waggons, and artillery train now blocked the route. The smoke from the bivouac curled through the trees, and the hum of thousands of voices became suddenly audible. We were up at last!

"It is all owing to the *Intendance*," answered Donnellan, "it is impossible that one department can successfully muster the troops; manage the pay list; issue provisions, fuel, forage, and clothing; supervise hospital service; manage the whole transport of the army, and take charge of all the materials of war."

"The greatest wonder of the German system appears to me to be its perfection and its economy. Prussia conducted two European campaigns, 1864 and 1866, at about the same expense that England incurred in the expedition to Abyssinia. Her soldiers only cost £29 10s. per head, per annum, while each Frenchman costs his country £41 10s., and the English soldier costs upwards of £90 per year."

"And withal the Germans are so splendidly equipped," said Donnellan, looking down at his tattered raiment, "but they don't compel their men to carry the useless lumber which is heaped in our knapsacks; look at that wretched boy staggering under 70lbs weight,

"LA COMPAGNIE IRLANDAISE." 181

half of which is pure rubbish," and Donnellan called my attention to a weakly-built youth, who was drawing his limbs along with painful efforts.

"Well, this war has proved that centralization is a failure. Each corps should be complete in itself, and be able to move in any dire .- tion without the necessity of reference to a central authority. The simple *piou, piou* of the French army, would be rendered an efficient soldier under the system pursued by Germany, while now he is only an incumbrance, and a delusion. But it is the same all through the service. The system of 'substitutes' is most nefarious. When the providing of those men was entrusted to private companies, the regiments were always full; but since the Government undertook the job, there has been nothing but peculation and deceit. It is monstrous to think that France, with all her military renown, would allow men to purchase 'exonoratives,' by paying a certain sum of money into the military chest."

"Do you remember how much it cost to purchase a substitute?" asked Donnellan, as we passed through the village of Dung.

"Oh, that varied; £100 was the general price, for which, however the 'substitute' was scarcely ever provided. Consequently France had a big army on paper, and a very small one, indeed, on the actual muster-roll."

"To what do you attribute the unparalleled successes of the German troops, Captain," asked Donnellan, a few minutes before we halted, and while the enemy's batteries were occasionally sending their shells over our heads.

"To the one broad fact, Donnellan—that in Prussia the army is made a profession, and its minutest details studied with care; while in France the life of a soldier is merely an occupation, where officers and men depend upon *prestige* and *élan* to carry them through all difficulties. Why even in Italy, one of the most fertile countries in the world, I have heard the officers of this regiment say, that the men were often without bread. The French have fallen away, they want a Carnot, a Mareau, or a Napoleon. Every great man who has handed his name down as a military genius, succeeded by adopting some new method of mobility. The genius of Carnot saved France at the plains of Fleurees, won twenty-nine victories in a year, captured nearly 4,000 guns, and dissolved the European coalition, and all by creating an army capable of being moved with rapidity and order. Alexander, Cæsar, Frederick the Great, and Napoleon—all the same—conquered by similar means. There is, however, one thing I admire in the French regimental economy—I mean the *ordinaire;* only for the three sous each of the men contributed to that, every five days, they would be in a state of chronic starvation."

"Yes; that keeps them up certainly, Captain, but perhaps the military authorities depend too much upon it, and consequently relax the efforts they would otherwise make, if it were not in existence."

"Perhaps so; but still I like the system."

"But the forty francs recruits get on joining their regiments is useless, for when kit and everything else is deducted, he generally finds himself in debt. But," he continued, looking to his direct front, "we are nearly up, the *musique de la guerre* is belching away. Do you think we shall have much fighting to-day, captain?" he asked, after a moment's pause.

"Oh, it is impossible to say, sergeant. I suppose we are in for a little of it in any case. If Villersexel be really carried, as we heard at Clarval, I don't see how the Germans can hold Montbelliard, for they would be crushed between the two wings of the army. If Villersexel is not taken, however, Montbelliard will hold out at all cost, for the fall of either place would in all probability enable us to raise the siege of Belfort.

"If anything happens to me will you write to my mother, Captain?" he asked, without betraying the shadow of emotion, and with a tone as cool and firm as if he was speaking of a ride across his native heath in Galway.

"Nonsense, old boy. But if it should of course I will—that is, if I am not wiped out myself."

Suddenly I heard a heavy footstep behind me, and turning around I saw Sergeant Carey holding something in his hand, and rushing towards where I was.

"Captain, captain, take it, take it; mind it is hot, sir," said the sergeant, as he offered me something that in the dark looked like a sausage.

"Take what?" I said, looking anxiously at the indistinct outline of what he held in his hand.

"A herring, sir, a red herring," and he held up a delicious fish just from the fire. I never asked Carey how he obtained the herring, but Dr. Macken had a standing joke against me afterwards that the fish was his, and that Carey had taken it from his orderly, and carried it in the cap of a boy who was down in smallpox.

"Is it clean, Carey?" I asked.

"Oh, as Glenfield starch, sir;" and I soon consumed the delicious morsel, holding it by both ends, and picked it clean. Just then we wheeled into a field, and took up our place in line of battle.

It was just daylight. About 50 yards behind where we stood a stripe of wood stretched right and left as far as the eye could see; before us lay an open undulating country, a kind of a rolling prairie, beyond which were dark blotches of timber, where we truly guessed the Germans lay. A little to our front and left, lay the village and chateau of Montbelliard, before which, and sheltered by the undulating ground, lay 100,000 of our troops in position. It was a glorious sight! There were, indeed, no bayonets glittering in the morning sun, no banners fluttering in the breeze; but there was a quiet, calm look about those lines of battle that inspired a sternness of purpose in every man's heart.

"*Bon jour*," said Lieutenant Kuess, taking off his kepi in salute to the first *fiegende zuekertsute*, or "flying sugar loaf," as the Germans call the shells, as the first of the messengers came hissing from the chateau, and rushed away miles behind our position, just as if the enemy wished to show us the length and range of their pieces. The play began then, and our battalion was ordered into the wood to light fires and cook their breakfasts, and I was seriously assured by the Capitaine-Adjutant-Major that at noon it would be our place to lead an attack upon the German batteries! But we were to take our "death feast" first.

"Where's Mr. M'Alevey?" I asked of his orderly.

> "' Just before the battle, mother,
>   When I am thinking most of you.'

I'm here, captain, what is it," said the object of my inquiries behind me.

M'Alevey and I walked over the rise in order to have a better view of the play. Around our position the dead of the enemy were somewhat thickly strewn. Every one of the Germans were barefooted, having being stripped of their valuable boots, and the stony-looking feet looked as they had been chiselled in yellowish marble. But the cannon belched away, a few prisoners marched by, escorted by those theatrical-looking warriors—the pompiers. Noon came! "*Sac-a-dos! Sac-a-dos!*" We were to march by the left. *La Compagnie Irlandaise* led the way, and was the first of 20,000 men who formed the third line of battle. Two lines were already in position upon our left, sheltered behind a rise in the ground, upon the uppermost slope of which our batteries were sending their "flying sugar loaves," at the Chateau of Montbelliard. We had about one kilometre to march yet before we would be in position, and when about half way across a round shot passed through our ranks between the files, and ploughed up the ground at the feet of General Pitevern and staff whom we were just passing at the time. Shall I confess that I ingloriously ducked my head, and that our *Commandant*, who walked beside me, called out *"pas gymnastique, pas gymnastique,"* while Sergeant Donnellan showed me better conduct by walking as coolly and as erect as if he was a moving landmark. We were ascending a slight rise in the ground at the time, and the ranks were more than usually open, which accounts for the ball passing through without injuring any of the men.

The General quickly changed his position, while our fine old Colonel, always on horseback, checked the *Commandant* for ordering the "double." Before us lay a wood, upon which the left of the line was to rest, and once up to the place we were face to face with the foe. About two hundred yards in our direct front lay one of our own batteries, behind which the first and second line of battle was formed, and to both of which we were drawn up in a parallel line. Not a German was to be seen, but their ugly concussion shells burst in and around the battery, and sent their splinters quite thick enough about our ears. It was miserable work, standing behind our guns coolly looking at danger without any of the excitement which turns it into a desire for blood. But it was a splendid lesson in training the troops to coolness under fire. The shells burst before us, we knew that each flew into twenty particles, flying off as if seeking a victim, and then to stand stone still, not a muscle moving, to hold the breath, expecting every second to get a blow, and then to draw a long sigh of relief when the pieces "bir-r-ed," and left you untouched, was a somewhat trying task. With the old shell there was often time to avoid the danger by lying upon the ground while the fuse burned out and the shell burst, the pieces flying upwards and around. But with the breach or segment shell the pieces fly to the front, and must act as a powerful propeller upon retreating troops. James Grant, in his "Constable of France," tells of the aged Conde de Fuentes who charged at the head of the infantry at the battle of

Rocroi in Spain, 1643, seated in an arm chair, and I often thought that the feeling of men standing behind a battery with ordered arms, while the enemy's shell is playing about their ears, must be somewhat akin to the feelings of the men who carried the chair in which the Conde de Fuentes was seated. It may have been very fine for the Conde, but I could pity the men. But there was no help for it, there we were, and there we should remain, and some of the officers of the regiment smoked their cigars, stood before their men, and let it rain away.

"First blood, captain," said Sergeant Terence Byrne. I turned around and saw the blood trickling from the face of Corporal Paul Cullen, who was just grazed by a splinter hitting the malar bone. Towards two o'clock the firing slackened in our front, and orders came for the *Regiment Etranger* to occupy the wood upon which the left of *La Compagnie Irlandaise* rested. The Irish Company alone was to cover 200 yards of the front; the place was pointed out by the *Commandant*, and we moved to take up our new position. We came, however, in view of the German batteries, and had no sooner entered the bush than a hell of fire broke around our ears. The shells fell at the rate of one a second, crushing, bursting, and tearing everything in their course, the splinters throwing the snow into our faces as we crouched low behind the shelter of the wood, or sent "limbs" of small trees upon our backs as we lay full length upon the earth.

For a minute or two the fire slackened, and I ventured to dodge from tree to tree to see how things were going on along the line. We had one man of somewhat peculiar mental mould in our ranks; and as I was passing the scattered files I saw this man upon his knees sheltered behind a large tree, his rifle by his side, his hands raised in prayer, while his lips moved as if in articulation. I thought there was a time and place for everything, and if I spoke harshly to the praying soldier, it was not because I thought less of the influence of pious acts, but at that moment, more of the necessity of every man at that time, looking to his proper front. But the soldier was down in an instant, looking in the direction of the enemy, his rifle in his hand, and I passed on. A few seconds afterwards I saw the same man engaged in devouring a good sized piece of horseflesh, which appeared to be but slightly done, but which was, no doubt, well sauced by hunger, for the pious Irish soldier. But, contrary to expectation, no attack was made upon our position, nor were we called upon to attack as we had been told in the morning. News had arrived during the day that Villersexel was not carried, and that Bourbaki with his left wing of the *Armée de l'Est* was in full retreat towards the Swiss frontier. Daylight merged into dusk, and dusk lapsed into night, before the cannon from the enemy's batteries ceased to play upon our position. A few of our men were wounded, none seriously, and as the last shot from the German position passed over our heads, many of the officers bade "*bon soir*" to the flying shell that, like the herald of the morning's strife, was sent miles over our position. The work had ceased for the day.

Beyond the open space that divided us from the enemy, the fires from their bivouac illumed the night with their livid glare, "while the stars up above, with their glittering eyes, kept watch while the army was sleeping." Beside our position a horse that had been killed during the day, and which had been partly devoured by the famished soldiers, afforded a substantial meal to such of the men as were not too choice in their food, and to the medical students of the company an opportunity of exercising their skill in cutting sections from its quarters. The dew fell heavily upon the wearied troops, and the thin foliage of January afforded but poor protection against the damp cold air, loaded with pain-creating moisture. A sickly fire, more smoke than flame, struggled through a few logs beside which some of us, stretched upon twigs pulled from the branches of the trees, in vain tried to court a few minutes of repose. There was no moon, and all around was as dark as Erebus.

"*Aux armes, aux armes,*" was shouted along the line, as the roll of musketry swelled throughout the camp at midnight.

"Fall in, fall in," M'Alevey called out.

"A night attack, Captain," said Lieutenant Cotter. "Fall in men, fall in. *En avant, mar——.*"

"*Cessez le feu, cessez le feu,*" blew out three regimental bugles.

"*Cessez le feu, cessez le feu,*" echoed along the line.

"See what's up now, Mr. M'Alevey."

"All right, captain," said M'Alevey, returning in a few minutes, "it was only an old artillery horse that had broken loose and strayed between the lines, which some d—— Mobiles had mistaken for an Uhlan."

Long before the dawn next morning, Tuesday, the 17th, before the sun's all-ripening wings swept the cold sweat of night from earth's dark breast, the troops were again upon their feet, cowering in the cold, with hunger gnawing at the vital thread that still held them to existence. The hum of 100,000 men raised around us a murmur, such as streams make when their waters meet in embrace. The clouds scudded over the giant trees under which we lay, and gave us but an occasional glance at the stars that blinked away as if they had nothing else to do. The snow was melting, and had made miniature pools over the plateau upon which the greater part of the troops had lain, the tramp of whose feet had converted the plain into a sea of mud. Batches of shivering soldiers stood around the embers of the half-burned logs of wood that fizzed and would not blaze. The chill north-east wind penetrated to the marrow of the famished soldiers of the army, whose miserable clothing could afford no protection against the keen biting blast. Hundreds of men were there around the choked camp-fires of the bivouac barefooted, thousands frost-bitten and almost without shoes—every man of whom would be compelled to take his share in the work of the day. But association with hardship had hardened the heart of every one, and there was little or no pity in men's thoughts. Our hearts had become steeled against compassion, and day by day we were becoming more brutalized in our ideas.

I suppose I must have been in a somewhat dreamy mood, as M'Alevey stood by my side and looked into my face, just as a Jew might look at a suspicious bank cheque. "Here comes our good morning," said he, as a shell flew over our heads kilometres to our rear.

"*Bon jour, bon jour,*" cried a thousand voices, while kepis flew off in salutation to the airy messenger. And then our own batteries sent the return shell of defiance over the German lines, and the play began for the day. Before this time we were in line, just behind a battery, before which a curtain had been thrown up during the night, and the shell from the enemy's lines swept through the embrasures and tore up the earth everywhere about our feet. We had no shelter, as the space between us and our guns (about 100 yards) was as flat as a dining table, and as the shell struck the ground, and burst, the ugly pieces again bir-r-r-ed and passed our ears. Several of the men had been hurt the day before—one or two were missing —but, on the whole, the chances of war were singularly favourable to the soldiers of *La Compagnie Irlandaise*. Behind us the ground sloped upwards, upon the summit of which two field officers' orderlies were sitting upon their horses, indulging in some quiet chatter of their own, perhaps planning something that should, of course, have been done—a shell hissed close to the rifles of our men and passed through one of the horse's legs—a singular evidence of the precision of the German artillerists, who at a distance of about 1,500 yards, at the first shot, shaved the mark at which, no doubt, the shell was aimed.

"Hold up your head," said somebody to one of the soldiers upon the left of the company a few minutes afterwards, and who was seen ducking without any apparent cause.

"I will, sir, when there's room for it," was the half-laughing rejoinder of the man whom, I afterwards heard, had just stooped in time to allow the heel of a shell from coming in contact with his head. About this time the fire grew hot again, and the firing from the enemy's batteries became continuous. We occupied a useless and a dangerous place. To our right and and to our left there was shelter, and it was culpable folly to expose men without any object to be gained. But worse still! About 10 a.m. a change was made in the disposition of the company, and I was ordered to face the wood, thus placing my men at right angles with our own battery, and open to an enfilading fire from the enemy's guns. It was butchery! One shot would have swept the Irish company off its feet, and as the shells from the enemy's batteries were falling quite thick enough about us at this time, there was some danger of this calamity happening. But as obedience is the first duty of a soldier, we took up our position, and then pointed out to our *Commandant* the uselessness of exposing the men in so dangerous a place where a single shell would sweep through the company from flank to flank, and the *Commandant* allowed me to remove the company to a place of comparative security under the slope of a hill about one hundred yards to the right of where we then stood. Here we had quite a joyous time of it. The men gathered *marmites* full of snow water, put it upon the almost dead fires, and used their last grain of coffee. Noon came again. The troops had their packs off, and had formed *façeaux*, and tried to snatch a little comfort from the tobacco that nestled in the corners of their pockets.

"*Sac-a-dos! Sac-a-dos!*" was shouted along the line. Down comes the colonel, his hardy grey Arab bespattered with mud.

"*En avant—marche!*" and off we went, the Irish company leading the way. We passed in rear of the exposed battery, behind which we had stood in the morning, and then skirted a wood that lay before us, keeping well under the shadow of the trees. Inside the wood a road, or rather a footpath, ran in a parallel line to the course we were walking along its outer edge, and why the movement was made in full view of the German lines, instead of moving under cover of the trees, I never could understand. But whatever was the cause, many a good life was lost by the exposure to useless butchery. I often think it a pity that officers are not in some degree more responsible for useless bloodshed, whether caused by incapacity, indifference, or neglect. Sir Charles Napier said that an incapable general was a murderer. If so, there are many such in the armies of Europe. The enemy appeared to allow us to march on until about 2,000 of us were fairly exposed to their fire, and then they brought a couple of batteries to play upon our line, and opened upon us simultaneously, throwing their shells amongst the men with great precision and driving some of the soldiers like crushed frogs against the trees beside which they walked. Then the *Commandant* indeed, shouted, " To the wood, to the wood." I stood beside an opening in the timber, which allowed the men to pass through, and as I looked along the line I saw shell after shell plunge amongst the ranks, and scatter the limbs and bowels of the soldiery about the place, as effectually as if the poor wretches had been blown from the mouth of the cannon. At that moment, too, I experienced the most sickly sensation I had ever felt under fire. As I stood with my *back* to the enemy, while the men were passing into the wood, a cold sensation, as if a bar of iron was passed down my back, appeared to creep over my spine. To turn about and *face* the bursting shell was nothing, but even a few seconds of coolly standing with one's back to the fire while the particles are bir-r-r-ing past our ears in flocks, was to avoid the extravagant, excessively unpleasant. But it was only for a few seconds, the men passed under the shadow of the trees, and, as the ground sloped downwards, the position was one of shelter and security to all.

"God be with the ould times when it was sabre, pike, and skian that decided a battle, and not these murtherin' *obuses* that brakes a man's leg a mile away," said a soldier when we had again halted and faced about under the cover of the trees,

"What's sauce for the duck is sauce for the drake," replied another taking his chassepot in his hand and moving the "garde mobile" to see if it was in good order.

"Well, by gorra, an' I'd like to see the blackguard that id hit me, anyways," said another. "Then there might be some chance of returnin' the compliment, if one could only get a peep at the white of their eyes."

"By dad, an' I'd rather be looking at the back of their heads, but listen," and the speakers looked steadily at their front, while the roll of musketry swelled, volley after volley, before our post. The silky sound of the rifle bullet made music in our ears as they kissed the air above, beside, around us. The enemy's batteries shelled our post with their usual accuracy and vigour, and just beside us a battery of mitrailleurs was growling death upon the advancing line of Germans.

"*Le Regiment Etranger—en avant—marche,*" shouted the *Commandant*.

"Now, boys, a blow for the old land," said somebody to the soldiers, and we moved up to the edge of the wood, expecting to take part in the coming struggle.

CHAPTER XII.

> "What though the field be lost?
> All is not lost; th' unconquerable will,
> And study of revenge, immortal hate,
> And courage never to submit or yield."
>
> MILTON.

YES, we thought we were "in for it," as I heard some of the soldiers say, while we moved towards the edge of the timber to meet the expected advance of the Germans. Our pickets were driven in, and rushed into our line in breathless disorder. They almost broke our ranks as we advanced under a sprinkling of rifle bullets to cover their retreat. The mitrailleuse growled away on our right, while the shell from the enemy's batteries burst around us in terrible rapidity. They flew into the wood behind our position, and exploded with a noise like the springing of a mine. But it was only a feeler! The Germans retired under cover of their batteries, while scarcely a head was to be seen where we expected to see battalions and brigades. The enemy wanted to find out whether we still occupied the position in front of Montbelliard in force. They expected, or knew, that the main army was in retreat, and thought to drive us into confusion, by forcing all from the field. The affair, however, cost both sides a few lives, and in the wood around and on the open plain before us, many fresh, dark, motionless objects were dotting the patches of still unmelted snow, or lying half covered in the pools of water. Shortly afterwards a regiment of *Chasseurs-a-pied* of our division, worked bravely up to within three hundred yards of the enemy's lines, suffered severely in their trial, and retreated minus half their number. The object of the movement was a feint too, and probably impressed the enemy with the belief that we were still in force, and even meditated becoming the aggressors.

At the foot of the slope upon which we were posted a road traversed the wood, along which troops were passing, and generals aides-de-camp, and their orderlies were hurrying backwards and forwards during the day. It was well sheltered from the fire of the enemy's guns, except when an occasional shell, aimed at our position, would overtop the mark, and drive through the files that at times were passing along. Once, as I turned round to trace the progress of a shell that plunged between the trees, beside which we were placed, I saw a mounted trooper, horse and all, blown yards across the road into the scrub that lined the route upon either side. The shell had struck the horse and exploded, sending beast and rider into atoms, spattering blood in every direction. But listening to the bursting shell became a passion so strong that when about three o'clock the firing slackened a little, there was a sense of loneliness around us, to be soon unpleasantly relieved, however, by a further sprinkling of shell as another feint was made upon our outposts, and led us to expect more serious work on hands. In the meantime our battalion had not come off unscathed. A dreary procession was flowing from the ranks, as man after man was carried to the rear, amongst the rest one or two of the men of my own Company. The *Commandant* sent round for the list of casualties, and for the names of such men as had distinguished themselves during the day, but as we had not been closely engaged, I had no names to recommend for the military medal—the soldier's reward for distinguished conduct in the field.

I could indeed have named half-a-dozen men who well merited such a high distinction for their gallant coolness under a withering fire, and for the example of *sang-froid* they showed to soldiers for the first time in action. But I hoped for a better opportunity, as I saw that there were men around me who would encounter any as it passed through the tube, thus, as it appears to an inexperienced artillerist, giving it more accuracy in its rotary motion, and a better fit in the grooves of the gun. In the French shell the pins are already made to correspond with the gun; in the Krupp shell, the grooves are made on *en passage*. But we were too weary that night to study questions of guns and gunnery. Even M'Alevey ceased to joke, and for the only time during the campaign I heard him grumble as he lay with the hood of his great-coat over his head, and a log of wood for his pillow. The men sat upon their knapsacks in fours, back to back, in preference to stretching upon the ground, and dozed to sleep as best they could. As I strolled down to take a last look at the company that night, I could see the work of the past two or three days written as plainly upon the countenances of the men, as if it were stereotyped upon my brain. Sergeant Donnellan was already giving way, his once giant form having dwindled into that of a shivering, starved, and hungry-looking man, with cheek bones almost cutting the air. Sergeants Terence and Frank Byrne were much the same, but Sergeant Carey bore up with wondrous good humour, and must have had a constitution as durable as wrought iron. He was everywhere. If a dispute broke out between the men, Sergeant Carey was sure to be first upon the spot, and was equally sure to put a stop to it in such a manner as was likely to satisfy all, either with the rigour or impartiality of his dealings.

As the petals of the flowers in early spring open to the refreshing influence of the sun's rays, as if in gladdened salutation, the soldiers of the Irish Company were, on the morning of the 18th, joyously refreshed as the sun shone above and around them. The sky was beautifully clear, the air was motionless, and the flush of comfort coursed merrily through our veins as we again stood in line of battle. We had, as usual, taken up our position an hour or two before daybreak, cold, wet, and hungry; but when an hour after daylight the sun came out of the funereal envelope of clouds that most ennobles a man." It may be so, but it alone is not at all times the best test of the highest type of a soldier.

"Well, here's to try the efficacy of the cold water cure," said M'Alevey, as he rolled himself in his blanket and stretched out upon the slimy ground, sinking into its embrace as effectually as if he lay upon a bed of feathers. Food there was none, unless, indeed, some of the men had a morsel of biscuit, which in many cases it was impossible to gnaw. Before us lay a farm-house, into which the officers crowded in heaps, amongst the rest Dr. Macken and our colonel. Beside us an old well gaped through the ground, from which the only hedge upon the plateau ran up to the house in front of us. About a dozen fires blazed over the plain, around which the officers of the various regiments stood and talked over the haps and mishaps of the day. The troops, not literally, but actually lay half buried in the melted snow, the wet eating into their bones, and making many a brave soul wish for that sleep that knows no waking. About us lay the bodies of the few men who in the sheltered place had been killed during the last two days, acting as grim reminders of the work in hands. Just a little to my right, and beside a pool as large as a plunge bath, but not deeper than a shoe-tap, lay a young artillery man, his hand and arm partly hid in the water. The moon's rays shed a liquid pathway of light across the watery surface, and I could easily fancy with Charles Dickens that along that track the released soul of the soldier was making its way to heaven. The wind made ripples upon the little waves and moaned a requiem over the corse, while the passing clouds drew momentary palls over the spot, as if hiding man's work from the eye of God.

Beside where I lay a battery of artillery was posted, and one of the gunners brought a Krupp shell, which had not exploded, and showed it to us, as we sat upon the ground. Unlike the French shell it was not "pin grooved," but must have had a smooth surface before fired. Its leaded coating was cut by the groves of the gun shell flew through the damp, cold atmosphere. But night was beginning to fall upon the scene. We had been all day standing in snow, rocking from one foot to the other, or stamping and splashing the water under our feet, as the only means of combating that deadness which steals over bodies that are inactive. We were indeed supplied with brandy during the day, the only time I saw it served upon the campaign. But the misery of the men was perfect. No enemy of the human race could desire to see more active suffering, than what was endured by the *Armee de l'Est* for three days before Montbelliard. Nothing but the excitement of active warfare could sustain men through such a trial. In the Irish Company there were a few weakly boys, not more than seventeen or eighteen years of age, weak with hunger, haggard with misery, almost frozen with cold, loaded down with pack, ninety rounds of ammunition, and a rifle, and their spirits were unalterably the same—indomitably Irish.

"*Bon soir, bon soir,*" was again shouted in salutation to the shell that, after a short lull, flew high over our heads away into the quiet fields that lay for miles behind our position. Then orders came to move into the place we occupied that morning, so that even the poor shelter of the wood was to be denied us. There was, I suppose, a reason for the order, but I never could make it out. We left the batteries to take care of themselves, obeyed the last command, and were soon floundering along, ankle deep in snow water. If there be limits to human misery they were reached that night of the 17th January, 1871. The entire plain was a gigantic pond—water, water everywhere. The troops had been on foot an hour before the earliest streaks of dawn, and were worn out with cold, famine, and misery. The highest quality a soldier can possess is that of a hardy and obedient campaigner, for in action every man must do some share of the fighting, undergo some share of the danger, without necessarily possessing any other qualification but that of brute courage. To be sure, some poet sings that bravery "Is the brightest virtue, and danger at my command. There was a cool, stern purpose in their conduct; a calm, easy determination in their countenances, that spoke of a resolve to do their duty to the letter.

In the meantime the first battalion of our regiment had been engaged in the attack upon the Chateau of Montbelliard, and had been beaten off with much slaughter, only 300 returning out of 700 that had left us in the morning, and the officers gave us the depressing assurance that the Chateau could not be carried without a more vigorous bombardment than had yet been seriously attempted.

"What's that?" I asked of Lieutenant Kuess, who had just returned from the attack upon the Chateau, as I perceived a hole in his blanket that looked as if it had been made by a rifle ball. The lieutenant looked suspiciously at the spot, unrolled his blanket, and there through the coat, just under the region of the heart, a similar hole had been made through the tunic, which was quickly opened, waistcoat, too, and there lodged in his watch a flattened bullet had smashed the works, and lay between the cases.

"*Vive la chance*," said the lieutenant.

"Saved in the nick of time," said M'Alevey at our side, who had come up and leant upon my shoulder while the Frenchman was searching for the bullet. Another officer had the skirt of his tunic torn off by a piece of an *obus*, a third had a bullet lodged in his tightly-folded blanket, a fourth had the *galon* on his kepi cut by a rifle bullet, while a fifth, all of the one battalion, had had a ball flattened against a five-franc piece that was in his waistcoat pocket. But it was all "*vive la chance*." Four officers had been killed in the attack on the Chateau, while the battalion had been decimated in the rank and file.

All the while the shells kept tumbling in and about our position, occasionally killing a soldier or two, and wounding several others. Sometimes a sound, just such as a malard makes with its wings, when alighting near a pool, would be heard above, as the heel of a obscured its disc, we thought ourselves blessed, indeed. The firing, too, appeared to be even hotter than the day before, as if the artillerists were anxious to show the metaphysical influence of heat upon famine. The shells from the enemy's guns did not burst so easily upon the soft surface of the plateau, as they did upon the two previous days, particularly the first, when the frost covered the ground with its icy layers. Unexploded shells were not uncommon around our position, for many of them were buried in the soil without striking their noses against anything sufficienty hard to cause an explosion. But they fell and exploded quick and fast enough for all that. The guns of the Chateau were belching away as vigorously as ever, and a new battery erected during the night sent an oblique fire ricochetting through our lines. There were no trenches in our hastily-erected batteries, and the oblique fire from the near position of the enemy, did much damage. But the direct fire from the Chateau was even more strongly sustained than on the previous days, as they appeared desirous of giving us all we could take, for they must have known that before many hours we would be retreating. We had failed at all points to carry Montbelliard, and the German position on the left bank of the Lusine was stronger than ever. Chembrier, on his extreme left, was surprised by General Keller, and gave the finishing stroke to our chances of success. The Chateau at Montbeliard is in itself a place of considerable strength and vastness. It is built at the extreme limits of the town, and commands a view of fourteen villages. It stands upon a rock, and is, in parts, surrounded by a trench cut out of the rock, which trench is spanned by a bridge. The place, too, has much historical interest, and it is not a little singular that in 1422 it was the prison of Frederick of Hohenzolern, one of the ancestors of the present prince, to whom France can trace the darkest chapter in her history. In the Chateau also are the remains of Saint Mainbœuf, a Scottish missionary, who suffered nartyrdom under Louis le Debonnair. Much of the importance that Montbelliard has attained, has been owing to the number of pilgrims who visited the shrine of St. Mainbœuf, who is, even to this day, spoken of with veneration by the peasantry.

But it was still wet under foot, and when, at about 10 a.m., we were ordered to occupy our old position in the wood, the sun suddenly became overcast for the day, a penetrating wind swept over the open ground, and we were again cold, wet, and hungry. All this day we had nothing to eat except some equine steaks that the men had cooked for breakfast. It was often a matter of amusement to see the men advancing, sword-bayonet in hand, "with murderous thoughts intent," looking for poor Dobbin, the tenderest portion of whose carcase would shortly afterwards be flavouring the air, as it was being converted into *pot au feu au cheval*. But there was little time for cooking that day, even if we had had anything that required the aid of a fire to make palatable, which we had not.

"There was a time," I heard a young soldier in the ranks say, and whom I had seen four months before a stout, heavy man, "There was a time when it was easier to jump over me than walk around me, but by gorra I think that it is quite the other way now," and he looked down upon his attenuated limbs, as if appealing for their vindication of his words.

But while crossing in rear of our batteries, six companies of Turcos filed out before us in retreat, their colours fluttering in the breeze, the only flags, regimental or company, I had seen in France. There were but two regiments of the regular army with Bourbaki—our own and the 39th of the Line, and both had left their colours in Africa, and the 39th alone of the whole *Armee de l'Est* was provided with a band. There were, however, several *Regiments du March*. These are composed of men belonging to the various Line Regiments in the service, and who, having lost their own corps, are huddled into the first *Regiment du March* they come into contact with. Being all strangers to each other they must unnecessarily lack that *esprit du corps*, so essential to the soldier. The Turcos appeared singularly cool, although the shells were falling about them, and one passed through their ranks, killing in its course four or five of the soldiers, and rolling over one of the standard-bearers as well. But the ranks were dressed up immediately, the wounded were carried off the field, and I saw the Turcos no more. We had, however, one in the *Regiment Etranger* a man about fifty years of age, and who had risen to the grade of sous-lieutenant after about eighteen years' service. The officers called him *Mocosh bono*, and he was one of the best tempered men I had ever met with. He, like his race, was a fatalist, and held it as a crime to attempt to avoid what Providence had ordained. He was fond of telling stories of officers and men who sought shelter during the serious combats through which he had passed, and who only rushed into the jaws of death. *Mocosh bono* would no more think of ducking his head, than he would of cursing or of taking the name of Ali in vain. He was, in many ways, an exemplary man, and I often thought that the Christian soldiers of the regiment might profitably follow his example and advice.

But until noon our third day at Montbelliard was much the same as the two previous ones. Standing fire without returning it until the Capitaine-Adjutant-Major called out "*La Compagnie Irlandaise pour tirailleur*." Yes, we were in for it then! Our time had come to manœuvre up as near as we could to the enemy's lines. Moving along the rear of our batteries, we worked up to the place from which we were to step into the open ground that divided us from the enemy and about 400 yards of which we had to cross apparently under the clear sweep of their guns. Before us lay a plateau about 400 yards of which was a flat, and then it undulated for about 400 yards up to the enemy's lines. Just where the plateau became broken into ridges, there was a slight shelter from the enemy's guns, and it was there that we were ordered to relieve a company of our regiment that was already in position. The Capitaine-Adjutant-

Major was always kind to the soldiers of the Irish Company and generously recognised the difficulties they had to contend against. He was minutely careful in pointing out the position of the enemy's lines, and then took off his kepi and wished me "*bonne chance, Capitaine.*" By taking a careful look at the position of the enemy's batteries and the nature of the ground over which we had to travel, it appeared certain that there were portions of the plateau that were not under fire, and that with careful handling we could work up to our position with little or no exposure to ourselves, by taking advantage of the irregularities of the ground, and by making the men double across or over the most exposed portions of the way. The company was divided into sections, each under the command of an officer, the men was thrown into Indian file, ten feet between each man, in order to divide the enemy's fire, and we worked up to our post without losing a man. The position was much exposed to the fire of the enemy's batteries. It was on a neck or bend that almost penetrated the German lines, and the shelter was so low that the men had to lie flat on the cold, wet earth, to avoid the shells that just topped the gentle rise before them. But we had further instructions from the captain whom we relieved. We had to send out laying posts under Lieutenant Cotter, Sergeants Donnellan and Corr, upon the right and left slopes of our position, to command a view of the ravine on our either side. All the time the shells from the batteries before us were tearing upon the ground around us, one or two falling amongst the scattered soldiers and throwing the earth in showers over their bodies, and nearly blinding some of the men with particles of small stone or sand. As the smoke from the enemy's guns announced the passage of an iron messenger, Captain Trucho, the officer whom we came to relieve, sang out in a loud, clear voice, "*Garde la bombe, garde la bombe.*"

Once or twice when the men imprudently attempted to raise themselves from their position, the shells burst with a fury that proved the artillerists on our front were, in the language of Sergeant Carey, "keeping their eyes upon us." On our right was the Chateau showing its teeth occasionally as its guns nearly enfiladed our post. Before us were two batteries of field pieces, and to our left was a deserted village over which a new battery had been erected, and under all was a line of skirmishers well sheltered by the undulating ground, and sending their stumpy bullets with sickly sound about our ears. Just upon our left front there was a house, from which an impudent soldier occasionally walked and tried to pick off any of the men who imprudently showed more of their persons than was safe to themselves. He was an excellent marksman, and grazed the kepi of one of the officers while moving from post to post. It was cold, wet work, lying in that exposed post, and for about eighteen hours the men had not tasted food. It was just noon when we occupied the place, and as Captain Trucho took his leave he bade me " *Bonne chance, Capitaine*, I returning the salutation with the new-born sobriquet, " *Bonne chance, Garde la bombe.*" Captain Trucho took his company back over the plateau, having lost, I think, seven men, in three hours' duty. Our time was to expire at five ; the exhaustion of the soldiers was complete, and the hour of our relief was anxiously looked for. In the meantime I placed some of my best shots to watch the marksmen in the deserted house, and between them, I opine, they had a brisk time of it.

Five o'clock came slowly and wearily, and then about 2,000 Germans came out of their shelter upon our left front, and placed another battery in position, as if to give us a further sprinkling of their shells, and, perhaps, under cover of which to make some movement that could only be readily seen from the post of observation held by *La Compagnie Irlandaise*, for at that time we of the combined armies of the Loire and the East were up nearest the enemy's guns. Every hour after I had to send a written report to the colonel of the regiment—oftener if necessary. One man, Corporal M'Evoy, had to carry the news of the new movement from the enemy's lines to headquarters. Immediately another company of the Regiment was sent to support us in an expected attack, and they attempted to cross the plateau in close order, neglecting or hesitating to carry out the Indian file formation that had stood to us so well. But they had no sooner come well under the fire of the batteries, than the shot made lanes through their ranks, stretched ten or twelve of them dead, and left numbers yelling with wounds, and the remainder like a herd of affrighted sheep, ran over the plateau looking for shelter. All order was lost, all formation was gone, and the reckless indifference of the officers, brave men as I knew them to be, should have brought on their heads a censure they never received. The men were sacrificed to the sheer imbecility of that mysterious and blundering "somebody." But night soon closed around us, and no relief for the Irish soldiers. Everything along the enemy's lines indicated a movement. The spiked helmets of the Prussian line, and the shoe-brush head-dress of the Bavarians could be seen plainly enough marching and counter-marching to the right and left of their positions. As darkness set in I advanced the posts about fifty yards nearer the enemy's lines, where a few bushes offered a screen behind which our men could hide. Once or twice on the rounds the men told me that black objects were seeing moving in our front, and as the night was pitch dark, and our post isolated and advanced, a movement of the enemy would have come like a thunder-clap upon our men. Had we been attacked that night there would have been little record of *La Compagnie Irlandaise*, for we would in all probability have shared the fate of a company that was posted upon our left, less advanced than our own, and which, it was said, was bayoneted to a man. But the three days' work had hardened us to our task, and everything went down before the one thought— duty! The hours passed slowly and miserably, and to some of us, who knew that the army was in full retreat, and that we might expect to be attacked any moment, the time was an anxious one. About 10 p.m. the rattle of musketry broke out upon our right, then the field pieces blazed away, and a vigorous and well-sustained fire appeared to herald a general attack along the line. It was evident that Von Werder was about to assume the offensive again. Every eye was peering into the darkness, every finger sought the trigger of a rifle or a revolver, and every second we expected a shower of rifle bullets searching for death upon our post. Not only in front, but upon both flanks we were liable to attack, and if it were sudden and severe the enemy would have annihilated us. But the Providence that shapes our ends hath not so ordained it to be. The excitement and expected fight made us almost forget that for nearly thirty hours we had not tasted food, except, indeed, horse-flesh, and that for twelve hours we had lain upon the slimy soil, and the men were in no holiday or presentable attire when midnight came, dark as the grave, but mild as an evening in August.

During this time I was resting behind a knoll, expecting every minute to hear the rush of the enemy on our post, when suddenly I heard some one near me give a vigorous snore, which he repeated again and again, with a splendid effect. He was, however, quickly aroused, and as punishment, one of the officers brought him fifty yards in front of the entire line, and placed him in front of the entire army, to continue his nasal thunder, if he was so disposed to risk his life. The man could have been shot, nothing could save his life if he was reported to the Colonel; a court-martial would have disposed of him in twenty-four hours. Yet this fellow's gratitude took the direction of abuse when he returned to Ireland, as he attempted to screen his conduct by invidious efforts to make people believe that the officers were exceptionably cruel. But this is one of the few evils of a Volunteer Corps, indeed incidents of this kind were so few, that an occasional misdemeanour was a novelty in its way.

"You are relieved, captain," said Sergeant Terence Byrne, standing suddenly by my side, after coming from the post he occupied under Lieutenant Cotter, upon our left, and which rested upon the wood.

"Where," I asked, looking for the expected company to occupy our place.

"I came from the *Commandant* of the post, sir, who occupies a position in our rear, with word that you are to vacate your position at once."

"Are you certain, sergeant," I asked, with just a little shade of suspicion, not of his honesty, but doubt that, owing to his imperfect knowledge of the language, he might have mistaken the command.

"Certain, captain," he answered, assuringly; "It was Mr. Cotter sent me to you with the instruction."

"And why is it not written ?" I asked.

"Don't know, sir; I give you the orders as they were given to me," replied the sergeant.

But I knew Terence Byrne too well to doubt the truth of his every word. The men were thrown out in skirmishing order and followed the sergeant into the wood upon our left, and which brought us up to within speaking distance of the enemy's lines. It would have been to all appearances safer to return as we had come across the plateau. Under cover of the darkness we could retire unobserved by the most keen-sighted of their sentries, or the best of their night glasses. But, as we afterwards learned, a line of *tirailleurs* was stretched about 300 yards behind us, and the *Commandant* was told that we had been ordered through the wood, so that there were no French troops then between him and the enemy. Had we crossed the plateau it is more than probable that the *Chasseurs-a-pied* would have fired into our ranks and done some mischief. It was a lesson in the necessity of obedience to orders. But into the wood we went, and were just in time to fall in at the tail of the battalion that had occupied the post, and which was now moving away. We could hear the enemy's sentries cough plainly enough, but our object was to get away unobserved if possible. Occasionally the slovenly-arranged tins of the soldiers would rattle against each other, and the noise sounded as clear as thunder in the still, dead, atmosphere. The rattle of those tins threatened at any moment to bring a fire around our ears, and more lives might be at any moment sacrificed to the neglect of not attending to such trifles as make up the efficiency of a soldier. "Silence, silence," was whispered along the line. "Silence," as some incautious soldier stumbled over a log into the bushes that lined the route, and caused the sentry at the other side of the narrow belt of timber to cock his rifle as we could plainly hear the "click, click," of the spring. But we soon reached our line of *tirailleurs*, and then sought our battalion. This was a bewildering task; and although not fifty yards from where we were, we were fully an hour searching for our decimated regiment. They had been engaged at the attack upon the right of our line, and had returned the skeleton of what they were. But I reported to the *Commandant*, and then sought the comfort of a stretch upon the leaves that were abundantly spread underneath our feet. The army was all the time in full retreat. Troops were hurrying off in all directions, and it was expected that three or four o'clock would see the last of the army of Bourbaki away. To our regiment was left the honour of covering the retreat, and as we were the last company of the regiment, we should be the last to leave the field.

But tired nature should rest. Even in the presence of death exhausted nature must have repose. By the dim and flickering bivouac fire, with a heavy mist falling upon the already wet ground, I had a few sticks thrown together, a log of wood for a pillow, and had two hours' gorgeous sleep.

There was one man however, who with a perseverance worthy of success, contrived to string a few lines of poetry together, and with vivid reality, pictured his position and thoughts upon the occasion :

The Sentinel's Song.

(WRITTEN ON GRAND GUARD AT MONTBELLIARD.)

I STAND a sentinel to-night,
   Within a hundred yards or so
Of Prussian fires; the lurid light
   Revealing many an armed foe.
The cold wind whistles past my ear—
   My coat is white with falling snow—
As, dreaming of the faded years,
   I lean upon my Chassepôt.

A rover o'er life's dreary tide,
   Without one smile to light my way,
Without a home, a friend to guide
   My wandering footsteps when I stray,
Or cheer me on my weary way;
   Yet I had all long, long ago,
But they have fled, and I instead,
   Have got a gleaming Chassepôt.

And brother, lover, friend, and home,
   My Chassepôt is now to me;
And shall be wheresoe'er I roam,
   O'er smiling vale, or mountain free.
Ah! fortune was unkind to me;
   But I care not now, for well I know
That I've a trusty friend in thee,
   My faithful little Chassepôt.

One hope is mine—I guard it well,
   For it cheers my heart full many a day—
That I may stand a sentinel,
   Upon a green hill far away;
And if Heaven grants this wish to me,
   For liberty to strike one blow,
Dear Erin, I will give to thee,
   A true heart and a Chassepôt.

OWEN T. MULDOON.

CHAPTER XIII.

> " Mountains interpos'd
> Make enemies of nations who had else,
> Like kindred drops, been mingled into one."
>
> COWPER.

"CAPTAIN, captain," whispered somebody in my ears about 5 a.m. on the morning of the 19th, and after I had had nearly three hours' sleep upon my luxurious bed of sticks.

"What is it, sergeant," I asked, looking up at Sergeant Frank Byrne, who bent over me, the butt of his Chassepôt resting upon the ground, while the light of a sickly camp fire fell upon his face and enabled me to trace at a glance the effect of the last few weeks of famine and fatigue, upon his frame. Sergeant Byrne was in every way a clean and exemplary soldier, yet even he appeared in no holiday or presentable attire that still morning in January, 1871. For weeks the men had had no opportunity of washing hands nor face, and for the last four days even the officers of the army were compelled to allow the dirt to accumulate upon their persons, except, indeed, what could be removed by a vigorous application of snow-water. Byrne's eyes were sunken, his cheeks were hollow, and the cheek-bones protruded so as almost to speak "hunger." His once well-proportioned body was attenuated, and as he stooped over me with blackened hands, a face well tanned by exposure, and made darker still with a less cleanly dye, I could not help smiling at his appearance, or in his own words, "at the figure he cut." His uniform, too, was covered with dirt, the clayey soil upon which we had lain when out on *tirailleur* the day before, having left dark blotches from his kepi to his gaiters.

"The *Commandant* wishes to see you, sir; the adjutant has been here," whispered the sergeant, straightening himself as he delivered his instruction.

"I was soon upon my legs, much refreshed after my three hours' repose. I could see by the flickering camp-fires that some of our troops had departed, and that preparations were everywhere being made by the men of the *Regiment Etranger* to follow the retreating *Armée de l'Est*. The men were falling in, and the *sous officiers* were busy calling the roll in a hushed under tone, and "*disparued, disparued*," was the most common answer I heard as I passed along the line. I soon found the fire, beside which the *Commandant* sat engaged in putting a fresh round of cartridge into a splendid double-barrelled breech-loading pistol which he held in his left hand.

"*Bon jour, mon Commandant*," I said, as I took off my kepi in salutation.

"*Bon jour, Capitaine*," replied the *Commandant*, as he looked up for a second, before placing his pistol in his belt.

"Captain," continued the *Commandant*, "of course you know we are to form the rear-guard for the army, and it is more than likely that before we get away we shall have the Germans down upon us. As your company is the last of the battalion, you will be required to act as rear-guard to the regiment. Last in last out, you know," said the *chef*, with an apologetical expression, which might mean "It's just your luck."

"All right, *mon Commandant*, I'll do my best," I replied.

"Well," said he, "if you are pressed hard, retreat along the road towards Sainte Marie, where, if the enemy press you, you will be sure to overtake the battalion."

"But are we to remain here?" I asked, hoping for a negative reply.

"No, no, you'll follow us into the open: it is there we shall possibly encounter the Germans, for they are massed on three sides of us. If we are not attacked, you'll continue to retreat with us; if we are attacked in force, we shall all have to fight; but if only slightly, you will engage the enemy and give us time to get away. You understand ?" he asked, looking into my face, and raising himsel from the ground.

"Perfectly."

"Very well, *Capitaine*, if God pleases we shall meet again," and the *chef* extended his hand to me, and then moved away to bring the battalion "out into the open."

The Irish Company was quickly in line and prepared for the route. The head of the battalion soon after commenced to move, and then with cautious steps we followed in the wake. "Silence, silence," was the whispered command, as we made towards the gate-like passage in the end of the wood, which lead to the open plain beyond. The effort to march quietly was painful in its intense anxiety. The least noise would betray our presence to the enemy. Those villanous tins rattled again, and sounded like the discharge of artillery upon our strained senses. "Silence, silence," hisses the *Capitaine-Adjutant-Major*, as some incautious soldier stumbles into a bush, and his comrades fall over him to be companions in the catastrophe. At this time the entire army of Bourbaki was two days before us in full retreat towards Besançon. We were the last regiment in the field. If we were attacked in force it would have been another Orleans for the *Regiment Etranger*. The Germans, however, knew what they were about, and appeared to judge our movement with mechanical accuracy. But just as the head of the Irish Company was about emerging from the wood, we halted and listened for anything that could indicate the advance of the enemy, but all was as silent as the grave. It was perfectly dark. Objects twenty paces away were undistinguishable. We were commencing to congratulate ourselves upon our probable success in avoiding the wary foe, when suddenly like a clap of thunder, a volley, then another and another was thrown upon our ranks, and the musical " Hurragh, hurragh, Vorwarts, vorwarts," of the Bavarians came ringing upon our ears. Before us a line of *tirailleurs* was stretched across the plain, and they quickly gave way before the advancing enemy, and came pell-mell upon our ranks. I had not been told that the *Chasseurs-à-pied* were in our front, and we were about to pour a volley into the ranks, but that we fortunately discovered our mistake in time. The *tirailleurs* however retreated, and left us once more nearest the foe. For a few minutes the battalion hesitated, as if expecting to be attacked in force, and then they marched away leaving us behind in the post of honour. We lined the wood and awaited the enemy. Hap-hazard fire was then thrown into our retreat, and a hap-hazard fire was returned. The Germans hesitated to advance in the dark, and we should engage them in order to enable the battalion to escape. If the enemy moved on a little in our front they could have effectually cut off our retreat and brought us up like a beast at bay. The dropping fire was vigorously sustained on both sides, each aiming at where the flash of their enemy's guns indicated their presence. At this time the Germans could not have been more than one hundred yards in our direct front. Both our flanks were exposed to attack, and in our front alone could we have made a vigorous resistance. The enemy fired at random, along a considerable portion of their line, while we, in turn, sent random volleys in the direction of the fusilade, which told us of where the Germans were. The bullets from the enemy's rifles cut through the timbers, and hissed above and around us. Suddenly however, the firing in our front ceased, and I was preparing to take *La Compagnie Irlandaise* away when I heard the stock of a rifle come into contact with somebody's head, and which was quickly followed by a low, hissing order of "Keep up to your work, you dog." As I turned around to ascertain the cause I could trace the dim outline of Sergeant Carey's well-proportioned form, standing over the prostrate figure of a fallen man. The stricken soldier was tumbled into one of the many thorny bushes with which the wood was abundantly dotted, and the efforts he made to save himself from the effects of the thorns, were amusingly dramatic. A revolver at his head quickly brought him up to toe the line with his companions, by whom he was afterwards known under a *soubriquet* neither complimentary to his courage, nor his sense of honour. But as there—

> "Is no flock howsoever watched or tended,
> But one dead lamb is there,
> There is no fireside howsoever defended,
> But has one vacant chair."

So is there always to be found one truant amidst a school, one coward amidst a company. Few indeed of the Irish soldiers ever stooped to waste a coward thought on life, but fewer still ever boasted of indifference about the dread uncertainty. True courage fears, but still faces the dreaded portal of eternity.

> "'Tis not the brave man that feels no fear,
> For that were stupid and irrational,
> But he whose noble soul that fear subdues,
> And bravely dares the danger nature shrinks from."

But the unfortunate wretch was punished with sufficient vigour to convince him that obedience to orders was in his case the better part of valour. Carey stood over him like a chained lion, and never parted from his side until he saw the unhappy man sheltered behind a tree, and blazing away at where the continuous firing from the enemy's rifles indicated their presence.

It was still quite dark, our battalion had gone, and the Irish Company, then reduced to about sixty-five rifles, was still behind upon the field of Montbelliard. The fighting of the past three days had indeed been of a singular nature. With the exception of the twelve hours we were on *tirailleur,* our duty was simply to stand in line of battle, and see our friends on every side, being sent to eternity. In the distance a cloud of smoke is seen, the noise of a discharged cannon quickly follows, then the shell strikes beside you, some of your men are down, their last reckoning has been rendered, and they have passed from time into eternity. There was much of the danger of a vigorous engagement, without any of that excitement or craving for blood, which to some extent deadens the feelings of soldiers when in close quarters. When we were on *tirailleur,* although exposed of the enemy's fire on all sides, still we were comparatively happy. The excitement sent the blood coursing through our veins, and we took a vicious, and a legitimate or human pride, in picking off our enemies. Now things were much the same, only we were expending our ammunition on thin air. The Irish Company had remained long enough behind. It was evident the Germans hesitated to advance in the dark; they were not in sufficient force to press us that morning. Von Werder had already accomplished one of the most brilliant feats in the history of military warfare. He had succeeded in doing at Belfort what Napoleon the First failed to do at Mantua. Von Werder had with 45,000 men, held a position between the army of Bourbaki, numbering at least 100,000 men on one side, and had held in check the garrison of Belfort on the other. Like an old British Regiment in Egypt, Von Werder had placed his troops back to back, and succeeded with less than half the force of the attacking troops, in beating off both. But it was not so much the men, as the means that accomplished this brilliant result. Individually the Frenchman is equal to any soldier in the world; in dash, in *esprit,* in gallant daring, in *élan,* in all that constitutes courage and enterprise the Frenchman has no superior. In chivalrous conduct he even surpasses the man who stands to-day before the world as his conqueror. But shoeless, foodless, almost nude, with the clothes hanging in tattered fragments from their persons, the raw levies of Mobiles were unequal to the task of endurance which a demoralized *Intendance* asked them to encounter. It was even more than the troops of the regular army could bear. In the entire army of Bourbaki there were but two line regiments intact—the 39th and the *Regiment Etranger*. Much of the hard work fell to the lot of these two corps. All the dangerous positions were entrusted to their keeping. Yet, even they succumbed to the hardships, and sank in hundreds beneath the fatal system which left them without supplies. Everywhere around us men lay dying of famine and cold. Hundreds stopped *en retraire*, and declared they could "go no farther." The Irish Company was no exception to this general break up. Six or seven of the men remained upon the field of Montbelliard completely broken down. As I took *La Compagnie Irlandaise* out of the wood that morning, there were a few names missing when we next called the roll, and the melancholy record " disappeared, disappeared," was too often the simple epilogue of their career. But our work was still before us. Day would soon be breaking, and we stole away while it was still dark, leaving the ghastly field behind, and taking the route indicated by our *Commandant*. But while yet in danger of attack, the men being out in skirmishing order, and making for the road, while we occasionally halted expecting to see the dark blue uniforms of the German soldiers bursting through the gloom; a voice which I thought a familiar one, called out "Is that the *Regiment Etranger ?*" For the instant we thought it might have been a *ruse de guerre* of the enemy, and the men were down upon their knees, every finger was upon a trigger, awaiting the order to fire, when the familiar voice sounded again, there was no mistaking its owner, it was our gallant old Colonel, whom we had left behind. Just then the earliest streaks of the coming day pierced the sombre envelope above, and I could trace deep thought upon the face of the fine old man as he came and walked beside me. He was visibly effected by some incident, and I anxiously asked him if he had been wounded.

"No, no, *Capitaine*," he replied with a tone of sorrow which even perplexed me more, and then turning his handsome, battle scared face towards me, he continued: "I told your *Commandant* that I should remain behind with your company, *Capitaine*, and be the last away, and I tried to take a few hours' rest at the farm-house, which has been our headquarters for the last three days. You might have seen that it was not more than five hundred yards from the German lines, but so sheltered by the inequalities of ground as to be safe from the enemy's artillery. Well, you remember the officer you relieved yesterday on *tirailleur*."

"Yes, *mon Colonel*," I answered, "Trucho, or as we christened him ' *Garde la bombe.*' "

"Well, when we were attacked this morning, another officer and myself rushed from the house—the enemy was within twenty yards of us, but we tried to escape nevertheless, and as our figures were relieved by the snow, the Germans fired at us, and I am here."

"But the other officer, *mon Colonel*," I said, now suspecting the truth, while the colonel shook his head, uttered the simple word *Tue*, mentioned a name, it was Trucho, poor, brave, much regretted '*Garde la bombe.*' "

Foodless, and in many cases shoeless, we commenced that disastrous retreat. The main army had been moving from the field for the last two days. The country around was devastated. Horseflesh had been for days our only subsistence; bread nor wine could not be had for any price, nor for any cause. The woods and fields around Montbelliard were strewn with corpses. Every house had its wounded soldier, and the simple *cortege* which marked the end of a soldier's career, might be seen moving from many an humble dwelling.

The *debris* of war was strewn along our route in prodigal profusion. Broken waggons, dismounted guns, dead and dying horses hacked to pieces by the passing troops, were everywhere to be seen. For about half-a-mile the dead men were as thick as berries, and not a few wounded, crawled into the shelter of the ditch, which, in too many cases, they probably never left alive. As if conscious of their approaching fate and our own position, they looked wildly at us as we passed along. Their distended countenances told of the mental agony they were enduring. They felt that appeal to us was useless, except, indeed, now and again, one of the Irish sergeants stopped and poured a mouthful of water into the parched and fevered lips of a wounded Frenchman, as he lay gasping upon the snow. The route we had passed four days ago full of hope and dreams of victory, we now re-passed, dispirited, and almost demoralized. Beneath us the little village of Dung nestled upon the border of a stream, and, as we crossed the bridge, we took up position to dispute the passage of the stream. The enemy shelled the woods behind us with their usual vigour. Their *eclaireurs* exchanged shots with us from the belt of timber that skirted the upper bank of the rising ground beyond the little river. Our colonel was still with us. The river was only fordable in one or two places, and if attacked we were to check their advance. We had an excellent position. The general of our division—Rebillard—left two mitrailleuses and two six-pounders to help in the defence of the stream, and said he entrusted them in our keeping knowing that we would defend them "*à la mort.*" The Germans shelled the wood in our immediate front, and their *eclaireurs* exchanged shots with us, as they worked their way to the edge of the trees before us. It was, too, a glorious day. The genial atmosphere had already commenced to feel the reviving power of the new year's sun. The snow was melting under the influence of the heat, and the weather contributed much to revive the drooping spirits of the exhausted soldiery. There is a sensible improvement in the weather about the end of January in Central France. Much of the frost has gone, the air becomes warmer, and the genial and balmy influences of Spring commences to render existence out of doors more comfortable, than in the trying month of December. The village of Dung where we halted, had a population of 381 souls, and the majority of the villagers took refuge in the woods and in the cellars, when they saw that we were prepared to dispute the possession of the place with the advancing foe.

"*Allez, allez, allez,*" I heard an affrighted peasant call out to a woman who was evidently his wife, and who was running before him, while he followed with rapid strides, protruding eyes, and distended jaws. With all his hurry, the peasant was not indifferent to his creature comforts, for I noticed that he was engaged devouring a gorgeous piece of meat, which to me seemed to have the hue of horseflesh.

A small inn stood beside the place allotted to *La Compagnie Irlandaise*, the door stood invitingly open, and I entered to try and buy or beg a drink of wine.

"Not a carafon, *Capitaine*," said the old man, who floundered about apparently in a state of mental torture, his deep set eyes and flurried countenance betraying the emotions he failed to express. "Everything I have in the world," continued the proprietor, "I buried under the three crosses you see outside the garden, and which I intend to make those piggish Germans believe have been erected over the remains of some soldiers who have been killed in the great battles of the last three days."

"We may be here an hour yet," I replied, "and you can make a harvest if you unearth your treasure and sell it to the officers, at your own price. Come, I'll take twenty francs' worth for my own company to begin with."

"No, no," hurriedly answered the old man. "No, no; there, there, *Mon Dieu, mon Dieu,* we shall all be killed," he almost screamed as a shell burst before the door, and I hurried out of the house expecting every minute to see the enemy burst through the timber in front or flank. But the Germans were slow, very slow that morning.

Had they pressed us in force, thousands of the dispirited troops would have fallen into their hands. However, as events proved, they had a better game on hands, and left us to continue our disastrous retreat.

Foodless, almost shoeless, with empty haversacks and heavy hearts, we commenced our harrassing march. There was no disorder, no broken ranks, no crowding, everything was conducted with soldierly precision. Skirmishers moved upon our flanks, occasionally turning to check the advance of the enemy when too closely pressed. Discipline was as rigidly enforced as ever, and the men were thoroughly in hands. But famine had done its work, and the emaciated and ragged troops looked wretched indeed. Men fell out of the ranks to die in the ditches. It was, indeed, *la misere*. It was very common to see men from whose toes the flesh had actually rotted from frost, limping in agonized wretchedness, over the broken and flinty road. There was nothing but retreat or death. The field Ambulances were crowded, the mules had all more than their legitimate burthen. I think it was on the first day of our retreat that poor Sergeant Donnellan came to me and declared he could go no further. He was worn to a skeleton. His giant and splendidly proportioned figure was attenuated, and his handsome face was shrivelled, while his eyes protruded with a ravenous-looking expression. Dr. Macken had already told me that he feared it was all up with Donnellan. Hardened as men's hearts become in a rough campaign, I was moved to compassion by the wretched plight that that gallant Irishman was in, as he stood before me during a short halt, as with soldierly grace, and ever prompt respect, he brought his rifle to his shoulder, and declared that he "could go no farther." He had, as was customary, made a hole in his blanket, through which he put his head, and the folds of the shoddy covering fell over his shoulders, and gave him some little protection from the weather.

"Come, Donnellan, make another effort," I said, as he sat upon the bank beside the road, and I saw that the troops were about to move on again. "Come, old fellow, try again, just one more halt, and I'll do my best in the meantime to get you a lift."

"It is no use, captain," he answered, every place is full, there is not the ghost of a chance of getting on either a mule or anything else, and I may as well give up here," and he held out his hand to me in firm resolve. "Wont you write to my mother, captain," he continued, after a moment's pause. Just then I saw a man taken out of one of the chairs, which was carried by the mules, and it was evident from the way the soldier was handled, that he was dead. I rushed over, and fortunately stumbled across Dr. Macken, through whose aid I succeeded in getting Donnellan into the vacant seat. But he did not appear to mind much whether he went or not, and as he was strapped in the place, and looked around with an expression which I interpreted to have a grave misgiving, whether or not he would ever see the morrow's sun. But the "fall in" was sounded, the command *en route* given, and we were away once more. I remember turning around to see if I could distinguish the gallant sergeant amidst the ruck of carts, and waggons, and mule teams, and I remember waving him an adieu, which he courteously returned. Poor fellow! I never saw him again, and he must have died of pure exhaustion, or rapid consumption, brought on by excessive hardships. Every man in the Company had the greatest respect for Donnellan. He was the *beau-ideal* of a chivalrous man. He was a perfect Bayard in his way, and what was left of *La Compagnie Irlandaise* regretted the loss of his soldierly experience. I fell into one of my dreamy moods, as we trudged along, and if I speculated upon how a poor lady in Galway would bear the sad tidings of her son's fate, and found time amidst the trials of that retreat, to tender a sympathetic feeling of respect for her sorrow, it was but the natural outpour of my respect towards a man whom I was proud to call my friend. Fate had been unkind to Anthony

"LA COMPAGNIE IRLANDAISE." 221

Donnellan, but withal I could'nt help asking myself " was France worthy of such a sacrifice ?" Even the honours he won upon the hard-fought field of Orleans, he never received. The cross which should have decorated his breast he never got, while Gambetta with prodigal hand distributed decorations to many a carpet hero of the Republic. But as a quaint old New England primer says with simple force—

> " Xerxes did die,
> And so must I."

The dead past buries its dead very quickly in this world of ours, and amidst the excitement of a campaign, the dead past is soon forgotten.

But we should press on, for Von Werder's cavalry occasionally pressed upon our rear. The 20th and 21st corps were already two days' march before ours. They had passed the fortifications of Besançon, and were in full swing for Lyons. But it was then that Manteuffel came down upon our broken and dispirited troops, and drove them across the Swiss frontier. He accomplished, perhaps, one of the grandest achievements of the war. He came full swing from the east of France to assist Von Werder in his resistance against Bourbaki. He saw the position of the two armies with that quickness that had distinguished the German commanders during the campaign. Bourbaki had hoped that Garibaldi, with his corps of Republican Volunteers at Dijon, could check the advance of the German commanders coming from the East. Dijon stood directly before the German troops. In the hands of an able commander the garrison could have seriously impeded the German advance, and saved the French troops. But Manteuffel measured his man. He left a small force to look after Dijon, and hurried on himself to overwhelm the dispirited and defeated French. He succeeded to the letter. He blocked the retreat to Lyons, and forced the famished soldiery of the Republic into neutral territory, and the 20th and 21st corps were huddled pell-mell across the border.

But our turn was coming. Von Werder was too much weakened to follow us with vigour, for he should still press on the siege of Belfort, the gallant little garrison of which held out with persistent valour. For four days, however, that desperate retreat was continued. The men were falling away in batches, but the Irish Company held together with wondrous perseverance. Their distinct nationality induced the men to keep intact. If they fell out they would be more completely lost than a Frenchman. But my pen fails to describe the hardships of that retreat. It was simply horrible. I would not like to see an Irish dog endure as much again. Men will, of course, risk life and limb for the bubble reputation, but to endure all the hardships of a winter-running campaign in a cold climate, is an undertaking which every man should well consider, before voluntary encountering. An officer can always make ends meet, but for the rank and file, it is another affair. For my own part, France will always have my sympathy and my sword in a war against Germany; but if there be any aspiring youths who feel desirous of following the fortunes of *La Grande Nation* in such a struggle, if it ever takes place, it is well that they should understand the trials they will have to pass through. It would damp the ardour of many a would-be hero if he could have seen the Irish Company on their retreat from Montbelliard, or if some enterprising photographer had taken a proof of the shoeless, foodless, and starved creatures they at that time were, as they shuffled on, over hill and dale, on the 20th of January, 1871.

CHAPTER XIV.

"O suffering, sad humanity!
O ye afflicted ones, who lie
Steeped to the lips in misery,
Longing, and yet afraid to die,
Patient, though sorely tried!"

LONGFELLOW.

IN the meantime the disasters which befel the armies of France were irreparable. The army of Bourbaki had been completely destroyed; Paris was giving indications of the coming surrender. A sortie on the 19th of January had been repulsed. Montretout was captured by a gallant effort of the besieged, but had to be abandoned. General Faidherbe was defeated at St. Quinten on the same day, and all hopes of relieving Paris from the north was at an end. The war was practically at an end, and France subdued. There might still, indeed, be some desultory fighting in positions favourable for defence, some more blood might flow from the already bleeding combatants, but organized resistance was at an end, and the nation recognized the fact. There were, indeed, a few men insane enough to think that France might still fight on, but there were interested speculators, who traded upon the blood of their countrymen. Men who witnessed and encountered the hardships of the campaign, knew that the game was up. For us, indeed, we might be compelled to fight again, but already speculations were rife as to an armistice, which we well knew was but the prelude of a necessary but humiliating peace. As we retreated through the beautiful country watered by the Doubs, over hill and through dale, in wet and cold, dropping with fatigue, and exhausted by suffering, I could not help speculating that to man alone is left a power of endurance which the beasts of the field could scarcely endure. But we had four hard days on that desperate retreat—days of famine, of cold, of hunger, and of danger; from early dawn until long after dark, it was a trial of speed, and then but little repose could be found on the slimy soil, torn up with thousands of horses and waggons, and the tramp of tens of thousands of men. Everywhere we had to sleep was converted into an ocean of mud; and yet men will live on, except here and there scattered amongst the regiments, some unfortunate ends his career by sending a bullet through his distracted brain. But the retreat continued through Roulens and Baume-les-Dames, and on the fourth day our advance guard was working through a defile in the Vosges, about eight miles from Besançon, and just beside the little village of Busy, when the astonished soldiers were stopped by the German challenge "*Wer-da-ish?*" sounding upon their ears. We were surrounded! I think that was on the 23rd of January, and I well remember how indifferently the troops accepted the challenge, as most would rather fight than march any further. On that day we had been on foot from six in the morning until nine in the evening, marching at a break-neck pace, and it was without exception the most harrassing day we had spent in France.

"We are in for it again, captain," said Sergeant Carey, coming and standing by my side, his iron frame, of all the men of *La Compagnie Irlandaise*, presenting the least trace of the misery he had endured. "And I am glad of it," he continued, "this retreating makes a man hungry, and I should like to exchange haversacks and boots with some of these friendly Germans before us." Carey's boots were indeed a study in their way. Originally they were too small for him, and he was compelled to squeeze his feet into the narrow limits of his shoes. Without socks, and being incessantly on the march, he was unable to guard against painful and ugly sores which formed upon his feet in consequence. Then he resorted to the expedient of cutting the shoes in order to remove the pressure, and give him ease. The frost penetrated the sores, caused them to fester, and protrude out of the limits of the orifice, and ultimately to present a sight from which even hardened soldiers turned in pitying horror. On one occasion he attempted to take his shoes off, and the efforts he made would have killed many a less determined man. At last, however, he succeeded, but as he often told me, "I looked down, sir, and saw my feet swelling so quickly, that I thought unless I put my shoes on at once, I would have to go barefooted." But he had to cut his shoes in order to get them on, and they became even worse than before. Yet Carey was as full of life and merriment as ever, and as he bustled about executing some orders for the better disposition of the Company, no trace of the agony he was enduring was visible either in his gait, his accent, nor his soldierly bearing.

That night we bivouaced behind the shelter of a friendly wall, which, in some measure, broke the keen, piercing air that blew in fitful gusts through the narrow mountain passages everywhere around us. But it was miserably cold. The rain fell in torrents, and the troops were thoroughly drenched. It was in every way a wretched night. At any moment the enemy might depart from their usual tactics of not attacking at night, and throw their well-provided men upon our weakened and famished lines. But we were not disturbed until the following morning, when the troops of Manteuffel advanced to the attack.

The rattle of musketry was well sustained in front of the village of Busy, and the adjoining village of Ornans. Behind the enemy's lines the Doubs coursed merrily along; the wily Germans, however, having constructed a "bridge-head," or *tete-de-pont* to cover their retreat, if that unusual resource was found necessary. Just at the re-entering sinuosity of the river they constructed the work, in order to enable the guns to play in harmony with the supporting batteries on the other side. Openings were left to allow the retreating troops to file through with guns and carriages without confusion, and the parapets were so disposed as to flank those openings effectually. But retreat for them did not become necessary. They had the game in their own hands. They played the attack, we the defence. Busy was hastily barricaded; the houses were crenelated, banquettes were made, and our mountain-pieces so disposed as to defend those parts most favourable to an advance of the enemy. Yet everything was terribly bungled. I was commanded to occupy a position which was contrary to all military rule. The Irish Company was to hold the "last ditch." After the village was won by the enemy we were to stand behind the last brick edifice in the place, and there check their advance, in order to enable the battalion to escape over the fields to our rear. Behind our position there was a stretch of unbroken ground, across which we would be compelled to fly. There was no shelter on our way. If the enemy won our position, which we regarded as a matter of certainty, they could have picked us off at their leisure as we were making across the open space behind us. Nor was there any disposition made to cover us, either with artillery or musketry fire. Once the village was won, the Germans could line the outer works, fire from the houses with security to themselves, but certainly with discomfiture to us. But it was not so to be. The blunder was averted. The order was countermanded, for we were wanted in the front. The musketry fire was meantime rolling along the line like an avalanche of rockets, while we traversed the streets of Busy, moving towards the other end of the village where our troops were engaged. In our direct front nothing could be seen of the enemy but the smoke from their small arms, and which was the only mark for our troops to aim at. It was a game of "hide and seek." Our men fired at where they thought the Germans were, or where the smoke from their guns indicated their position. Occasionally, indeed, a soldier more imprudent than his companions, would expose his person, and he immediately received half-a-dozen bullets through his body as recompense for his hardihood. But fire answered fire, and the leaden shower battered against the wall, or buried itself in the ditches, behind which our troops were sheltered. The bullets fell thick and fast enough around the men, when, with their accustomed tactics, the enemy sought to gain our flank, and compel us to retire. At this time our line extended over the hill upon our left, where some *Chasseurs-a-pied* were engaged in defending the wood through which the enemy threatened our flank. Between us there was an open space, across which no enemy would attempt to move, and we retreated through the village and sought the hills, which skirted the village on flank and rear. The Germans had driven us out of Busy. We now made for the high ground behind the village. The Irish Company was sheltered behind an " *auberge*," when General Rebillard rode along the post, escorted by a troop of Lancers, while he endeavoured to map out our new line before the enemy too closely pressed upon our position.

" What regiment are you ?" the General demanded, pulling up before our post, looking indifferently at the guard that had turned out to do him honour.

" *La Compagnie Irlandaise, Regiment Etranger, mon General*," said Lieutenant Cotter, to whom the words were addressed.

" Ah," replied the General, with an approving smile, while he more keenly looked at the line of Irishmen who stood before him, " Ah, I would rather have your company than a battalion of Mobiles," and a welcome Irish cheer caused our French companies to stare in amazement at what they, no doubt, considered the frantic conduct of the Irish soldiers. 'Tis true, indeed, that " praise undeserved is scandal in disguise ;" but I had other proofs by which I ascertained that General Rebillard was genuine in his laudation of the *Regiment Etranger*. He had more than once complimented them for their gallantry in the field. The *Regiment Etranger* was, above all others, his favourite corps. Every position of importance was entrusted to its care. That a Frenchman should compliment foreigners and disparage his own countrymen is not so strange, when the history of the Foreign Regiment proves it to be one of the best corps in the service of France. Then, too, the Mobiles were merely regarded as mob soldiery. The officers of the regular army had very little respect for the capacity of the Mobile commanders. It was in their capacity as campaigners and hardy soldiers that General Rebillard preferred the volunteers of the *Regiment Etranger* to the conscript Mobiles. He knew both, and he judged accordingly.

But the enemy were drawing their lines still closer upon our position. They knew they had us trapped, yet they even more effectually guarded every outlet by which we could escape. Our division had retired under the guns of the fortress and the outlying forts of Besançon. We were still the rear-guard of the army. To us was left the honour of checking the German advance. Even the other two battalions of our regiment had retired and left us up nearest the enemy's lines. The country was admirably adapted for defensive operations. Belts of timber cut the hills into divisions, and gave good cover to our troops. Before us the Doubs still murmured on its way, until its waters met the more turbid current of the Rhone. Upon a rocky eminence, in our direct front, the shell of what was once a baronial castle stood out sharp and clear against the cloudless sky. The people in the neighbourhood told weird stories about the "Chateau" and its once lordly inhabitants. Time was when the proprietors of the once lordly dwelling exacted black mail from the travellers through the valley of the Vosges, and gnomes and ghosts of defunct cavaliers still trod the deserted chambers of the ruined building. Along the outer boundary of the structure might still be seen the spirits of the departed dead moving with majestic mien through the amply wainscotted hall which so often echoed to the thread of a hundred gentlemanly desperadoes. The form of a female, too, was—

> "At twilight seen to glide,
> Smiling o'er the fatal tide"

of the river that still kept coursing on, ever on, to the sea. To the country people around the old castle was a tabooed spot, not to be desecrated by the foot of man. Immediately opposite the ruined castle, but divided by a deep ravine, through which the German commanders advanced their men, the enemy had a post of observation, which took in a range of our new position, and enabled them to distribute their troops as to effectually block us in under the guns of Besançon. The German outposts pressed us on all sides. Before our position the light from their bivouac fires illumined the boisterous nights of the latter end of January. For some days we occupied a wood in front of the German outposts. The foliage of the trees was strewn upon the ground, and formed a gorgeous bed for all that remained of the wearied soldiers of the *Armée de l'Est*. As usual we lined the skirt of the timber, in order to give a clear sweep for our guns in the event of attack. But reaction set in amongst the men again. The rattle of musketry no longer kept them from drooping with exhaustion. Poor Sergeant M'Crossin became emaciated. I scarcely ever saw such a deplorable and famine-struck man. His eyes actually protruded from their sockets, while the bones nearly cut through the remnant of flesh that was left upon his face and person. He was tottering with pure weakness, and at last his limbs refused to obey the effort of his will. But "misfortunes rarely come in single file, but in battalions," and at last M'Crossin was afflicted with small-pox. Yet, even then, under the damp air of January, stretched upon the moisture preserving leaves of pine trees, almost naked, with "famine" written upon every lineament of his features, the brave fellow refused to go to hospital because we were likely to be engaged any moment. I had absolutely to command him to leave the field, and as his emaciated figure disappeared behind the thickly matted saplings which abundantly interlaced our encampment, I thought I had seen the last of my sergeant-fourrier.

"Another good man gone," said Mr. M'Alevey, when M'Crossin and his escort had disappeared. "Poor fellow, it is hardly possible that he can pull through, for he is already half dead; but *mais a la guerre, comme a la guerre*," and the lieutenant gave an additional twist to his well trimmed mustache, lit a cigarette, and was soon enveloped in a cloud of smoke.

In the meantime the enemy had been feeling our position on all sides. They pressed our outposts, and their advance-guards had continual encounters with our troops. The rattle of musketry was rolling along our entire front. They still hesitated to occupy, although they had compelled us to retire from, Busy. The slopes of the hill, the edges of the timber, the sheltered ditches, every available and protected position was occupied by our men, while the Germans tried on all sides to outflank our lines, or to drive the flanks in confusion in upon the centre. There was, indeed, but little or no exposure on either side, but the Germans were manœuvring through every inch of ground before us. For five or six days we lay in the wood in front of Busy. Our grand-guard and the outposts of the enemy were constantly engaged. Our men had meantime become still more reduced in numbers. *La Compagnie Irlandaise* could only muster fifty-five rifles under the trees in front of the German position before Busy. The casualities from the bullets of the enemy were few, but famine had reduced our ranks to nearly half its original strength. The time passed pleasantly enough, too, as the reviving sun of January sent the flush of comfort merrily coursing through our veins. But the end came at last! Our troops retired closer still to the fortifications. Behind our position every hill had suddenly been capped with field works. To our battalion was left the honour of being the last to retire. We were still left nearest the German lines. The wood was vacated, and a commanding position taken upon the summit of a hill about 400 yards in our rear. We had lost our *Commandant* at Montbelliard, and our new *Chef* was more strict in his attention to the letter of military law. Our new post commanded the village of Busy, and our outposts occupied the adjoining wood. But the duty was terribly severe. It was a continual round of grand-guard and picquet, picquet and grand-guard. Every morning, an hour before daybreak, the battalion turned out and formed in front of our position, prepared for an attack. Even the poor comfort of a night's uninterrupted repose upon the dew-damped soil of mother earth was denied the men. Rumours of the armistice had reached us, and the fall of Paris was generally believed. In other parts of France the Celt and the Gaul faced each other in grim quietude, the hush of arms was stilled, the shock of battle was over, the record of blood was nearly full. Peace, at least for a while, settled upon the disastrous homesteads of France, and the armistice brought mingled feelings of joy and sorrow to every creature's heart. But it was not so for us. We were to fight on. The Germans refused to grant us the luxury of an armistice, they thought we should be entirely destroyed. Three days after the ring of the rifle had ceased in France, the troops of Manteuffel again advanced to the attack upon our position.

I think it was on the 2nd of February that we were aroused from our comparative lethargy, by the shout of "*Aux armes! aux armes!*" ringing along our line. For a whole week the enemy had been manœuvring along our front, and had completely succeeded in blocking up every route by which we might hope to force an exit. Every day we were engaged at some portion of our lines, and all with varying results. We had taken a few positions from the enemy, while we had to abandon a few in return. It is, indeed, somewhat singular how quickly the ring of a rifle rouses the latent spirit of soldiers. The men who, after the long and trying marches which followed their retreat from Montbelliard, were scarcely able to draw their weary limbs along, suddenly became possessed of *élan* which nothing but being face to face with the foe could effect. On this day, however we were destined to see this *esprit* more fully developed. Before our position a line of *tirailleurs* was irregularly, and as I thought, imprudently disposed in an open space, which could be readily enfiladed from a position which could be easily carried by the enemy. Our left was protected by a country-house called the "Red Farm," while on our right flank a battery of six-pounders gave some security to our position in that direction. A battery of mountain-pieces crowned the height upon which the main portion of the battalion was posted, and the Irish Company was placed behind a well-protected swell in the ground. Out of our entire division the 5th battalion of the *Regiment Etranger* was still nearest the enemy's lines. The rest had for some days retired under the guns of the numerous forts, which protected every avenue of approach to Besançon. The Uhlans scoured the neighbourhood, and came with gallant impudence within 400 yards of our lines. They had to feel the way for the attacking force. From out some well-sheltered bushes, however, into which many of our skirmishers had made their way, a smart fusilade was opened on the advancing horsemen, saddles were emptied, and the remainder turned and fled, madly pressing on each other as they scampered away. But they advanced again with recruited ranks, and cautiously moved in detachments towards every place likely to conceal our men. They rode with easy grace, and sat their horses like true soldiers. But many a brave fellow for the last time spurred his unfaltering charger onwards, as from out the sheltered slopes of bush and brake our men sent volley after volley into the advancing squadrons. Horses and riders rolled upon the earth, saddles were emptied, and riderless steeds rushed frantically over the plain sniffing the air with wide distended nostrils. Then the small arms came into play, and the *music de la guerre* was for a while merrily sustained. In the meantime our left was threatened and we were compelled to change the position of our troops in that direction to meet the tactics of the enemy. The field guns of the Germans had by this time come into position. Our pieces were admirably disposed upon an elevated platform beside the " Red Farm," and as the head of the enemy's infantry column wound its way through the streets of Busy, making towards our lines, the first *obus* was sent upon its mission. It was a splendid shot ! The shell cut a clear and well-defined lane through the German lines and caused a deep gap in their ranks. They were evidently unprepared for such good practice, but they quickly closed up, and advanced rapidly in open order, to gain some cover in their front the while. Our line of *tirailleurs* had meanwhile become engaged, as the enemy pressed closer upon our position. The rattle of small arms was by this time vigorously sustained on both sides. The Germans hesitated to advance across the open space that divided them from our lines, while we were satisfied with holding our own without attempting to dislodge the foe, while they tried to gain our flank upon the left, they were met by a well directed fire from the shelter of a friendly ditch which checked their advance and left us staring at one another in grim and anxious determination. The groans of the wounded were already audible amidst the din of the combat, when suddenly from out the wood upon our right a troop of the enemy's dragoons charged upon our line of *tirailleurs* and threatened to ride over them. But our men quickly rallied by fours and successfully resisted the onslaught, while the number of dismounted troopers told how steadily the men of the *Regiment Etranger* had done their work.

But the enemy still pressed upon us. They won position after position in spite of all our efforts. In every place in which we encountered them they mustered fully three to our one. The plain still divided us. One portion of the open space was not more than 100 yards across, and it was supposed that it was at that point they would in all probability attempt to cross in order to carry our post at the point of the bayonet. We were not mistaken in our conjecture. Another and a more formidable attempt to turn our left flank was an indication of their intention, and just as they made some slight advance to success upon our left, the troops in front rushed out from under the shelter of the trees and made straight for our lines. It was a wild, exciting moment. Many a gallant fellow bit the dust in that short run. Their officers led them on with chivalrous daring, and again that really musical " Vorwarts, vorwarts," sounded upon our ears. The bayonets of the French and Germans glittered in the sunshine, and in another instant would have been reeking with each other's blood. But the record was full, the cup had overflown. With a singular and, indeed melo-dramatic effect, a horseman bearing a white flag, was seen riding furiously towards the combatant lines. It was a message of peace ! Every lip uttered the cry of *" Drapeau blanc, drapeau blanc."* The shout was carried along the line, the combat ceased, and then louder than ever was heard the thankful sentence *" Drapeau blanc, drapeau blanc."* All eyes were turned towards the trooper and his white flag. *" Cessez le feu, cessez le feu."* rang out the bugles, *" Cessez le feu, cessez le feu,"* shouted the officers in command, and in a few minutes the strife had ceased, the harvest of death was at an end, and the white flag with all its peaceful significance waved above the victor and the vanquished. That was certainly the happiest moment I experienced in France, and I allowed my thoughts to wander homeward, and I freely speculated upon meeting old friends and relatives again. We had grown sick of our continued disasters, and to suffer on in hopeless agony, without the shadow of success to cheer us to new exertions, was trying in the extreme.

Yes, the troops were thankful. They may have experienced the

"LA COMPAGNIE IRLANDAISE."

sad reflections of a lost cause or a defeated nation, but there was that sudden release from danger which pleases all men. To a soldier there is nothing so pleasant as the feelings he experiences after a fight in which he has done his duty. Every man in the *Regiment Etranger* had played his part, and the compliment that *La Compagnie Irlandaise* received from General Rebillard is sufficient proof that the men of the Irish Contingent took their share of warlike danger, and acquitted themselves to the satisfaction of all.

Soon afterwards, however, there was a *parlementaire*, and then we heard that the armistice had been extended to us, and we might rest in peace.

"Well, *Capitaine*," said our *Commandant* to me, during the evening, "the war is probably over, and to our battalion remains the honour of having fired what was probably the last shot. When you return to Ireland it may be something to remember." And so it is! We cannot forget that if we were late in the field, we were last out of it. We must treasure it as one of the most satisfactory of our reminiscences, that we heard the last shot and saw the last German souls sent to eternity, during the Franco-German war of 1870 and 1871.

CHAPTER XV.

> "In peace there's nothing so becomes a man
> As modest stillness and humility."
>
> SHAKSPEARE.

THE beginning of February, 1871, brought mingled feelings of joy and sorrow into the homes of the people of France. Around many a hearthstone national humiliation must have been more than compensated for by the assurance that the darling son or brother had survived the bloody campaign, while many a home was shadowed over by the dim cold shade of death. Yes, the love of kind is, in the old at least, stronger than the love of country. There are few Spartan mothers, although there may be many Spartan sons, in those days. Preach as we may about devotion to country, let the manhood of a nation pronounce as it will its willingness to sacrifice life in its country's cause, yet the parents of that nation's manhood would, unlike the Spartan mothers, rather see their sons return *without* their shields than *upon* them. As we grow old, that patriotic fire which animated us in our youth, gives way to a more temperate spirit; we may still be truly patriotic, but it is a patriotism of a different stamp from the sacrificing and generous impulse which possessed us in our youth. Passion gives way to reason, and the hero of the past becomes the cautious counsellor of the present. The old are never brave. Even *Napoleon le Grand*, the man who, when a youth, was first to cross the bloody bridge of Lodi, when his grenadiers hesitated to advance, was, in his latter days, not free from the imputation of being careful to preserve his anatomy entire. As we advance in life, the love of existence and the cares and responsibilities of age in a great measure, deaden all other feelings. The thousands of associations and family ties which age conjure up and create, make it harder for the old to leave the world, than for the youth whose ties are but the creation of yesterday, and whose plans or prospects in the future are in all cases but indifferently arraigned. The youthful soldier full of patriotism, alive with animation, and buoyed up by the hope of returning to the paternal roof, with all his new-born honours thick upon his head—falls—and there is an end to all his greatness; but the parents survive but to sanctify his death, and to carry along with them the sorrowing recollection of his end. Yes, they are the real victims of the war! Amidst the excitement of a campaign, soldiers have little time for reflection, while their parents and relatives think of nothing but the dangers which are attendant upon the war, and are for ever speculating and praying for the absent ones. But the armistice enabled all to speculate on meeting old friends again; and an Order from the General of our Division, soon after, released many of the soldiers from their engagement, and brought with it associations of lost companions, and the recollections of a lost cause.

ARMY OF THE EAST.

DIVISIONAL ORDER.

Officers, Non-commissioned Officers, and Soldiers:

"A decision of the Administration obliges many amongst you to return home. Before their departure, I am anxious to express to them the deep regret I feel at parting with them.

"If since Coulmiers, success has not followed our arms, you have not the less continued to show an example of courage, discipline, and devotion. During the retreat upon Orleans, in presence of a great force, the Second Division of the Fifteenth Army Corps, distinguished itself by courage and coolness, while defending Arteney, Chevilly, and afterwards the heights of Mountjoie, on the 2nd, 3rd, and 4th of December.

"Your conduct in the East does you the highest honour. You have bivouaced on the snow when the thermometer marked fifteen degrees below zero, often without fire, and sometimes without provisions, in consequence of the impossible arrival of the convoys.

"At Mount-Chevis (Montbelliard), you stood up bravely for three days, under the murderous fire of a powerful artillery.

"You fought before Busy, to cover the fatal movement of the army upon Pontarlier.

"During the armistice, you cut out a new line of defence before Besançon, to supplement the insufficient fortifications of that place.

"*Officers, Non-commissioned Officers, and Soldiers of the Second Division:*

"I shall ever remember with pride and happiness, that I have had the honour of marching with you against the enemy for a period of five months.

"Under the grievous circumstances in which our country is placed, endeavour to maintain order, and guard the national dignity in presence of the foreigner, who is to occupy our soil, until we can take revenge.

"(Signed) "REBILLARD,
"*General of Division.*

"*General Headquarters, Berne, (near Besançon),*
"MARCH 9TH, 1871."

Day by day it was evident that the armistice brought joy to the troops. *La Compagnie Irlandaise* was still quartered at the Red Farm, and were able at last to rest and be thankful. The weather became warm, and the sun, as if in gladdened splendour, shone with redoubled vigour upon the earth. Everything promised a joyous time of it. The troops occupied their time when off duty by sewing their tattered raiments, and putting their worn and dilapidated kits in order. Books were posted, accoutrements polished, and all the appurtenances of camp life underwent a vigorous overhauling. The men were looking themselves again, and their home-bound fancies ran riot with their joyous speculation. Everywhere around us the sword was turned into the ploughshare; the cavalry horses were working on the farms, and preparing the productive soil for another crop of cereals or grape.

Yet the men were not idle all the time. Every hill around Besançon was converted into a fortress. Fatigue parties were constantly at work, and the Irish soldiers had some good opportunities of learning some of the mysteries of the Sappers' art. Walls and trenches were made, barricades and banquettes were constructed in the villages of the neighbourhood, and the troops in general were preparing for a renewal of hostilities which we all knew would not occur. However, the Irish soldiers were expert enough at the use of the pick and shovel. It was an agreeable change; constructing lunettes, redoubts, bastions and demi-bastions, curtains, gorges, and rifle pits, was after all better than the misery which was attendant upon our experience under Bourbaki. Gabions for revetments, mantlets for guns, platforms for gun carriages, facines sunken and half sunken, and all the methods of defence against vertical, direct, ricochette, or oblique fire, were carefully attended to, and anxiously learned by the men of *La Compagnie Irlandaise.* Sergeant Carey was particularly at home in his new vocation, and was for ever wandering amongst the works, and asking pertinent questions from the engineers. At last, however, we were relieved, and were to take up our quarters at a deserted chateau near the village of Pugy, about five miles from Besançon, where we still pursued our occupation assisting the *génie.* The officers were still *comme a la guerre.* Their uniform was torn and soiled, and occasionally was not quite *à la militaire*, at least in the dandified opinion of those carpet heroes, the *Garde Nationale.* I remember once having run the gauntlet of *Chef de Battalion*, colonels and generals, and ultimately succeeded in getting a pass to Besançon, and entering its historic gate in all the *dishabille* of my campaign dress. My tunic was patched and soiled, my kepi was battered and dirty, and my trousers was covered with mud stains. I must have cut a sorry figure, and the interest with which the dandified *Garde Nationale* took in my costume, caused an occasional surprise on my part that my clothes were, perhaps, coming to pieces. But it was not so, and I was able to see the town without having recourse to a tailor for assistance. Dr. Macken accompanied me, and he, with philanthropic longing, visited the hospitals, which were crowded with sick and wounded. I, however, went the round of the town, and was interested in hearing the military history of the place, of being told that it was in the neighbourhood Cæsar defeated Ariovistus, that Louis XIV. took the town in 1660, and that it was successfully defended against the Allies in 1814. There were of course fussy members of the *Garde Nationale,* the fireside champions of the Republic, who would insist on seeing my papers when they heard my foreign accent. There were, as an equal matter of course, the strutting officers of the same useless body, covered with lace, and treading the earth with an air that would take Theophile Gautier to do justice to. The divinity of such a form could only be successfully treated by a master hand. Then there were the neat French·girls, dressed with that exquisite taste which one hardly ever sees out of *La Belle France.* But above all there was an excellent dinner at a *café,* which Dr. Macken and myself enjoyed with voracious relish. After all, true enjoyment consists in sudden release from pain. There is no pleasure so exquisitely fine as that which enables us to contrast the two extremes, while enjoying the better—contentment, that parent of delight and physical comfort on the one hand—and famine, frost and misery upon the other. The sun itself appeared brighter under the new aspect events had taken, the landscape more beautiful, and all Nature seemed to harmonize with the herald of Peace. Yes, Peace, bright, joyful Peace, what thousands of associations you bring to the battle-stained soldier; he alone feels the full measure of your mission; he alone appreciates, in all its immeasurable depth, the ocean of happiness you bring in your wake. It may, indeed, damp the ardour of a soldier's spirit to know that his national banner is trailed in the dust, but still Peace is welcome to the wearied soldier, who has despaired of redeeming the fallen fortunes of his flag. It is not that men fear death for their country's cause, but what heart so dead to the influence of home, so indifferent to the clinging love of wife, parents, sisters, or brothers, as not to experience joyous emotions when he feels thoroughly free to speculate upon seeing them again, and to be the recipient of their unfathomable love, when he returns with all his new-born honours fresh upon his head. But I am becoming pathetic, and can imagine my cynical reader turning with irritating indifference on to the next page.

Besançon, however, was, like all French towns at that period, in mourning. The authorities had donned sackcloth, preached peace, and talked of revenge. The carpet heroes were loud in their protesttations of treachery, and even swore that Bourbaki attempted his own life, because he was discovered in the fact of selling his country, and his country's cause. While I wandered about the town, I had a thousand speculations to make, and as evening was throwing its giant shadow upon the battlements which capped the hills around me, I made towards the gate, passed out of the town, and took the road for Pugey. I remember it was a glorious day; the Doubs coursed merrily along beside the road I traversed, and on every side the fortress-crowned hills looked defiantly upon the many passages below. It was, indeed, a place worth fighting for, and I returned to our quarters impressed with the assurance that France, with all its faults, was still flowing with milk and honey. But the defects of the French military system became more painfully apparent during the armistice. Immorality amongst the officers was openly practised, and upon one occasion I was somewhat surprised at seeing a female of questionable repute, quizzingly scanning the soldiers of *La Compagnie Irlandaise* from the windows of an officer's quarter close by. I remember too, Sergeant Carey drawing my attention to the fact, and smarting under the criticisms which the woman's protector and herself, indulged in.

"Captain," said Carey coming to my side, "the men are being insulted by that hussy in the window."

"Well, sergeant," I replied, "what can I do? the quarters are not mine, and how can I interfere?"

"Will you give me liberty, sir," said Carey, "and I'll get rid of her."

"Certainly," I answered in thorough confidence, knowing well that my trusted sergeant would do nothing contrary to military law or to the strictest interpretation of military regulations.

Carey was drilling a squad at the time, and without casting a single glance towards the window, he so manœuvered his men that he brought them face to face with his critiques, while he was supposed to be encountering an enemy. I suddenly saw the squad going through all the motion of loading, then quickly falling upon their knees. At the command "fire," from the sergeant, the triggers were pulled, and the obnoxious occupant of the window retired in forcible anticipation of an accidental cartridge being hidden in the breech of some of the Chassepôts of the Irish soldiers. Carey succeeded, and eventually had the satisfaction of driving the woman out of our neighbourhood by a strategem, which did infinite credit to his judgment, and even more to his keener penetration. But the officers were, as a rule, an ill-conditioned lot of men. They were quick enough to resent and to punish the most trivial act of misconduct in the men, while they caroused and outraged many of the provisions of military law. They were, too, often guilty of that "choleric word," which, in the captain, means nothing, but in the soldier is rank mutiny. Individually they were brave enough, indeed I was many times forced to admire their gallant bearing under fire, but collectively they were a sorry lot, and understood but little of the actual duties appertaining to their calling. I find it hard, indeed, to censure men from whose I was the recipient of many favours, and to whose kindness and consideration the men of *La Compagnie Irlandaise* owe some recognition of esteem; but I must express my opinion of their general incompetency, and want of military knowledge. There were, of course, exceptions. Our fine old Colonel, for instance, as gentle as a child, as brave as a fanatical Turco. He always had a kind word for the Irish soldiers, and was often amusingly demonstrative in trying to make them understand his "leetle" English. But time passed quickly in our comfortable quarters at the Chateau at Pugey. Occasionally some misdemeanant from the *Regiment Etranger* was shot in the grey of the morning, and it became quite a study to see how men of various mental culture met their fate. Then, too, the melancholy ordeal of selling the effects of officers that had been killed, caused some painful recollections, and set many a brain wandering over past scenes, and past associations. Then came a parting dinner from the officers of the battalion, to the officers of *La Compagnie Irlandaise*, all of whom had fortunately pulled through the campaign with whole skins. Then there were two inspections, a change of quarters, and we once more found ourselves near the "Red Farm," and could see the very spot where the last shot was fired. Our new post was at a cross road, and disbanded Mobiles and Franc-tireurs passed every hour of the day, in groups. They were going home, and sang patriotic chants, by way of individual joy at the fact. They wished to appear sorry, but were really glad. They swore vengeance, and indulged in the telegraphy of the arms, but they were merry all the time, and were evidently picturing the welcome which awaited them at the threshold of their homes. I remember one poor fellow who attracted my attention on one of those occasions. He was a young man, and carried himself with a quiet *hauteur* which commanded respect by its easy force. A simple gold band which ran obliquely across the cuff of his tunic, proclaimed his rank to be that of a sergeant, and as one arm was in a sling, it told its own tale without any varnish. There was something in the bearing of this sergeant that attracted my attention, and as he stood before me, his attitude and manner forced me to regard him as a man of superior culture. His story, as I afterwards learned from himself, was a simple one, common enough to the sons of France at that date. He was the son of a noble in Alsace. His father's chateau had been bombarded and razed to the ground. His mother died, his only brother was killed, and he was then winding his way to Switzerland, where his heart-broken and ruined parent had taken up his temporary abode. "But we will always be French, *mon Capitaine,*" he said, addressing me, "it is impossible that Alsace can be made to accept the government of Germany. We are French in character, in idea, in habit, and above all in sympathetic force. As for me and my poor old father, we return to Alsace only to dispose of the remnant of our estates and then we shall start for Algeria, where we shall await the day of reckoning with the victors of to-day." It was a common enough story of the time, but was rendered doubly interesting by the method of its telling, and the quiet and gentlemanly manner of the sergeant. But days passed on with the usual routine of military duties, and military promenades, and we had on one occasion the poor satisfaction of marching into the village of Busy, from which the enemy had been induced to retire. The men were once more clean, and had the luxury of indulging in a vigorous application of soap and water every morning. Days passed on in a monotony that became a pleasure, owing to the recent hardships we had passed through. For four months the men had not taken off their uniforms, and it requires no student of entomology to picture the state of their clothing. But all this was rapidly changing. Needles and thread were everywhere at play, and working became a regular duty, while an occasional inspection of the kits rendered competition in cleanliness, a healthy and soldierly pastime. About this time the journals in Besançon sounded our praises, and elevated us upon a kind of chivalrous platform for the admiration of the bourgeoise of the town. They claimed us as brothers and as friends, said we were fine fellows generally, and swore undying attachment to what they variously called "Catholic Ireland," and "Green Erin."

La Franche Comté, is one of the most influential journals in that part of France, and one morning we were flattered by noticing the following paragraph in our favour:—

"Amongst the volunteers who have come from all parts of Europe to place their swords at the services of France, when she was invaded, and her independence threatened, we cannot forget the Irish Company, which formed part of the army of the East. Officers and soldiers, sons of green Erin, they remembered in the hour of our danger the ties of strong sympathy which have for a long time united Ireland and France. Having been the first to come to us, they are the last to leave us, after having borne a brilliant part in the different combats of the East. At Montbelliard they were the last to leave the field of battle. At Busy they were complimented by General Rebelliard. In the name of our poor France thanks, once more thanks to our Irish brothers, we shall take care faithfully to remember their courage and their devotion."

Other journals were equally complimentary, and showered praises upon our heads with prodigal profusion. But all this had its results. Visitors occasionally enquired for our whereabouts, and demonstrated their friendships in some neighbouring *café*, into which they generally invited the too willing soldiers.

In the meantime the peace negociations were being pushed forward and the armistice was to extend until the 24th of February. Paris had been occupied by the Germans, and the war indemnity had been settled at 5,000,000,000 francs, or £200,000,000 sterling. This, however, is but a portion of what that disastrous war cost France. The number of "bons" signed by officers for goods requisitioned, must have been something fabulously large. For *La Compagnie Irlandaise* I must have signed "bons" to the tune of many thousand pounds. Every officer commanding a company or a detachment, must have done the same, and the poor peasants and shopkeepers often looked with suspicious dread at the stamped order which compelled them to part with their goods for what to them was a doubtful piece of paper. But they were mistaken in their suspicions. France paid her debts to friends as well as to foes. Belfort capitulated on the 16th of February, and the garrison reduced from 16,000 to 12,000 men, marched out with full military honours, and took away with them the armaments and the archives of the fortress. The heel of the French Achilles, as Vauban called Belfort, had done its duty nobly, and if the *Intendance* had been equal to the occasion, Belfort would have formed a base of operations for the army of the East, which might have given a new complexion to the campaign. Belfort opens the road to Paris, overawes Lyons, threatens and neutralizes Strasburg, and turns the entire line of fortresses constructed to guard the frontier. So wrote the great engineer of Louis XIV., and so the experience of the Franco-German war proved it to be. Then there was a further extension of the armistice for two days, and on the 28th of July, the preliminaries of Peace were agreed to, and the national pride of *La Grande Nation* was trailing in the dust.

Our time was drawing to a close. We were volunteers *pour la dureé de la guerre*, but the colonel with generous intent asked us to remain in the service, all ranks holding their position. I declined hearing that it was likely that I would be taken down a peg, and Mr. Cotter was the only one who accepted service. For my own part, I was much pleased at the unanimous determination of the men to return to Ireland. It proved to the French officers that the soldiers of the Irish Company did not go to France as mercenaries. When their work was done they desired to return home, and it was easy to detect that the spirit which evinced itself in the ranks of *La Compagnie Irlandaise*, contributed to their elevation in the opinions of the colonel and the officers of the regiment in general.

"We would like to have you with us in Africa, *Capitaine*," said the colonel to me as I informed him of the men's decision, " but I suppose your men are too comfortable at home, to wish to serve in such a country."

" It is not that, *mon Colonel*," I replied, " we Irish always give our sympathy, and many of us will again give our services when France goes to war, but many of these Irish soldiers have professions to follow, and then there is no glory in your African campaign to compensate for its trials and its hardships."

"Ah, *Capitaine*, I fear France will not be able to fight Germany for many a long year to come. Three million and a half of our people taken from us, an enormous indemnity, twice as much in itself as it cost England for the two years war in the Crimea, and then our own debts contracted for the war, our *prestige* gone, our national pride humiliated. Ah, *Capitaine*," continued the old man, visibly effected by the picture he had created; "do not mind the cries of revenge you hear, we are not able for the Germans at present; but," he added, straightening himself in his chair, and rattling the decorations which hung from his soldierly breast, while his eye emitted that genuine fire, I had seen it give out more than once under fire; "but who knows, this is an age of complication, and France may wake up still, may wake up still."

"You marched through Prussia as if you were on a promenade, and your eagles were planted under the Lindens before, *mon Colonel*," I replied, "and you may do so again. You have a bead roll of victories before which the triumphs of Germany of to-day must pale. Nations, like families, have their troubles, and each in its turn dictates to its neighbours."

"Very well, *Capitaine*, call to-morrow at nine in the morning, and I shall have all your papers ready, and the next day you can leave for your own country. And," he added, standing up and extending his hand to me, "may God bless you, and if we ever meet again, I hope it will be under better circumstances, and brighter auspices both for your own country and for mine." I shook the old man's hand, and left him, with mingled emotions of joy and of sorrow, for that fraternity of brotherland, which grows amongst companions in arms, had rendered our Colonel dear to every officer in his command. At last, however, our time was drawing to a close. Day by day preparations were being made to send us home, and on the

26th of March, we received final orders to prepare to leave our quarters on the morrow. Arms were delivered up, accounts settled, books posted, and we were mustered out of the army, carrying with us the good opinion and the kind wishes of every man in the *Regiment Etranger*. The peace was, however, gall and wormwood to many of the officers.

"This peace is a bitter pill, but we'll have it out some day, *Capitaine*," said Ceresole to me the day before we parted, "and then, perhaps, we shall see your face in the *Regiment Etranger* again."

I hope so, but "Hope whispers a flattering tale," which, I fear, I shall never see realized.

Well to-morrow came. I parted with the officers early in the morning, and I remember turning around to wave a salute to the knot of war-worn heroes who stood upon a small knoll behind me, where they had congregated to bid me adieu; and I heard the familiar phrase of my late companions in arms for the last time calling out in general chorus as they waved their kepis above their heads, "*Bonne chance, Capitaine, bonne chance.*" I must confess to a feeling of sadness upon the occasion, and I wended my way along the beautiful valley of the Doubs, where the connecting canal of the Rhine and Rhone join in mutual embrace. I gave way to speculation, and drew melancholy pictures of the past on the one hand, and joyous anticipations of the future on the other. At last my face was towards home, sweet, sweet, home. That love of strange attractive force which guide the feelings in its narrow channel, soon claimed and obtained entire possession over my mind, and I gave way to the coming happiness which anticipation brought upon its hopeful passage.

I reached Besançon about noon. Mr. M'Alevey was to follow with the Company the next morning, while I saw the *Intendance*, and tried to make preparation for our conveyance by rail if possible. No conveyance was to be had for love or money. Here was another dilemma. There were about twenty sick, and it was impossible that they could march to Dôle or Dijon, a distance of eighty kilometres. I spent two days in vain endeavours to induce the authorities to make some effort to enable me to keep the Company intact; but it was all in vain. The General appeared to have an electric battery at the end of his feet and hands when I made the request, and declared that it was "impossible—impossible," while he demonstrated his words by shrugging his shoulders, extending his hands, arching his eyebrows, and indulging in theatrical grimaces that would do justice to a circus clown. If he had the disposition, he certainly had the means of being our friend upon the occasion. The *Intendance* was, indeed, civil; he even took pains to try and see us provided for. He gave me an order to the station-master, to try and have our sick conveyed by rail, but all was useless, and the sick had to be left behind.

I think it was on the 30th of March we left Besançon for Dijon The reviving sun of Spring made our route pleasant enough, and we trudged along in our own time. The villages along our way were occupied by German troops, and I had a few opportunities of inspecting the drill and bearing of the soldiers of the Vaterland. It was marvellous to mark their precision on parade, as it was really magnificent to observe their promptitude and soldierly bearing. Their movements were as mechanically true as the beating of a chronometer. Accustomed as I had been to drill with some of the crack regiments in the English service, I never saw anything so precise in all its minutest details, as the movement of a Prussian regiment on parade. More than once I saw several thousand men drawn up in columns of companies, and in the manual and platoon, the entire mass moved as if they were automatons, working by the electric influence of the officers in command. Not a boot was placed one inch beyond another, nor a rifle was a fraction out of its direct angle. To me it appeared simply marvellous that such precision could be attained. I had indeed tried, and I think succeeded, in making *La Compagnie Irlandaise* the best drilled company in the *Regiment Etranger*. They marched better, manœuvred with more precision, and went through their formations, in general, with more regularity and order than their French companions in arms. I took a natural pride in seeing them the best company in the regiment, and was more than a dozen times congratulated by French officers on the fact. But they bore but a poor comparison to the clock-like precision of the German troops. Without being positively stiff or rigid, still the Germans were perfect in their movements, and inspired me with a degree of respect, which I confess never to have experienced when looking at the best troops of the French line. The kits of the Germans were well provided, and their comfortable boots, warm clothing, well filled haversacks, wonderful organization, and general healthy appearance, told the plain unvarnished tale of their splendid successes.

Everywhere traces of the war were evident. Rude crosses marked the scene of many a combat, where French and German, Franc and Teuton closed in the embrace of death. Here and there some companion of the slain had carved the name or names of the occupants of the earth beneath, upon the wood, while rude, and, indeed occasionally creditable epitaphs told the simple story of a lifetime. All the villages and towns along our route were occupied by the Germans, little *petites postes* dotted the country at every point likely to afford shelter and protection to the invaders. To men wearing the uniform of the regular army, both officers and soldiers of the enemy were marked in their respect, and I well remember the surprise it caused me when marching along a road, cut into deep furrows by the numerous waggons that had passed over it, when meeting three Saxon officers who were promenading quietly before their quarters, they saluted me with military and, indeed, courteous promptitude, which I endeavoured to as courteously return. Victors however can afford to be civil, and they were even so to the privates and non-commissioned officers of the regular army. To the Mobiles and Franc-tireurs, however, there was no such respect shewn. I remember when passing through Dôle, a town of 4,000 inhabitants, romantically situated in a narrow rocky gorge, seeing the band of a Prussian regiment turn from their direct front, and play for a passing regiment of Mobiles as they marched *sans armes* into the town. Here, too, I had a little *recontre* with the Prussian guard. I had picked up an old Prussian gun at Montbelliard, and wished to take it to Ireland as a *souvenir* of the war. It was one of the old pattern, and had in all probability seen service in the war of 1866. It was a heavy, cumbersome, long, unwieldy weapon. It was nearly double the weight of a Chassepôt, and the escape of gas from the breech was so great that provision was made on the stock, by its peculiar formation, to rest on the thigh, from which position the gun was often fired. I found it, too, a convenient way of punishment *en route*. There are always some misdemeanant in a company, and " carrying the field-piece" became a recognised means of punishment on the line of march. When I entered Dôle, the patrol demanded the gun, and against all my remonstrance took it and the man who carried it, to the guard room. A crowd collected, the townspeople became excited, a row appeared to be brewing, when again I had an opportunity of witnessing the wonderful promptitude of the Prussian military system. In one minute every post in the town was under arms, and the spike helmets of the German troops, inspired a feeling of awe, which subdued the effervescent outburst of the bourgeoise, and at once threw oil on the troubled waters. However I succeeded in bringing the gun with me.

" It is contrary to regulations, *Capitaine*," said the captain of the guard, " we are not to allow any gun through our lines; and you know," he said, almost apologetically, " that orders *must* be obeyed." I, of course, acquiesced in this determination to carry out his instructions to the letter, but on pointing out an injury the gun had received which rendered it useless as a firearm, I succeeded in setting at rest his troubled spirit, and was allowed to bring my trophy along with me, the Prussian, however, merely asking me for my name and the regiment to which I had belonged, as a guarantee, and then with courteous salutation bidding me "*bon voyage.*" If I am to confine myself to personal experience, I must confess I found the Germans both courteous and civil, and conducting themselves towards the inhabitants with dignified and soldierly reserve. I have no doubt but cases of individual hardships did occur ; I have no doubt but ruffians committed outrage, and robbers plundered property, when removed from the surveillance of their officers, but I did not see it, nor do I think, with a few notorious exceptions, that the conduct of the German troops in France, was more severe than would be the conduct of a French army in Germany. Napoleon the Great's march through the Vaterland was not unmarked by that severity, which is to a great extent, necessary in a country fanatically hostile to the invading force. The first duty of a General is to protect the lives of his own men, and in France this was impossible without resorting to measures which, with a few disgraceful exceptions, I think perfectly justifiable. But it was Germans, Germans everywhere. Dijon, with all its old associations, where the Dukes of Burgundy lorded over the adjacent country, was full of the enemy; all along the road to Paris villages were ruined, every house appeared to be crenellated, while the tottering walls of many a homestead, which I could see from out the window of the railway carriage, told of ruin and of woe. For the time being the Germans lorded it with erect heads yet calm demeanour. There were few swaggerers, and it was only when I arrived in Paris, that I saw the spirit of rowdyism, when I was surrounded and taken prisoner by a Communist guard, first as a German spy, and then charged with the obnoxious crime of being an officer of the *Armée Regulaire.* The gallant champions of Liberty, Equality, and

Fraternity, thought my uniform a matter of suspicion, and brought me in durance vile before the officer of the guard, who hesitated to dispose of my sacred person, and sent me on to the *Commandant.* He, too, generous soul, should give me a further promenade, and I was sent under recruited escort to the general in command of the district, and was ushered into his august presence with little ceremony, and with less respect. I regret I forget this fellow's name, or that I cannot put my hand upon the official *laissez passer* which he ultimately gave me. He was not, however, a *distingué* looking individual. His subordinates treated him with a familiarity which was generally communistic in its way. However, he overhauled my papers, and when satisfied with my character, generously invited me to accept service under his filthy-looking rag.

"I will give you command of a regiment this very day, *Capitaine,*" he urged, moving towards the chimneypiece, on which several black bottles labled " cognac" were standing in quiet anticipation of having their contents emptied by the General and his staff. No doubt he wished to soften my obdurate heart, as he invited me to some of the brandy and helped himself after a fashion I had very seldom seen practised in France—a flowing full bumper.

"It is not my affair," I replied, "against the Germans I am always at the service of France, but a foreigner has no right to interfere in domestic affairs of another nation."

"Ah, you are mistaken, *Capitaine,*" replied the General, as I hit upon one of the favourite arguments of the heroes of the Commune. "Ours is the cause of humanity," he continued, as he helped himself to convenient sips at the contents of the glass, "wishing to establish a fraternity of nations to elevate the poor, and to curtail the wealth of the rich. Law, sir, should protect the weak, the strong can generally protect themselves. Legislation in the past has been made by one section of society, to the discomfiture and degradation of the other. Come," he continued extending his hand towards me, " come and join us, and be one of the regenerators of the human race." But it was no use, and my unsympathetic nature could not appreciate the utopia the ardent brain of the general, assisted by ardent spirits, had conjured up. At last he gave me a *laissez passer*, and even provided an escort to see me safe at the station, giving me, however, a parting instruction to quit Paris at once. I did so! It was not safe for any one wearing the uniform of the *Armée Regulaire* to be found strolling about the streets, and I took the first train for Havre. *En route*, the Germans were still everywhere, they crowded all the stations, were posted at all available points, and their spiked or shoe-brush head-dresses, were visible all along the way.

At Havre, there was, as usual in all French towns at that period, the hum of *"encore la guerre."* Revenge appeared to have entered the hearts of all the people in the town. The soldiers alone were silent, and more than once I was forced to notice the contemptuous sneer that passed over the face of some men, who bore the traces of the campaign upon his person, when he was listening to the flippant bombast of a bourgeois, or a National Guardsman. In the *cafés*, in the streets, in the theatres, it was all the same; the cry of *"encore la guerre,"* was repeated everywhere. Even the Mobiles occasionally indulged in the prediction. Men, whose term of service had been made up behind the fortifications, were above all others, the most uncompromising heroes, the most determined advocates for another war. The carpet heroes of the Republic—the darlings of the Commune, were one and all loud in their determination, to see the issue out with the German "hordes," at no distant date. These men, however, knew little of French military organization, and they knew less of German administrative power. But I found that each political party blamed every other party with being the cause of the disasters. The Legitimists "saw it all from the commencement." It was impossible that the Imperialists could succeed. The exit of the Emperor was, in their opinion, a just *denouement* to his entry. Sedan was the retribution for the *coup d'état*. But *Henri Cinq*, the legitimate claimant to the throne of his ancestors, would restore the faded honours of France, and once more burnish her worn and battered armour. So argued the Legitimists, who generally accompanied their opinion by a virtuous denunciation of everything that was not tempered to their political tastes. The Republicans were even more boisterous. They were merely biding their time, just waiting to consolidate their policy, and then the manhood of the nation would settle accounts with the "barbarians" of the North. When the political structure of "Not I the king, but we the people," was once fairly an its legs, the Republicans were to seriously set about another war, the result of which would assuredly be, to march across the Rhine, to the victorious shout of "*à Berlin, à Berlin.*" But this was all swagger. It was the effort of a foolish bravoism, which will not acknowledge itself worsted. "No matter from what cause, France has been beaten," Marshal MacMahon said to me months afterwards, when I had the honour of an interview with the illustrious chief; he acknowledged openly and fairly, that France had been humiliated, and he is too much the soldier, too open in his chivalrous soul, not to candidly admit what is patent to the whole world. But the gentlemen of the garrison towns would scarcely admit the fact. It was a mere temporary depression in their opinion, and a few months would make matters right again. To men unmoved by prejudices, even Hope appeared to have fled from France, for military, social, and political life, was in a state of chaos.

It was refreshing, indeed, amongst the crowd of swaggering bullies, to meet an occasional soldier, men who had seen service in the field amidst the frost, the famine, and the hardships of a midwinter campaign, and to hear *them* speak in terms of immeasurably disgust of the *bravache* gentry with whom they came into contact.

Even the Garabaldini were not free from the braggart spirit of the day. They contrasted most unfavourably with the unassuming *piou, piou* of the French line. I met one of their captains in Havre, who, if all his words were to be accredited, had performed prodigies of valour; he told such stories of hair-breadth escapes by flood and field, that I was induced to believe that the toga of Jack Falstaff had fallen upon his shoulders. " Garabaldians never run, sir," he said to me with the air of Don Quixote, while he strutted about with measured strides, and a swaggering gait. He looked upon me with a sneer worthy of Mars himself, when I replied that I was very often glad to run away, and that the feeling, next to a desire to do my duty, which possessed me, was to keep my precious anatomy entire, from the effects of villanous saltpetre. I disgusted the here of Dijon, when I told him that I tried to emulate the flight of an electric current upon such occasions, and was desirous of leaving not even a wreck of me behind, as I vanished " like the baseless fabric of a vision." He evidently thought we Irish made poor soldiers, although he did not tell me so, perhaps he hesitated to offend a late companion in arms, or perhaps he had some other reason more patent when applied to swaggerers of the Falstaffian type. However Havre was crowded with Volunteers. The Government generously gave each man a month's pay and a free pass to his destination. The Irish soldiers had already departed for Dublin *via* Liverpool, and on the 6th of April I left Havre *via* Southampton for London. The distant lights of *La Belle France* faded in the gloom, as we spun on across the channel, and more than once I conjured up many happy associations which had sprung into existence, during my six months' campaign in the country. Yes, France is the premier country of the world. With all her faults she has her virtues. Monarchy has not made her sycophantic, Imperialism has not made her unchivalrous, nor has Republicanism made her uncourteous. Where will you meet with the easy courtesy, the refined tone, the generous impulse, the chivalrous conduct, which is so universal in France. Nor do I believe that France was the aggressor in that disastrous war. She was not the aggressor when Denmark was assailed, and dismembered by those "peaceful Germans." She was not the aggressor when those "peaceful Germans" planned and worked out the campaign of 1866 against Austria, and which resulted in the subjugation of the Union States of Germany. She was not the aggressor when Prussia forced the South German States to accept a military convention, which was secretly convened in contravention to the articles of the Treaty of Prague. France was not the aggressor when those "peaceful Germans" set at nought the same treaty with reference to the Danish population of Holland. She was not the aggressor when Bismark, in conspiracy with Prim, sought the elevation to the Spanish throne of a scion of the house of Hohenzollern. The sin of France ever has been that she was, and is, too chivalrous. In her the oppressed nationalities of the world have ever found a champion. Instinctively she leans to the weak. Her virtues more than counterbalance her faults. France has ever been the pioneer of civilization in Europe, the home of sages, and the cradle of chivalry. To-day the kingly grace of the court of Louis XIV. sits as easily upon the Republican *ouvrier*, as it does upon the coroneted brows of those long line of *noblesses* who look at you from out their gilded frames on the walls of the picture gallery in Versailles. When France found herself thrown from the pinnacle of military fame, pushed from the pedestal of her greatness, into the mire of degeneracy, it was natural that some burst of indignation, and threats of revenge should sweep like an avalanche over the country. At such a time all due allowance must be made for a nation of chivalrous men. But take her all in, all and nowhere will you find that courteous civility which is equally perceptible beneath the *blouse* of a labourer or the fine cloth of a *homme distingué*, whose home is France. Comparisons may be odious, and yet even what is odious, may be also healthy. "Look upon this picture and then upon that" may be the means of tempering many a man's conduct in life. From France to England is but a short journey, at least geographically, but it is a very long way if all the amenities of life were to be the gauge of distance. I was not two hours on English soil until I was insulted, and simply because I wore a bear-skin coat as a protection against the weather. In France I had not seen six drunken men during the six months I was in the country, in England I saw a dozen before I arrived at the metropolis. I heard, too, from the men who were compelled to travel in their uniforms, that they were everywhere received with uncourtesy, rudeness, nay, with positive insults; even men wearing the uniform of her Majesty did not hesitate to offend a few of the men of *La Compagnie Irlandaise* who had travelled *via* Southampton, and we were all glad to shake the dust of England off our feet, and to once more stand upon Irish soil, after six months' absence from our native land.

APPENDIX.

NOMINAL ROLL

OF

THE IRISH COMPANY

AS IT STOOD AT THE FORMATION AT CAEN.

NO.	RANK AND NAME.	REMARKS.
	Captain M. W. Kirwan.	
	Lieut. F. M'Alevey.	
	,, B. Cotter.	
	Assistant-Surgeon R. Macken.	
1	Sergeant-Major Albert Dunsford	
2	Fourrier-Sergt. Henry M'Crossin	
3	Sergeant Terence Byrne.	
4	,, Frank Byrne.	
5	,, M. H. Carey, ...	Promoted lieutenant.
6	,, John Myers.	
7	,, James Quinn.	
8	Caporal W. D. Carmichael ...	Promoted fourrier caporal at Bourges, 5th Dec. 1870.
9	,, John Foran.	
10	,, Andrew O'Reilly.	
11	,, Matthew French.	
12	,, Patrick Corr ...	Promoted sergeant.
13	,, Patrick Manning.	
14	,, C. B. Brennan.	
15	,, John O'Brien.	
16	,, Richard O'Brien.	
17	,, William J. Dwyer.	
18	Soldat Michael Bain.	
19	,, Thomas Bannon.	
20	,, James Barry.	
21	,, Joseph Begley.	
22	,, James Boulger.	
23	,, James K. Bourke.	
24	,, Patrick Boyle ...	Promoted to 1st class soldier.
25	,, Philip Branagan ..	Promoted caporal.
26	,, Patrick Brien.	

APPENDIX.

Nominal Roll of the Irish Company as it stood at its Formation at Caen.

NO.	RANK AND NAME.	REMARKS.
27	Soldat Laurence Breen.	
28	,, Andrew Callwell.	
29	,, John Carey ...	Promoted to 1st class soldier.
30	,, John Claffey.	
31	,, James Clinch.	
32	,, Andrew Carroll.	
33	,, William J. Clinton ...	
34	,, George Coleman ...	Promoted to 1st class soldier.
45	,, Timothy Conroy ...	do.
36	,, John Conway ...	do.
37	,, Michael Coyne.	
38	,, John Cronin.	
39	,, Philip Crute.	
40	,, Paul Cullen ...	Promoted caporal.
41	,, Kearn Delany.	
42	,, Thomas Delany ...	Promoted to caporal of the 1st class.
43	,, Bernard Dullaghan.	
44	,, James Eustace.	
45	,, Michael Galvin ...	Promoted caporal.
46	,, Daniel Gilfedder ...	Promoted to 1st class soldier.
47	,, Patrick Gorman ...	Promoted 1st class caporal.
48	,, George Graham.	
49	,, William Grace.	
50	,, Peter Griffin.	
51	,, William R. Haughton ...	Promoted to 1st class soldier.
52	,, Edward Hayden ...	Promoted caporal.
53	,, Denis Hayes.	
54	,, William Hoey.	
55	,, Gerald Howard.	
56	,, James Hyland.	
57	,, William Kelly.	
58	,, George Kennedy.	
59	,, Thomas Knowles.	
60	,, Timothy Larkin.	
61	,, Michael Lynam ...	Promoted to 1st class soldier.
62	,, James M'Kenna.	
63	,, James Madden.	
64	,, Daniel M'Evoy ...	Promoted caporal.
65	,, George Malone.	
66	,, Hilary M'Dermott ...	Promoted caporal.
67	,, Laurence Mahony ...	Promoted caporal.
68	,, Timothy Marks.	
69	,, Thomas Marum ...	Promoted to 1st class soldier.

APPENDIX.

Nominal Roll of the Irish Company as it stood at its Formation at Caen.

NO.	RANK AND NAME.	REMARKS.
70	Soldat John Meehan.	
71	,, William Millar.	
72	,, Owen Muldoon.	
73	,, Gerald Nolan	Promoted to 1st class soldier.
74	,, Charles Nordell.	
75	,, Francis O'Brien.	
76	,, Timothy O'Connor.	
77	,, Edward O'Keeffe.	
78	,, Cæsar O'Doherty.	
79	,, E. J. L. O'Hanlon.	
80	,, James O'Neill.	
81	,, Jeremiah O'Neill.	
82	,, George O'Shaughnessy.	
83	,, Patrick O'Reilly	Promoted caporal.
84	,, Michael O'Toole.	
85	,, George Pope.	
86	,, Daniel Scanlon.	
87	,, Patrick Sheehan.	
88	,, James Smith.	
89	,, Joseph Sutcliffe.	
90	,, James Walsh.	
91	,, Augustus Underwood	Promoted caporal.
	SUBSEQUENTLY JOINED THE COMPANY AT BOURGES.	
92	Sergeant Anthony Donnellan.	
93	Soldat Patrick Mahony.	
	FRENCH SERGEANTS ATTACHED TO THE IRISH COMPANY.	
94	Sergeant H. Amaud.	
95	,, G. Mazaine.	
96	,, G. Malouski.	

NOMINAL ROLL

OF

THE IRISH COMPANY,

TAKEN AT THE "RED FARM," ON THE 24TH JANUARY, 1871.

NO.	RANK AND NAME.	REMARKS.
1	Captain M. W. Kirwan	Duty—wounded first day at Montbelliard.
1	Lieutenant F. M'Alevey	Duty—wounded second day at Montbelliard.
2	,, B. Cotter	Duty.
1	1st Class Assistant-Surgeon R. Macken	Duty.
1	Sergeant-Major Albert Dunsford	Duty—wounded first day at Montbelliard.
*2	Fourrier-Sergeant Henry M'Crossin	Ambulance.
*3	Sergant Terence Byrne	Duty.
*4	,, Frank Byrne	Duty.
*5	,, M. H. Carey	Duty.
6	,, Anthony Donnellan	Wounded second day at Montbelliard — missing second day on the retreat.
7	,, Patrick Corr	Duty.
8	,, Henri Amaud	Died in hospital from the effects of wounds received on the second day at Montbelliard.
9	,, G. Mazaine	Shot second day at Montbelliard.
*10	Fourrier Caporal W. D. Carmichael	Duty.
11	Capora' Andrew O'Reilly	Ambulance.
12	,, George O'Shaughnessy	In hospital—wounded second day at Montbelliard.

Nominal Roll of the Irish Company, taken at the Red Farm, Jan. 24, 1871.

NO.	RANK AND NAME.	REMARKS.
13	Caporal Hilary M'Dermott	Duty.
14	,, Patrick Gorman	Duty.
15	,, Laurence Mahony	Duty—wounded first day at Montbelliard.
16	,, Michael Galvin	Duty.
17	,, Daniel M'Evoy	Duty.
*18	,, Paul Cullen	Duty—wounded first day at Montbelliard.
19	,, Thomas Delany	Duty.
20	,, G. Malouski	Shot second day at Montbelliard.
21	Soldat Michael Bain	Duty.
22	,, Thomas Bannon	Hospital (frostbitten).
23	,, James Barry	Hospital.
24	,, Joseph Begley	Reported missing second day of Montbelliard, turned up in Switzerland.
25	,, James Boulger	Duty.
26	,, James K. Bourke	Duty.
27	,, Patrick Boyle	Duty.
28	,, Philip Branagan	Duty.
29	,, Patrick Brien	Duty.
30	,, Laurence Breen	Died at Bourges (small-pox).
31	,, C. B. Brennan	Reported shot at Orleans.
32	,, Andrew Caldwell	Duty.
33	,, John Carey	Duty.
34	,, John Claffey	Duty.
35	,, James Clinch	Hospital (small-pox).
36	,, Andrew Carroll	Wounded second day at Montbelliard. Reported shot first morning of the retreat.
37	,, William J. Clinton	Hospital.
38	,, George Coleman	Duty.
39	,, Timothy Conroy	Ambulance — wounded at Montbelliard second day.
40	,, John Conway	Duty.
41	,, Michael Coyne	Hospital—fracture of the leg.
42	,, John Cronin	Ambulance (frostbitten).
43	,, Philip C. Crute	Shot second day at Montbelliard.
44	,, Kearn Delany	Duty.
45	,, Bernard Dullaghan	Duty.

APPENDIX. 267

Nominal Roll of the Irish Company, taken at the Red Farm, Jun. 24, 1871.

NO.	RANK AND NAME.	REMARKS.
46	Soldat William J. Dwyer	In hospital — wounded third day at Montbelliard.
47	,, James Eustace	Hospital—(small-pox).
48	,, Matthew French	Reported shot third day at Montbelliard.
49	,, John Foran	Staff employ (Tours).
50	,, Daniel Gilfedder	Duty.
51	,, George Graham	Duty.
52	,, William Grace	Duty.
53	,, Peter Griffin	Duty.
54	,, Edward Hayden	Ambulance (frostbitten).
55	,, Gerald Howard	Missing second day at Montbelliard — turned up in Switzerland.
56	,, Denis Hayes	Duty.
57	,, William Hoey	Duty.
58	,, James Hyland	Duty.
59	,, William Kelly	Missing second day at Montbelliard.
60	,, George Kennedy	do.
61	,, Thomas Knowles	Duty.
62	,, Timothy Larkin	Duty.
63	,, Michael Lynam	Duty.
64	,, James Madden	Hospital (frostbitten).
65	,, George Malone	Missing—wounded third day at Montbelliard.
66	,, Patrick Manning	Duty.
67	,, Timothy Marks	Wounded—missing first day at Montbelliard.
68	,, Thomas Marum	Duty.
69	,, John Meehan	Hospital (wounded).
70	,, William Millar	Missing — reported shot second day at Montbelliard.
71	,, Owen Muldoon	Duty.
72	,, John Myers	In hospital (frostbitten).
73	,, Gerald Nolan	Duty.
74	,, Charles Mordall	Missing second day at Montbelliard.
75	,, Francis O'Brien	Missing first day at Montbelliard.
76	,, John O'Brien	do.
77	,, Richard O'Brien	do.
78	,, Timothy O'Connor	Duty.
79	,, E. O'Keeffe	Hospital.

Nominal Roll of the Irish Company, taken at the Red Farm, Jan. 24, 1871.

NO.	RANK AND NAME.	REMARKS.
80	Soldat C. O'Doherty	Duty.
81	,, E. J. O'Hanlon	Missing second day.
82	,, James O'Neill	do.
83	,, Jeremiah O'Neill	Duty.
84	,, Patrick O'Reilly	Duty.
85	,, George Pope	Hospital.
86	,, James Quinn	Duty—wounded.
87	,, D. Scanlon	Reported shot second day at Montbelliard.
88	,, Patrick Sheehan	Duty.
89	,, James Smith	Ambulance.
90	,, James Sutcliffe	Duty.
91	,, James Walsh	Duty.
92	,, A. Underwood	Shot first day at Montbelliard.
93	,, John Malony	Hospital.
84	,, William R. Haughton	Duty.
95	,, James M'Kenna	Duty.
96	,, M. O'Toole	Duty.

NOTE.—The names marked with an "asterisk," were recommended by the Colonel of the Foreign Legion to receive a service medal for distinguished conduct in the field.

THE END.

www.ingramcontent.com/pod-product-compliance
Lightning Source LLC
Chambersburg PA
CBHW031137160426
43193CB00008B/170